Encountering God
in Tyrannical Texts

Encountering God in Tyrannical Texts

Reflections on Paul, Women, and the Authority of Scripture

FRANCES TAYLOR GENCH

WESTMINSTER
JOHN KNOX PRESS
LOUISVILLE • KENTUCKY

First edition
Published by Westminster John Knox Press
Louisville, Kentucky

15 16 17 18 19 20 21 22 23 24—10 9 8 7 6 5 4 3 2 1

Except as otherwise indicated, Scripture quotations are from the New Revised Standard Version of the Bible, copyright © 1989 by the Division of Christian Education of the National Council of the Churches of Christ in the U.S.A., and are used by permission. Some bold or italic emphasis is added to the NRSV text.

Excerpts from Richard B. Hays, *First Corinthians*, Interpretation (Louisville, KY: John Knox Press, 1997) are reprinted by permission of Westminster John Knox Press. Excerpts from © Deborah Krause 2004, *1 Timothy*, Readings: A New Biblical Commentary (London: T&T Clark) are reprinted by permission of Bloomsbury Publishing Plc. Excerpts from *Presbyterian Understanding and Use of Holy Scripture*. Office of the General Assembly, Presbyterian Church (U.S.A.). 1983 pp. 11, 13. Used by permission.

Book design by Drew Stevens
Cover design by Lisa Buckley Design
Cover art: Mary Magdalene © *He Qi/www.heqiart.com*

Library of Congress Cataloging-in-Publication Data

Gench, Frances Taylor, 1956-
  Encountering God in tyrannical texts : reflections on Paul, women, and the authority of scripture / Frances Taylor Gench.
    pages cm
  Includes bibliographical references.
  ISBN 978-0-664-25952-5 (alk. paper)
  1. Women—Biblical teaching. 2. Bible. New Testament—Theology.
  I. Title.
  BS2545.W65G46 2015
  227'.06—dc23

2014050130

FOR MY HUSBAND
Roger Joseph Gench

Contents

Acknowledgments

This project has had a protracted birth process, and thus many people have contributed to it by providing invaluable feedback along the way. First and foremost, I wish to record my appreciation for the opportunity to deliver the Zenos Lectures at McCormick Theological Seminary in February 2011 and to thank its faculty and then-president Cynthia Campbell for their hospitality and for providing the initial impetus for this project. I am grateful to have had opportunities to share material in this volume as it developed further with other groups in a variety of academic, ecclesial, and retreat settings: the Ethics and Biblical Interpretation Section of the Society of Biblical Literature; the 2011 National Conference of The Covenant Network of Presbyterians; Presbyterian pastors in the Synod of the Southwest at Ghost Ranch, New Mexico; Ring Lake Ranch, Wyoming; Spring Academy at Gettysburg Lutheran Seminary; the Susan R. Andrews Lecture on Progressive Theology at Bradley Hills Presbyterian Church, Bethesda, Maryland; the John Haddon Leith Lecture Series at First Presbyterian Church, Auburn, Alabama; the Royster Lecture Series at First Presbyterian Church, Henderson, North Carolina; Theology Weekend at First Presbyterian Church, Spartanburg, South Carolina; Spring Symposium at First Presbyterian Church, Burlington, North Carolina; Enrichment Series Weekend at Sardis Presbyterian Church, Charlotte, North Carolina; Scholar in Residence weekend at First Presbyterian Church Howard County, Columbia, Maryland; and at a Congregational Retreat of Capital Hill Presbyterian Church, Washington, D.C. My ever-inspiring home congregation, The New York Avenue Presbyterian Church in Washington, D.C., also has provided a variety of lively forums for discussion of all the texts featured in this book throughout my writing of it.

I owe a debt of gratitude to Westminster John Knox Press and to Marianne Blickenstaff, Bridgett Green, and Julie Tonini for shepherding this project at different stages. I am deeply grateful to the administration and Board of Trustees of Union Presbyterian Seminary,

Richmond, Virginia, for a sabbatical period during which much of the research and writing was completed, and to my faculty colleagues for thoughtful collective feedback on this material as it initially developed. Students at Union Presbyterian Seminary have been primary conversation partners throughout the writing of this book, and I have been instructed in important ways by their close engagement with the biblical texts featured in this volume.

Finally, fine friends have provided encouragement and consultation at important points along the way: the Revs. Jenny McDevitt and Lindy Vogado; and the Rev. Drs. Cynthia Rasmussen, Holly Hearon, and Richard Carlson. This volume is dedicated to my best friend and beloved husband, Roger Joseph Gench, with gratitude for his unflagging encouragement and support and for the enormous blessing his partnership in marriage and ministry represents in my life every single day.

Frances Taylor Gench

Introduction

> If reading the Bible does not raise profound problems for you as a modern reader, then check with your doctor and inquire about the symptoms of brain-death.
>
> Robert P. Carroll[1]

I have loved the Bible and been in conversation with it for as long as I can remember. In fact, my relationship with it was established well before I could read, and my earliest impressions of it were formed by a song—one of the first taught to me by my parents and grandparents and legions of faithful Sunday school teachers: "Jesus Loves Me, This I Know, for the Bible Tells Me So." The words of that song impressed themselves upon my mind and heart throughout my Wonderbread years and led me to embrace the Bible as the story of a love affair—the story of the love that God in Christ had for me, for all people around the world, and for the whole creation. That conviction became foundational for all my later encounters with the Bible and is one I have never relinquished.

But loving the Bible and sustaining a lifelong relationship with it does not entail checking one's brain at the door. It does not require agreement with, or acquiescence to, everything it has to say. In fact, many thoughtful people who honor the Bible nonetheless relate to Robert Carroll's frank observation: reading an ancient document like the Bible cannot help but raise profound problems for them. And among those problems (and the one that will concern us in this volume) are "tyrannical texts"—that is, texts that have proved to be profoundly oppressive in the lives of many people. The Bible is a profoundly liberating document, but there is no denying that it also contains deeply problematic texts—indeed, "texts of terror"[2] that have adversely impacted the lives of women, slaves, Jews, Palestinians, Native Americans, and gays (to mention but a few). Such texts and prevalent interpretations of them may be described as "tyrannical" in the sense that they have legitimated the right of some to exercise unjust power or control over others. They are "tyrannical" in the sense that they have circumscribed human lives and possibilities, functioning (and in many cases, continuing to function) as instruments of oppression.

So what is a thinking person who honors Scripture and strives to be faithful to it to do with such texts? How might one offer alternative interpretations of them? And in what sense do they function "authoritatively" in our lives as "holy" Scripture—as media that bring us into encounter with the living God? These questions are at the heart of this volume, which has several objectives. One is to provide in-depth study of texts within the Pauline tradition that have circumscribed the lives and ministries of women throughout Christian history. Some are from letters that the apostle Paul himself wrote (from what scholars refer to as his "undisputed"[3] letters); others are from letters that are understood by most scholars (and in this volume) to have been written in Paul's name after his death in order to honor and update his legacy and bring it to bear on new circumstances. The latter (referred to as "disputed,"[4] or "deuteropauline,"[5] letters), which seek to continue Paul's heritage, are no less "authoritative" for the life of the church than the former, for their authority derives not from their authorship but from their canonical status. They achieved canonical status because the early Christian community, during the formative centuries of its existence, found them to resonate with apostolic teaching and came to revere them for the power they displayed in engendering, sustaining, and guiding Christian faith.[6] Our engagement with all of these texts, Pauline and deuteropauline, will be deepened and broadened by new questions, insights, and perspectives that feminist biblical scholarship has brought to a reading of them. We can learn a great deal from these texts and from this scholarship about early Christian women and their contributions to the formation and expansion of the early church.

A second objective is to provide strategies for engaging problematic, tyrannical texts with integrity—that is, without dismissing them, whitewashing them, or acquiescing to them—and as potential sources of edification for the church. While texts that have adversely impacted women's lives will serve as test cases, I hope the recommended strategies will prove to be helpful for wrestling with other texts that readers deem problematic and oppressive. I also hope they will encourage and facilitate direct and public engagement with texts that are often dismissed or ignored in mainline churches—precisely because they are regarded as "tyrannical" and, frankly, "canonical embarrassments."[7]

Finally, I hope engagement with the texts featured in this volume will help readers think deeply about the nature and authority of Scripture and how they live out their relationship with it. In fact, one of the most helpful things about wrestling with tyrannical texts is that they force us to articulate clearly how we understand the nature and authority of Scripture. When we avoid such texts, we deprive ourselves, and our congregations, of the opportunity to think through, and to think deeply about, our relationship with the Bible and how God is present in our engagement with it. In other words, we miss opportunities to grow in understanding, to mature in faith.

Six texts from the Pauline tradition will be featured in the pages that follow. The first chapter, "Beyond Textual Harassment: Engaging Tyrannical Texts," will introduce the study and recommend strategies for engagement with tyrannical texts, taking 1 Timothy 2:8–15 as a test case—the most frequently quoted text in the Pastoral Epistles and the pivotal biblical text in ongoing ecclesial controversies over the role of women in church and society. The second chapter, "Wives Be Subject? Articulating Biblical Authority," is also introductory and aims to help readers think through their understanding of biblical authority in conversation with Ephesians 5:21–33—the most fully developed argument in the New Testament for gender hierarchy and a text that has proved to be hazardous to women's health and survival. The third and fourth chapters, "Women and Worship Wars," will wrestle with 1 Corinthians 11:2–16 (the only assertion of gender hierarchy in Paul's undisputed letters and arguably the most obscure words he ever wrote) and 1 Corinthians 14:33b–36 (which for most of Christian history has been used to deny women participation and leadership in the Christian community). These chapters, necessarily the longest, will also address important shifts in recent study of "Paul and women" (as the topic has often been framed) that can expand our engagement with these texts. In addition, they will review classic principles of biblical interpretation that can help us argue with contentious texts with integrity. The fifth chapter, "Reining in Rambunctious Widows," will consider 1 Timothy 5:3–16, a text that represents the longest discussion of widows in the New Testament and aims to curtail their activity and diminish their influence in the life of the Christian community. Finally, chapter 6, "Women in Ministry," will engage Romans 16:1–16, a non-tyrannical and largely overlooked text that serves as an important counterpoint to all the other texts featured in this volume.

This book emerges out of my own wrestling with these texts and is written for those who, like me, have struggled with them and with what it means to speak of biblical authority in their presence. Who might such readers be? I have written the book with a variety of readers in mind: female and male, including church professionals (pastors and educators) as well as lay readers—any who engage in serious study of biblical texts. I hope, for example, that it will be a resource for preachers and teachers and encourage direct and public engagement with these texts in their practice of ministry. It can serve as a textbook for college or seminary courses dealing with women in the biblical world, Pauline and deuteropauline letters, or the nature and authority of Scripture. It is also designed for use by laypersons and groups interested in this topic and substantive Bible study of the texts in question. I try to present technical matters in an accessible fashion and include study questions with each chapter to facilitate group discussion or individual reflection. I encourage group study: reading the Bible in the company of others is always a richer and deeper experience than reading it alone! For those engaged in group study, chapter 3, the longest in the volume, can be divided into two manageable study sessions under the headings "Listening to the Text" and "Dialogue with the Text." I hope all readers will find this book a useful resource that will facilitate engagement with problematic texts and prompt reflection on their import for Christian life, faith, and renewal.

1

Beyond Textual Harassment: Engaging Tyrannical Texts

1 Timothy 2:8–15

I have been spending a good bit of my time of late musing over the question of what to do with problematic, offensive, downright tyrannical texts in the Bible—a book we describe as "holy" and revere as "authoritative," as "normative" in some sense for Christian faith and practice. And I'd like to pose a question for reflection that, I think, gets to the heart of the matter: *Is there any biblical text that you would reject?* Ellen Davis of Duke Divinity School says that when this question was posed to her by a colleague, she could not get it out of her mind: "What should we in the church do with biblical texts that do not seem to accord with a well-considered understanding of the Christian faith? . . . Is there a point," she asks, "at which we have to give up the struggle and admit that in this case edification is not possible? That this particular biblical text must be repudiated as a potential source of valid theological insight? That it is disqualified for public or authoritative reading in the church?"[1]

It seems to me an important question for mainline Christians to consider. I confess that it is one I have wrestled with my whole life. At one time I thought I had an answer, a solution to the problem—for there have been rough moments in my relationship with the Bible, particularly during my teenage years, when I began to read the Bible with some seriousness and found myself tremendously insulted by what I thought at the time to be Paul's view of women. For example, I didn't care for the fact that in 1 Corinthians we read that it is shameful for women to speak in church gatherings (14:35), or for the fact that Corinthian men appeared to be advised that "it is well for a man not to touch a woman" (7:1). Nor was I fond of 1 Timothy, which commands that no woman is "to teach or have authority over a man" (2:12). Women, rather, are told to be silent and submissive and to earn their salvation by bearing children (2:15). So much for justification by grace through faith alone!

I had a solution to this problem: it was simply to take my magic marker, "X" these portions out of my Bible, and then record obscene remarks about the apostle Paul in the margins for future reference. But even that did not suffice when I came to Ephesians 5: "Wives, be subject to your husbands as you are to the Lord. For the husband is the head of the wife just as Christ is head of the church, the body of which he is the Savior. Just as the church is subject to Christ, so also wives ought to be, in everything, to their husbands" (5:22–24). When I came to Ephesians 5, I got out the scissors. These were words that had to be forcibly removed—excised, banished from my personal canon of Scripture. It was, I suppose, my first experience of "textual harassment,"[2] though it was not my last, for the Bible is full of repellant, tyrannical texts—texts that have proved to be "texts of terror"[3] for women, slaves, Jews, Palestinians, Native Americans, gays (to mention but a few)—instruments of oppression. And early in my relationship with the Bible, it seemed to me that the best solution to this problem was to perform radical surgery on the canon. Of course, other and less drastic strategies, with much the same effect, were surely available and are more often employed by mainline Christians confronted with such texts: we can always simply ignore them, or dismiss them as antiquated relics and their authors as benighted savages.

But these no longer seem to me to be the most constructive ways of wrestling with tyrannical texts. *Is there any biblical text that you would reject?* I've been challenged by Ellen Davis's own answer to that question: "No biblical text may be safely repudiated as a potential source of edification for the church." She even goes on to say, "When we think we have reached the point of zero edification, then that perception indicates that we are not reading deeply enough; we have not probed the layers of the text with sufficient care."[4]

Not reading deeply enough—now there's a challenge! This challenge has compelled me to spend much of my time of late in the company of texts that raise my blood pressure to see if that might be possible—to read deeper, probe further, and perhaps find some word of edification for the church in tyrannical texts that I have failed to hear. I returned first, of course, to texts I used to tackle with my magic marker and scissors in hand, and I invite you to consider one of them, from 1 Timothy 2, as a test case. As you read it, listen for what the Spirit is saying to the church!

1 TIMOTHY 2:8–15

[8]I desire, then, that in every place the men should pray, lifting up holy hands without anger or argument; [9]also that the women should dress themselves modestly and decently in suitable clothing, not with their hair braided, or with gold, pearls, or expensive clothes, [10]but with good works, as is proper for women who profess reverence for God. [11]Let a woman learn in silence with full submission. [12]I permit no woman to teach or to have authority over a man; she is to keep silent. [13]For Adam was formed first, then Eve; [14]and Adam was not deceived, but the woman was deceived and became a transgressor. [15]Yet she will be saved through childbearing, provided they continue in faith and love and holiness, with modesty.

The Word of the Lord? Thanks be to God? It is hard to say that without gagging. Recently, when I assigned this text for exegesis (translation and interpretation) in a New Testament epistles course, every woman in the class showed up that day in braids and pearls. Few texts in the New Testament are more painful to our modern sensibilities, and few have had such far-reaching, fateful consequences for the lives of women around the globe, within both the church and society. It has frequently been used to silence all women, to exclude them from leadership, to confine them to domestic roles, to legitimate hierarchical relationships. Indeed, to this day, it is the pivotal biblical text in ongoing ecclesial controversies over the role of women in church and society, in many quarters still justifying the church's exclusion of women from certain leadership roles. These controversies, and thus this text, may strike members of most mainline denominations in the U.S.A. as irrelevant and passé, since we resolved our own controversies over women's leadership in the church decades ago. My own denomination, the Presbyterian Church (U.S.A.), has been ordaining women as ministers of Word and Sacrament,[5] elders, and deacons for some time and has long since moved on to other ordination controversies. So perhaps it is important to remind ourselves that some of the immigrant congregations within mainline denominations still struggle mightily with this matter, as do other Christian communions that remain adamantly opposed to the ordination of women. Moreover, the global communion of Christians more often than not does not share our sensibilities about this text or our struggles with it, finding in it normative guidance—a rather clear word about the universal will of God for relations between men and women and leadership in the church, grounded in the very orders of creation. All of this suggests that it behooves us to stay engaged with this text as well and to be part of the conversations it evokes rather than relinquish our opportunity—and our responsibility, I think—to make a contribution to it, for a lot of people out there *are* talking about this text, rather loudly, and if we are not engaging it seriously, we are not likely to be heard or to make any impact on that global conversation about a text that continues to circumscribe the lives of women to this day.

My own newfound willingness to try to stay in conversation with a text I have long despised, to keep company with it for a sustained period of time, is indebted not only to Ellen Davis but also in no small part to a recent formative experience on a denominational task force appointed to wrestle with issues uniting and dividing Presbyterians (issues related to sexual orientation and ordination, which have roiled most mainline denominations over the last decades). It was an experience in which twenty Presbyterians—as different from one another as we could possibly be, who under ordinary circumstances never would have dreamed of hanging out together for six years—found ourselves engaged in a profoundly challenging learning experience in the art of listening. An important part of our work was learning how to lower the decibel level of our conversations—to speak our truths with love and respect, but also to *listen* to each other, to really try to hear and understand the logic and integrity of other points of view—even if we considered them misguided. The biblical text surely requires no less of us, for we truly are every bit as related by baptism to the author of 1 Timothy as we are to disputatious believers in our own time and place. We are part of the same church, the same family of faith, for as Joel Green has astutely observed, "To speak of the church, theologically, is to speak of its oneness across space and time. There is only one people of God."[6] The writers and readers of Scripture constitute one community of faith. What that means is that, whether we like it or not, the author of 1 Timothy is part of that family, a brother in the faith, and that when we read his letter, we are not reading someone else's mail. We are reading our own mail, addressed to the one, holy, catholic, apostolic church, past, present, and future.[7]

It is an ecclesiological perspective, at least, that has helped me re-engage 1 Timothy 2 with a bit more charity and patience than I was first inclined to do. And Deborah Krause's observation in her brilliant commentary on 1 Timothy has also proved enormously helpful: "Rather than an enemy," she says, "I like to think of the writer of 1 Timothy as a distant great-uncle. While he may be strange and even creepy, he is a member of the family and one with whom I need to learn to converse. If I deny my relationship with him, I miss an opportunity to better understand who I am and what it is that I believe."[8]

It also turns out that if we deny our relationship with him, we stand to lose invaluable pieces of our family history, for as we listen to this text, his is not the only voice that we hear. Indeed, as we engage 1 Timothy, we need to bear in mind a very important distinction, now axiomatic in feminist biblical scholarship: the difference between *prescriptive* and *descriptive* literature. If a text is *prescriptive*, we should not assume that it provides a description of actual behavior or practices—a glimpse of the community addressed as it really was. Instead, it presents the author's *ideal*—that is, what a congregation *should* look like according to his vision. So listen again to verses 11 and 12: "Let a woman learn in silence with full submission. I permit no woman to teach or to have authority over a man; she is to keep silent." Is that description or prescription? It is clearly *prescription*, and prescriptive material is often the best historical evidence we have that the *opposite* is happening! As Deborah Krause has observed, "You don't tell women to shut up, unless they are talking."[9] You don't command them not to teach unless they are, in fact, teaching.

So between the lines of this text, we hear the voices of foremothers in the faith and perhaps other voices of those who listened to their teaching.[10] Maybe some of those men who, in verse 8, are directed to pray "without anger or argument" were inclined to dispute the author's prescriptions for church order and his silencing of women and thus were presented with a gag order too. Deborah Krause puts it this way:

I have come to see that rather than a megaphone commanding silence, 1 Timothy 2.8–15 is a site in which there is an argument about who has a voice and why. All of a sudden the text has opened up for me in new ways. Where it had seemed to close doors, it now presents possibilities. Rather than an edict to silence women, 1 Timothy 2.8–15 has become transformed into a debate about who can and cannot have a voice in the church. . . . The power to speak is . . . something women have fought about for a long time, from the very origins of the church. For its role, even unwitting, in preserving this argument I now affirm 1 Timothy 2.11–12 as "Holy Scripture."[11]

Indeed, 1 Timothy 2 is a space in which that argument continues in our own day and invites our participation. As I began to consider these possibilities, I found myself admitting that my old nemesis might have more edifying potential than I had imagined—that these Pastoral Epistles (1–2 Timothy and Titus), which have more to say about women and exhibit more anxiety about managing their behavior than any other New Testament documents, inadvertently preserve important pieces of our family history that would otherwise be lost to us, documenting the struggles of foremothers in the faith, straining against prescribed reality, from whom we can take courage.[12]

The effort to read more deeply, to try to discern edifying potential in tyrannical texts, should by no means ignore or attempt to whitewash the real problems they present. In the case of 1 Timothy 2, the problems are considerable. These are, after all, the best-known and most frequently quoted words in the Pastoral Epistles and the most well-known New Testament restrictions on women's behavior. Indeed, the text is remarkable for its stringency and the lengths to which it goes to prove the unsuitability of women for teaching and leadership roles—all the way back to Genesis. And there is no getting around the fact that the author's tendentious midrash of Adam and Eve's story makes three very problematic and questionable points. *Point number 1*: Women are not to teach or have authority over man, first, because of the order of creation. Look at verse 13: "For Adam was formed first, then Eve"—the first being more important. The author clearly assumes that the very sequence of creation, as he understands it, is a revelation of God's will that women are to be subordinate to men. *Point number 2*: Women are not to teach or have authority over men, second, because they are, by nature, more gullible, easily prone to deception. We see this in verse 14: "Adam was not deceived, but the woman was deceived and became a transgressor." Indeed, the Greek suggests that she was "profoundly deceived" (*exapatētheisa*), and the moral of this story, in the author's mind, is clear. Given this inherent character flaw, daughters of Eve ought not to occupy positions of influence and authority, or else all hell breaks loose: men who listen, like Adam, fall into transgression. But the author concludes on what he undoubtedly regards as a positive note, an important word of reassurance and mollification. *Point number 3*: "Yet she will be saved through childbearing, provided they continue in faith and love and holiness, with modesty" (v. 15).

There is no denying that all three of these points are downright problematic, even "theologically and morally outrageous"![13] Genesis, for example, by no means absolves Adam, nor does Romans, which says, "Sin came into the world through one man" (see Rom. 5:12, 16, 19), ascribing guilt essentially to Adam—as does 1 Corinthians when it affirms that, "as all die in Adam, so all will be made alive in Christ" (15:22). And 1 Timothy 2:15, most problematic of all, is unique in the New Testament in suggesting that salvation for women is different from that of men, requiring adherence to domestic, maternal roles. It is a highly selective reading of Genesis. The rhetoric is way over the top, and the logic is strained. But by means of it, the author mounts a devastating argument, insisting that women who teach in public or exercise authority over men violate the limits of their place in the fundamental order of things.[14] It is one of the very few theological arguments about anything in the Pastoral Epistles, and in the minds of many Christians around this world, it is an especially authoritative one because it derives from the creation ordinances, reflecting the divine will revealed in the very orders of creation. These deeply problematic affirmations of the text should by no means be ignored or whitewashed.

Yet this is not to say that interpreters haven't tried! Various whitewashing strategies have been deployed to defuse 1 Timothy 2, to argue that it's really not as bad as it sounds—but none of these arguments are convincing. One of the most common strategies is to celebrate the positive admonition to learn in verse 11: "Let a woman learn" (albeit "in silence with full submission"). Let a woman learn: one of the highest callings in the church! The author, in other words, should be congratulated for his recognition that women are capable of learning, and surely he implies that they may teach once they have acquired sufficient education. Some even translate verse 11 as follows: "A woman should learn in quietness" (e.g., NIV), or even, "They must be allowed to study undisturbed."[15] In other words, get this woman some childcare! I'm not convinced. At this point many commentators also observe that the admonition to learn represents a great advance for Christian women over their miserable lot in Judaism—an argument that, unfortunately, is inaccurate, bad history, and thus very bad theology.

"Blame it on the Jews" is another, far too common whitewashing strategy, for when faced with really tyrannical texts about women in the Pauline and deuteropauline epistles, commentators are often tempted to resolve the difficulty by bifurcating the apostle Paul, saying: "Oh, that's not the Christian Paul—that's the Jewish Paul—a place where he couldn't quite shake off his Judaism." The good stuff, like Galatians 3:28 ("There is no longer Jew or Greek, . . . slave or free, . . . male and female; for all of you are one in Christ Jesus")—that's the Christian Paul; but the bad stuff represents unfortunate lapses on his part back into Judaism—points at which the author is "more Jewish than Christian in his thinking."[16] This unfortunate strategy also conveys grossly inaccurate caricatures and continues to contribute to the long, sad history of Christians teaching contempt for Judaism.[17]

Other whitewashing strategies appear with some frequency in commentaries on this text: the argument, for example, that this is a temporary restraining order for a particular time and place rather than a universal norm—a word of advice for a specific church struggling with bossy interruptions in the worship service and obnoxious, domineering women. A surprising number of commentators argue that verse 15 is not as bad as it sounds, that it does not actually speak of salvation through childbearing. Women will be saved, not by childbearing, but by the birth of a particular child—by Jesus, of course! Eve's sin and that of all her daughters is thereby reversed with the coming and work of Jesus Christ. But the otherwise distinguished commentator who takes the cake, I think, is the one who insists, incredibly, that the injunctions in this text are a *blessing* from God, who *allows* women to be silent and thereby *frees* them from the onerous tasks of instructing and guiding the church[18] (though admittedly, women might be inclined to consider this a blessing when trapped late at night in an interminable church council, session, or vestry meeting). I put all these efforts to defuse the text in the whitewashing category and would not recommend them. Most of them strike me as efforts to put way too much lipstick on this pig.

It seems to me that mainline Christians are more often inclined to one of two dismissive strategies: either reckoning that the text is an antiquated, historically conditioned relic with which we need not concern ourselves, or that the apostle Paul did not write it. After all, most scholars agree that he did not, that 1 Timothy is a pseudonymous letter, written in the apostle's name by someone trying to interpret his legacy in a new time and place. But these are no solutions since the whole of Scripture, every text, is historically conditioned, as are we; and regardless of who wrote 1 Timothy, it is still in the canon. Its authority derives not from its authorship but from its canonical status.

STRATEGIES FOR ENGAGEMENT
WITH TYRANNICAL TEXTS

So if we're not going to whitewash tyrannical texts, dismiss them, or ignore the real problems they present, what in the world should we do with them? For the sake of discussion, let me recommend five things that at least are proving helpful, and more constructive than scissors, in my own effort to stay in conversation with them—five strategies that increasingly seem incumbent upon me as one who claims to honor Scripture and to take the Bible seriously as an authoritative guide for Christian faith and practice.

Recommendation 1: Remember that "the difficult text is worthy of charity from its interpreters."[19]
I am indebted to Ellen Davis for this first recommendation, who says that "charity does not mean pity but rather something more like generosity and patience toward the text"—a willingness to contend with the difficulties.[20] In the case of 1 Timothy 2, this has required a willingness on my part to sit down and listen to that distant uncle who penned this text, to whom I am related by baptism, to try to understand what motivated him: Why was he driven to such rhetorical extremes? This is a point at which historical-critical inquiry can be enormously helpful. If I stick around long enough and take the time to listen, perhaps I can empathize with real difficulties he may have faced—even as I find myself deeply regretting the choices he made as he articulated a response to them.

As I took the time to immerse myself in this letter and scholarly conversations about it, I gained a clearer sense that the historical circumstances in which the author found himself were complicated. To say the least, he faced complex problems. For one thing, he was mightily distressed about false teachers, whom he believed to be distorting Christian faith and endangering the well-being of the church, for the letter is filled with angry polemic against them. It is hard to ascertain the identity of his opponents because the attacks on them are vague and imprecise, on the order of name-calling, insults, broadsides, and conventional vilification. And we should never assume that polemic represents an accurate picture of opponents. But a few clues do present themselves.

In 1 Timothy 4:3, for example: "They forbid marriage and demand abstinence from foods, which God created to be received with thanksgiving by those who believe and know the truth." Elsewhere the author describes them as overly fascinated with cosmic speculation: myths, endless genealogies (1:4), and what is "falsely called knowledge" (6:20); and he castigates those who "have swerved from the truth by claiming that the resurrection has already taken place" (2 Tim. 2:18). From clues such as these, most commentators surmise that the author had some sort of early Christian Gnosticism on his hands. It also appears that the author's opponents and their teaching of rigorous asceticism, celibate piety, found a hearing especially among women—that the false teaching he counters had special appeal for them. We see this in 2 Timothy 3, for example, where the author says this about them (vv. 5–7): "Avoid them! For among them are those who make their way into households and captivate silly women, overwhelmed by their sins and swayed by all kinds of desires, who are always being instructed and can never arrive at a knowledge of the truth."

It is not hard to understand why ascetic teaching and celibate life had real appeal for many early Christian women as an avenue to freedom—freedom from patriarchal households and the hazards of childbirth, the leading cause of mortality among women in the ancient world. A close reading of the Pastorals suggests, in fact, that some celibate women and widows were banding together in all-female households—a development evoking a great deal of anxiety for the author, as shown by the urgency with which he instructs younger widows to marry, bear children, and manage their own households (1 Tim. 5:13–14). Perhaps these circumstances also shed light on the need he felt to emphasize maternity as a worthy vocation for women, albeit in overstated fashion as a means of salvation.

But the challenges presented by false teaching were not the only ones the writer faced. Clues to another complicating factor may be found in the dress code the author establishes for women, insisting that they "should dress themselves modestly and decently in suitable clothing, not with their hair braided, or with gold, pearls, or expensive clothes, but with good works, as is proper for women who profess reverence for God" (1 Tim. 2:9–10). Intriguing questions have been raised about the socioeconomic implications of these words: Doesn't it appear that some women in this congregation could afford expensive jewelry, extravagant clothing, and hairdressers to arrange the elaborately braided hairdos that were in style among wealthy women of the day? It is hard to imagine that many could afford such luxuries. Perhaps just a few women were in view, which raises a very interesting question: What if these wealthy women were major benefactors of the congregation, the ones paying the congregation's expenses through sizeable donations to the annual stewardship campaign? We know that patronage was an entrenched feature of life at all levels of Roman society. Socially superior patrons provided benefactions, and their socially inferior clients in return were obligated to enhance the prestige, reputation, and honor of their patrons with public recognition of their status.

So what if a handful of wealthy women in this congregation, upon whose generosity the congregation depended, expected a culturally recognized return on their investment? What if they assumed, for example, that their donations entitled them to leadership roles? They could certainly assume this in every other aspect of their lives. It is an intriguing possibility to consider: that a handful of wealthy women were asserting their power, wealth, and status, butting heads with the congregation's duly elected and installed, though socially inferior, leaders.[21] Maybe it is for their benefit that the author affirms, in chapter 6, that to *God alone* honor is due (6:16). Benefactors, in other words, should not usurp that honor and should expect reward for their generosity, instead, in the life to come (see 6:18–19). This sounds very much like a critique of the patronage system.

Elsa Tamez has made a compelling case that this kind of power struggle is reflected in this text, between wealthy women and church leaders named by the laying on of hands.[22] The author could have addressed such a conflict in a variety of constructive ways. But Tamez observes that he chooses, instead, to resolve it by invoking traditional patriarchal values to squash these wealthy women—to put them in their place. But by speaking in generic terms, rather than directly to the dominant women, he responds in a way that squashes all women, regardless of their class.[23] It is an intriguing scenario—one that suggests, at the very least, that the dilemmas facing the author of 1 Timothy were indeed complex and merit a measure of our empathy, for these kinds of socioeconomic tensions and expectations afflict the lives of congregations to this day.

One final complicating factor is worth considering: the pervasive anxiety reflected throughout the Pastoral Epistles about public opinion, the church's public image and reputation. In the text before us, for example, there is a notable emphasis on modesty and decency. In the chapters that follow, we hear a repeated concern that church officers be "above reproach" and "well thought of by outsiders" (3:2, 7). And in 5:14 the author insists that "younger widows marry, bear children, and manage their households, *so as to give the adversary no occasion to revile us.*" The world is watching and suspicious of new religious movements, and the author is anxious for the church's "family values" to be on display. And what I think I have begun to appreciate, however grudgingly, is that far more than the church's public image was at stake. Its mission is also in view—its concern that the gospel receive as wide a hearing as possible and that no obstacles stand in the way. For nowhere in the New Testament do we find so explicit a statement of God's desire to save all, as in 1 Timothy 2:4, God's desire that "everyone be saved and come to the knowledge of the truth." Observable Christian living that gives no offense, provides no stumbling block is, in the author's view, of inestimable importance for the validity and spread of the gospel.[24] So this dynamic too was likely at play: the missionary necessity of maintaining a dialogue with culture.[25]

If space allowed, more could be said about circumstances reflected in this letter—about the complex dynamics and varied power struggles its author may have faced. But I trust the point has been made: if we take the time to listen, to probe the layers of tyrannical texts with care, and try to understand the complex motivations behind them, perhaps we can cough up a measure of empathy for the challenges their authors engaged, even as we find ourselves regretting unfortunate choices they made as they articulated responses to them. "The difficult text *is* worthy of charity from its interpreters." But having said that, and having made a genuine effort to listen, remember that genuine conversation is always a two-way affair. This brings us to Recommendation 2!

Recommendation 2: Argue with the text, confident that wrestling with Scripture is an act of faithfulness.

By all means, argue with the text—engage it, address it, confident that wrestling with Scripture is an act of faithfulness, an act of taking the text with the utmost seriousness. Indeed, we have much to learn from our Jewish neighbors about this sacred practice of arguing with Scripture. As Amy-Jill Levine has observed, "The general sense in the

Jewish tradition is that one argues with the text and with fellow Jews about the text, and that in some cases multiple meanings are possible. Jews are more inclined to say, 'I'm right, and you may be right too.'" Yet Christians, she says, "more familiar with the word from the pulpit, the hierarchy, or the individual (not just Jesus, but Paul, Augustine, Aquinas, Luther, Calvin, Wesley, etc.), may be more prone to seek a single response."[26] Do you think she's right about that? I think she is, and that we may also be more prone to passive engagement with Scripture: we may be far more acquiescent before biblical texts than we ought to be. In fact, Walter Wink may be the only Christian I have ever heard speak forthrightly about his own loud wrangling with Scripture. He put it this way, as I recall: "I yell at the Bible about its sexism, its violence, its homophobia—it yells back at me about my attachment to wealth, my neglect of the poor." It struck me at the time as a remarkable image of the mutual address and critique that should characterize our engagement with Scripture.

Moreover, it is important to remember that the Bible argues with itself, providing a model for our own engagement with it. First Timothy's is not the only voice in Scripture, and as Walter Brueggemann has observed, "To give any one voice in Scripture the authority to silence other voices surely distorts the text and misconstrues the liveliness that the text itself engenders in the interpretive community."[27] So by all means *argue* with tyrannical texts! When confronted with one, don't check your brain at the door, for God has given us minds to think deeply. Argue in the context of the whole of Scripture, bringing other biblical voices into the conversation, for this is not the only text in the Bible that speaks of women in the church, of relationships between male and female, of the means of salvation. It is not the only text in the New Testament that makes claims about life together in the Christian community. What about the presentation in Acts of Priscilla's authoritative instruction of Apollos (Acts 18:26)? What about Paul's own witness to the full, authoritative participation of women in worship and the life of the church in 1 Corinthians 11 and Romans 16, or his rather emphatic insistence on justification by grace through faith alone (e.g., Rom. 3:21–31)? Cast as wide a net as possible, and know that the commitment to struggle with biblical texts—to wrestle with them, even angrily—is a sign of our faithfulness to this book.[28]

Argue also with other interpreters (and interpretations) of the text, for this, too, is a faithful practice by which we test alternative readings and discern compelling ones. It is surely worth inquiring, for example, about the practice of selective retrieval when it comes to 1 Timothy 2:8–15. The text's absolute prohibition of women's speech and exercise of teaching and leadership roles is viewed by many as the New Testament's definitive view on the matter. Verses 11 and 12, in fact, are the most well-known and frequently quoted verses in the Pastoral Epistles. But what about the text's elaborate dress code and restrictions on external adornment in verses 9–10 or its contention that salvation, for women, requires childbearing and adherence to domestic, maternal roles (v. 15)? Why aren't these admonitions viewed as equally decisive? What accounts for interpretive inconsistency on these points, for selective interpretive retrieval? Some regard the prohibition of women's speech and authoritative teaching as especially binding because it is grounded in the creation ordinances. But as we have noticed, the tendentious midrash on Genesis 2–3 is itself questionable in many important respects; and as Daniel Kirk perceptively inquires, isn't this giving "the last word to the curse of the fall rather than to the redemption of Christ"? Does not the subordination of women in the church "as a norm for all times and places undermine the scope and power of God's redemptive work and of our own calling to make the church the living story of new creation"?[29] These are important questions with which to grapple!

As we wrestle not only with the text, but also with other interpreters (and interpretations) of it, they, too, are worthy of our charity and generosity. In fact, Ellen Davis identifies charity, "evidenced first toward the text and second toward those who read it differently from the way I do," as a key interpretive virtue, declaring that a measure of "interpretive humility and charity" would go a long way toward fostering "God's work of reconciliation within the church" in our collective engagement with contentious issues.[30] Collective wrestling with both the text and the interpretations of others is central to the church's life, a means by which we discern what God is calling us to be and do. So wrestle with all your heart, mind, and strength. But as you do so, there is a third recommendation to bear in mind.

Recommendation 3: Resist the temptation to throw the baby out with the bathwater!

As deeply problematic and offensive as tyrannical texts may be, it is worth asking: Is there *no* blessing to be found here? Are there really *no* points of edifying potential? The practice of engaging them with charity, of listening closely, may surface more edifying food for thought than we might have imagined. In the case of 1 Timothy 2, for example, we have noted that it preserves the site of an important argument about who has a voice in the church as well as important pieces of our family history that would otherwise be lost to us. But are there not other points of edifying potential to be discerned? For example: Are what we wear and how we adorn ourselves in worship entirely petty issues?[31] Or should our apparel befit our identity as disciples of Jesus Christ? Isn't there something to be said for simplicity and modesty in a society desperately in need of these virtues? And are not matters of economic and ecological injustice implicit in the production of luxurious clothing and adornment?[32] How might ostentatious fashion statements distract attention from God in worship, flaunt our economic status, and obstruct our ministry to the poor? And in a culture that so often defines us in terms of our personal appearance, isn't there something to be said for clothing ourselves, instead, with "good works" that give visible expression to our faith (cf. Rev. 19:8; Isa. 61:10)? I do wish women had not been singled out for sartorial concern. Men, too, would benefit from such instruction. Still, there is food for thought here. There is surely also something to be said about the integrity of the church's struggle to live in the world, rather than withdraw from it, and to stay in dialogue with culture for the sake of the gospel—however imperfectly the church negotiates that tension. And we can be grateful for 1 Timothy's robust theology of creation—its insistence, in the face of opinion to the contrary, that everything that God created—including food, marriage, the bearing of children—is good.

But positive dimensions of the text are not the only points of potential edification for the church. We do believe that the books of the Bible are guides for us, and as Raymond Brown has observed, "Part of the guidance is to learn from the dangers attested in them as well as from their great insights."[33] This, in fact, is Recommendation 4!

Recommendation 4: Learn from the dangers as well as the insights that biblical texts present.

In the case of 1 Timothy 2, discerning the insights was the hard part; the dangers are all too apparent: the temptation, for example, that the church faces in every age to silence dissident voices among us or to sacrifice the good of some of our members for the sake of our reputation or mission. The dangers persist, for before us is a text that continues to wield enormous influence, circumscribing the lives of women around the world and throughout the church to this day. And can we not learn from the dangers as well as the insights? Can't we learn from evidence of painfully imperfect efforts to embody the gospel? I'd venture to say that we see a good bit of imperfection reflected in 1 Timothy 2, which (I pray) is not a cavalier judgment but one that emerges from serious wrestling with the text, in conversation with the whole of Scripture and the collective wisdom of the church, which now benefits from two thousand years of discipleship experience. It needs to be a judgment made with the reluctance called for whenever we find it necessary to critique and correct a family elder[34] (even a distant great-uncle who is, admittedly, a little bit creepy).

There is more to be said about this—about learning from both the insights and the dangers a text may present. But for now, I invite you to consider the former Archbishop of Canterbury's eloquent summary of this important point. Scripture, Rowan Williams contends, is the record of "an encounter, a contest, a wrestling":

> Here in scripture is God's urgency to communicate; here in scripture is our mishearing, our misappropriating, our deafness, and our resistance. Woven together in scripture are those two things, the giving of God and our inability to receive what God wants to give. . . . The gift of God, the liberty of God, is passed through the distorting glass of our own fears.[35]

He goes on to suggest:

> When we listen to a passage that is difficult, alien, or offensive, I think our reaction should be neither to say, "This is the word of the Lord, so the difficulty is my problem," nor to say, "This is rubbish, we ought to produce a more politically correct version of scripture!" Our task, rather, is to say that the revelation of God comes to us in the middle of weakness and fallibility. We read neither with a kind of blind and thoughtless obedience to every word of scripture, as if it simply represented the mind of God, nor with that rather priggish sensibility that desires to look down on the authors of scripture as benighted savages. We read with a sense of our own benighted savagery in receiving God's gift, and our solidarity with those writers of scripture caught up in the blazing fire of God's gift who yet struggle with it, misapprehend it, and misread it.[36]

It is important to name the points of misapprehension and misreading when we discern them, for errors, when acknowledged, are

indispensable to learning and have a role to play in the Bible's formation of the mind of Jesus Christ in us.[37]

***Recommendation 5: Don't let anyone tell you that you are not taking
the authority of the Bible seriously!***
Finally, if you are practicing the discipline of charity or generosity
toward the text, listening patiently and carefully to it, arguing with it,
being instructed by both the dangers and insights it presents—then
don't let anyone tell you that you are not taking the authority of the
Bible seriously! This, too, requires further comment in my second
chapter (below), for tyrannical texts, more than any others, force us
to articulate clearly how we understand the nature and authority of
Scripture—how God is present in all our engagement with it, which
is, after all, why we call it "Holy." God is present whenever we wrestle
with Scripture, both with and against its claims. So don't let go of it.
It is holy wrestling. Hang on to that text, like Jacob wrestling at the
river Jabbok (Gen. 32), and do not let it go until it has a chance to
bless you.[38]

QUESTIONS FOR DISCUSSION
AND REFLECTION

Is there any biblical text you would reject? What are some of the
biblical texts that have most troubled you—ones you might describe
as "tyrannical" or "oppressive" or "texts of terror" in your own
experience?

What do you think of the five recommendations for wrestling with
tyrannical texts presented in this chapter? Which do you find
the most challenging, and why? How might these recommendations inform your engagement with the texts that most trouble
you?

Which do you find more difficult: exercising charity or generosity
toward the text—or toward those who interpret it differently?
Why?

What has been your earlier experience with 1 Timothy 2:8–15? In
what contexts have you encountered it? Has it impacted your
experience? If so, how?

What strikes you most about 1 Timothy 2:8–15? What questions
does it raise for you?

What new insights about 1 Timothy 2:8–15 have emerged from your engagement with this chapter? Why are they important to you? What questions linger?

What questions would you like to ask the author of 1 Timothy 2:8–15—or the women and men who were first addressed by these words? What questions would you like to ask those who interpret it differently than do you?

Would you be inclined to preach or teach on 1 Timothy 2:8–15? Why, or why not?

Share your reactions to Rowan Williams's striking observations quoted above. What insights emerge? What questions do they raise for you?

2

Wives, Be Subject?
Articulating Biblical Authority

Ephesians 5:21–33

I have been keeping company with biblical texts that raise my blood pressure. So in the first chapter I recommended five things that are proving helpful in my own effort to stay in conversation with them—five things that increasingly seem incumbent upon me as one who claims to honor Scripture, to take the Bible seriously as an authoritative guide for Christian faith and practice. To recap: *Recommendation 1* was remember that "the difficult text is worthy of charity," of generosity, from its interpreters. *Recommendation 2:* Argue with the text, confident that wrestling with Scripture is an act of faithfulness. *Recommendation 3:* Resist the temptation to throw the baby out with the bathwater! *Recommendation 4:* Learn from the dangers as well as the insights that biblical texts present. And *Recommendation 5:* If you are practicing the discipline of charity or generosity toward the text, listening patiently and carefully to it, arguing with it, being instructed by both the dangers and insights it presents—then don't let anyone tell you that you are not taking the authority of the Bible seriously! In fact, one of the most helpful things about wrestling with problematic texts is that they force us to articulate clearly how we understand the nature and authority of Scripture. When we avoid such texts, we deprive ourselves, and our congregations, of the opportunity to think through, and to think deeply about, our relationship with the Bible and how God is present in our engagement with it. In other words, we miss opportunities to grow in understanding, to mature in faith.

So I was thrilled when I received a wonderfully honest letter from a bright seminarian, attached to her weekly reflection paper, in which she conveyed the genuine angst she was experiencing in my classroom as texts she had long held to be authoritative began to collide with feminist interpretations and her own feminist convictions.

Dear Frances:

I am writing to say that I hate the Bible, and you and your Christian feminist colleagues are driving me nuts. Truthfully, though, my issues aren't with you all. In fact, I really appreciate feminism's contributions to biblical interpretation. My problem is [that] deep down I want to be a Christian feminist too. I really, really want to like the Bible, but I just can't figure out how to do it. To me, being a Bible-toting woman feels the same as an African American flying a Confederate flag or a Jewish person supporting the Third Reich. While the causes may have had some higher purpose like states' rights or national advancement, a person really can't ignore the fact that they also advocated the destruction, or at least oppression, of entire groups of people. How can women call attention to all the grievances found in Scripture . . . but then still espouse the importance of Christianity?[1]

These are very important questions with which members of our congregations may also be wrestling. And given the existential investment in them, it is an opportunity to help people think deeply about their understanding of the nature and authority of Scripture and how they live out their relationship with it. What does the authority of Scripture mean? Does it mean complete truthfulness and accuracy in all it teaches, to which I am to submit without question? Or something else? What does it mean to affirm the Bible as both divine word and human word? And is obedience to it an all-or-nothing proposition? Can we wrestle with Scripture, question it, argue with it? What does it mean to call the Bible "holy"? How do we read it faithfully? And what is the role of the community in discerning in Scripture a word to us from God?

ARTICULATING BIBLICAL AUTHORITY

Tyrannical texts, more than any others, force us to grapple with such questions; so, for the sake of discussion, let me articulate some of my own assumptions in hopes that whether you agree with them or not, they will help you clarify your own thoughts. Perhaps it is important to start with a very basic one, in case anyone is wondering: I do take the authority of the Bible very seriously! (But then, one rarely meets a Christian who would say that they do not! As John Burgess tellingly observes, "Presbyterians are better at asserting the authority of Scripture than at actually opening the Bible"[2]—and the same no doubt holds true for more than a few Lutherans, Methodists, Episcopalians, and others.) But since varied notions of the nature and authority of Scripture coexist under my own denominational roof, let me try to clarify my own.

I suspect it is already clear that I do not adhere to a monological notion of biblical authority along the lines summarized by the bumper sticker that reads, "God said it, I believe it, that settles it." This sentiment reflects what is called a propositional notion of revelation,[3] which holds the Bible to be a repository of divinely dictated propositions—true assertions and moral absolutes. Those who incline toward this view sometimes describe the Bible's human authors as "infallible" (they recorded exactly what God wanted to say to us) and the propositions they transcribed as "inerrant" (how could it be otherwise, given the Bible's miraculous origin?). And there is, to be sure, only one way to respond to a package of divinely revealed propositional certitudes: what else can one do but assent!

However, I do not believe that the Bible was divinely dictated or faxed from heaven, but rather that it is every bit as fully, thoroughly human as was Jesus himself—and I am not inclined to make of Scripture something more supernatural and timeless than God's own self-revelation in Christ.[4] Thus I affirm, with the Confession of 1967 (included in *The Book of Confessions* of the Presbyterian Church [U.S.A.]), that "The Scriptures, given under the guidance of the Holy Spirit, are nevertheless the words of men, conditioned by the language, thought forms, and literary fashions of the places and times at which they were written" and that they "reflect views of life, history, and the cosmos which were then current."[5] Yet I also affirm that, through the power of the Holy Spirit, this fully human text is a privileged mediator of our encounter with God, and that our engagement with it is part of God's own work in us, forming the mind of Jesus Christ in us.[6]

So I incline toward a more dialogical, relational understanding of revelation in Scripture, rather than a monological, propositional one.[7] The Bible *is* a revelatory text in my view, not in the sense that it contains divinely revealed propositional certitudes, but because it has a unique capacity to draw us into the living presence of God—even when we find ourselves wrestling both with and against its claims. It mediates an encounter with God that discloses, not propositions, but God's very self, inviting us to share in God's own life and in its projected vision of the world as God's creation. The proper response to this invitation is not assent to propositions or doctrines but openness to this encounter and a willingness to imagine the world in a different way, in light of God's plans and purposes.

Perhaps this is why John Calvin spoke of the Bible as the "lens of faith,"[8] likening it to a pair of spectacles by which we are enabled to see the world with clearer vision as God's creation—a pair of eyeglasses that "brings focus and clarity to all aspects of our lives" and "lets us see what we otherwise would not."[9] It is the best image of biblical authority I know. It is worth noting that we do not look *at* spectacles, but *through* them.[10] And once we have them on, "there is nothing, absolutely nothing, that escapes their vision-framing power."[11]

What I have been wrestling with, then, is that at some points we may find that the spectacles are shortsighted. How could it be otherwise if the Bible was produced by real people in remote times and places under certain historical circumstances, who said what those circumstances permitted them to speak? To return to Rowan Williams's compelling point, noted in chapter 1 (above), "Here in scripture is God's urgency to communicate; here in scripture is our mishearing, our misappropriating, our deafness, and our resistance. Woven together in scripture are those two things, the giving of God and our inability to receive what God wants to give. . . . The gift of God, the liberty of God, is passed through the distorting glass of our own fears."[12]

First Timothy 2, I've had to conclude, is one such point at which the lens of faith is distorted, marked by the shortsighted perspective of its author as he tackled predicaments before him. I no longer advocate throwing it out, for not only does it preserve important pieces of our family history that would otherwise be lost to us; it also is not without insight—and I hope that in the first chapter I managed to retrieve a few insights. But the dangers it presents may prove especially instructive for us: its witness to painfully imperfect efforts to embody the gospel; and its sobering warning to us of dangerous temptations the church faces in every age to silence dissident voices among us or to sacrifice the good of some of our members for the sake of our reputation or mission. The text exercises authority by prompting us to reflect on these things, by providing an opportunity to learn about our checkered ecclesial history and to imagine how we might challenge injustice and faithfully embody the gospel in our time and place.[13]

The judgment that a text may be shortsighted, that it may represent a misunderstanding or even betrayal of the gospel, ought not to be a cavalier judgment or a solo one, but one that emerges from communal dialogue and discernment that is authorized by Scripture itself in several respects. For one thing, the Bible itself, with its multitude of voices, embodies "a sacred conversation between God and humanity, and a sacred conversation among believers about God, God's will, and what it means to be God's people."[14] As we have already had occasion to note, "There is not [just] one voice in Scripture, and to give any one voice in Scripture or in tradition authority to silence other voices surely distorts the text."[15] The Bible argues with itself in many instances. Voices with contrary opinions beg to be heard, which is why a classic principle of biblical interpretation is that we are to interpret Scripture by Scripture: the entire biblical canon is the context for understanding the fullness of Christian faith and life. So 1 Timothy 2 has a right to be heard, but its insistence that women should not teach or have authority over men, that they should keep silent and earn salvation by bearing children, needs to be placed in conversation with the presentation in Acts of Priscilla's authoritative instruction of Apollos (Acts 18:26) or with Paul's odd discussion of appropriate headgear for women when they are in fact praying and prophesying publicly in worship (1 Cor. 11:2–16), as well as his insistence on justification by grace through faith alone (Rom. 3:21–31; 5:1; 10:10). When 1 Timothy 2 is up for discussion, Galatians 3:28 usually gets tossed into the ring to complicate things, for how do you square 1 Timothy's insistence on women's subordination with the affirmation "There is no longer Jew or Greek, there is no longer slave or free, there is no longer male and female; for all of you are one in Christ Jesus"? The Bible itself resists any monological notion of authority given its multitude of voices. And because its witness is multivocal and multivalent, it requires faithful struggle on our part to hear and discern.

But listening is not all that is required. The ancient voices that speak in Scripture evoke an ongoing dialogue that requires our active participation. Their sacred conversation about life in God's presence begs to be continued among believers today, for the fact of the matter is, the Bible is not self-interpreting. It is a living word through which

God continues to meet us and speak to us in our own particular historical moment, and thus it demands to be newly interpreted for new historical situations. And interpretation is not simply reiteration of the text, repeating what was said before, but the hard work of bringing it into our own time and place. So every new generation of believers must join the interpretive conversation as it experiences the living God in relation to new circumstances.[16]

That interpretive conversation takes place in and with Christian communities that have themselves been formed and shaped by their engagement with Scripture in such a way that they may find themselves required to critique the biblical heritage at certain points. For, as Sandra Schneiders contends, a text, once fixed to the page, is cut loose from its author and can transcend its own psycho-sociological conditions of production. Indeed, a text creates a world that it projects in front of itself, and there is always the possibility of the text's exploding the very world out of which it came. Schneiders finds a compelling analogy in the American Declaration of Independence, another foundational document that formed, and continues to shape, our national identity and life. As she explains, a written text generates a history that qualifies and transforms its meaning, and a clear example of this is the gradual expansion of the meaning of the affirmation that "all men are created equal." We can be fairly certain that our founding fathers did not have women, slaves, or children in mind when they penned those words. Nor were they thinking of Native Americans, immigrants, the physically challenged, or the poor. But as Schneiders observes, the text "generated an historical experience in the new nation that gradually revealed to Americans the humanity and therefore the equal rights of all people." It produced a people finally capable of seeing that slavery, to mention but one example, was incompatible with the world of freedom and equality that the founding documents themselves projected. Thus "the text was susceptible of reinterpretation" as the world projected by the text "literally exploded the patriarchal world of its authors."[17]

"In much the same way," Schneiders observes, "the biblical text must develop. The meaning of the New Testament is not limited to the meaning intended by its authors. Nor are Christian believers of the twentieth century faith-clones of their first-century forebears."[18] The Bible has shaped and expanded our own historical consciousness, and over the course of twenty centuries it has generated an understanding of discipleship much richer than its authors imagined. We bring both to our practice of biblical interpretation, which involves engagement not only with the question "What does the text say?" but also with the question "What is the meaning of the text for the believing community?" And "part of that meaning," Schneiders contends, "may be that some of the beliefs held and positions taken by the community in the course of its history are untrue or immoral, a judgment based precisely on what the community has discerned through its formation *by this text*."[19]

If this contention initially strikes you as outlandish, it should not upon a moment's reflection. To give but one example: when mainline denominations finally decided (after endless decades of collective discernment) to lift prohibitions on the ordination of women, did they do so in violation of Scripture? Did they decide to ignore Scripture? Were they throwing Scripture out? No! It was precisely *because* of Scripture's witness that a new collective judgment emerged that the Holy Spirit calls both women and men to all ministries of the church—and that they had erred in restricting women's leadership. It was Scripture itself that reformed the church, projecting a vision of male and female as equally created in God's image, and claiming that in Christ "there is no longer male and female" (Gal. 3:28). Thus, in obedience to what they discerned as the broader, more fundamental witness of Scripture, many denominations reversed themselves on the question of women's ordination.

Scripture itself, by the power of God's Spirit, continues to form and reform us, shaping our vision of the world and guiding us to new understandings of what God is calling us to be and do. This is why Presbyterians and other Reformed Christians take as their motto the ancient words "church reformed, always reforming" (*Ecclesia reformata, semper reformanda*)—a motto that is better and more fully translated as, "The church reformed, always to be reformed according to the Word of God" in the power of the Spirit (*Ecclesia reformata, semper reformanda secundum verbum Dei*).[20] This important point—that Scripture itself continues to form and reform the church—too often fails to be appreciated in the midst of ecclesial debates over contentious issues, whenever one "side" claims faithfulness to Scripture and declares that the "other side" has abandoned it—when in fact there may well be a biblical logic and integrity to an opponent's point of view!

Now if you believe that the Bible was divinely dictated, verbally inspired, you might be hard pressed to make or accept the claim that formation by Scripture may require us to critique the biblical heritage (for example, a text like 1 Tim. 2) at certain points. But if you believe that the Bible was produced by real people in remote times and places under certain historical circumstances, people who said what those circumstances allowed them to speak, you are less likely to suffer an existential crisis over biblical authority: you can roll with the punches. For despite the shortsightedness of the biblical spectacles at some points, Scripture, by the power of the Holy Spirit, continues to bring us into the living presence of God and to shape our vision of the world in light of God's plans and purposes. I've always appreciated Letty Russell's eloquent testimony to this fact:

> In spite of the patriarchal nature of the biblical texts, I myself have no intention of giving up the biblical basis of my theology. The Bible has authority in my life because it makes sense of my experience and speaks to me about the meaning and purpose of my humanity in Jesus Christ. In spite of its ancient and patriarchal worldviews, in spite of its inconsistencies and mixed messages, the story of God's love affair with the world leads me to a vision of New Creation that impels my life.[21]

What I have been trying to emphasize is that wrestling even with the mixed messages, the shortsightedness of a biblical text, can draw us more deeply into the living presence of God, for errors, when acknowledged, are indispensable to learning and can play a role in the Bible's formation of the mind of Jesus Christ in us. As Schneiders has observed, human relationships can grow through misunderstanding and struggle and even infidelity and betrayal, and so can our relationship with God through honest wrestling and confrontation with oppressive dimensions of Scripture.[22] And I contend that when we accept the Bible, with all its inconsistencies and ambiguities and mixed messages, as the world in which we live, being instructed by both the dangers and insights it presents—when we stay in critical, discerning conversation with it, always taking it into account—then it really cannot be said that we are not taking the authority of the Bible seriously!

LISTENING TO EPHESIANS 5

So for all of these reasons, I have arrived at a point in my relationship with the Bible at which I no longer perform radical surgery on the canon. Even a text like Ephesians 5, which I first tackled with scissors in hand, now stands undefiled in my NRSV. Indeed, I am now of the opinion that we should never throw anything out, since we can be instructed by the dangers as well as the insights that biblical texts present; we can grow into deeper relationship with God as we wrestle with them. Moreover, new historical contexts may produce new insights about biblical texts that earlier generations were not in a position to see. As Phyllis Trible sagely observes, you never know when a text you consider a curse may prove to be a blessing to someone else or in another setting.[23] So I direct your attention to Ephesians 5 as a second test case and briefly highlight some of the ways in which my relationship with it has been undergoing rehabilitation. As you read it, listen for what the Spirit is saying to the church:

EPHESIANS 5:21–33

[21]Be subject to one another out of reverence [lit., fear] for Christ.

[22]Wives, be subject to your husbands as you are to the Lord. [23]For the husband is the head of the wife just as Christ is the head of the church, the body of which he is the Savior. [24]Just as the church is subject to Christ, so also wives ought to be, in everything, to their husbands.

[25]Husbands, love your wives, just as Christ loved the church and gave himself up for her, [26]in order to make her holy by cleansing her with the washing of water by the word, [27]so as to present the church to himself in splendor, without a spot or wrinkle or anything of the kind—yes, so that she may be holy and without blemish. [28]In the same way, husbands should love their wives as they do their own bodies. He who loves his wife loves himself. [29]For no one ever hates his own body, but he nourishes and tenderly cares for it, just as Christ does for the church, [30]because we are members of his body. [31]"For this reason a man will leave his father and mother and be joined to his wife, and the two will become one flesh." [32]This is a great mystery, and I am applying it to Christ and the church. [33]Each of you, however, should love his wife as himself, and a wife should respect [lit., fear] her husband.

I used to take comfort in my conviction that the apostle Paul did not write this text—that someone who was as much of an advocate for the freedom and equality of all people in Christ as he was would surely have been horrified by it and might even have approved of my own surgical inclinations. Many do seem to take the text's pseudonymity as license to dismiss it. But as we have already had occasion to note, this is really no solution to the problems the text presents, for whoever wrote it, it is still in the canon. And though I continue to believe that Paul is not the author of Ephesians 5, I am not as convinced as I once was that the household codes we find in the deuteropauline epistles are entirely inconsistent with Paul's own letters, which at points do reflect genuine ambiguity on his part about social conventions related to women (as we will see in later chapters). But I do think the author of Ephesians, whoever he may have been, sought to bring Paul's legacy to bear in challenging new situations that Paul himself could not have foreseen and did not face, and I am now persuaded that *the text is worthy of a measure of charity from its interpreters*—worthy of generosity (Recommendation 1 in chap. 1 above). It deserves our willingness to try to imagine what may have occasioned it and to contend with the difficulties it presents.

After much study, we still find it hard to say for sure why the authors of deuteropauline epistles felt compelled to include household codes in their ethical instruction and why the author of Ephesians, in particular, felt compelled to provide such theologically elaborate instructions for husbands and wives. The text reveals little about its social setting or circumstances, and its function is a matter of scholarly debate. But most of the proposed scenarios warrant perhaps a measure of empathy. Some contend that the codes grapple with the delay of the Parousia. Paul, after all, had anticipated Christ's imminent return, convinced that the structures of this world were on their way out. But by the end of the first century, the churches he left behind must have realized that they were going to be around much longer than Paul had expected. And how were they to live as Christians in a world that was not quickly passing away? Some would say this is why we find household codes in later New Testament epistles (Col. 3:18–4:1; Eph. 5:21–6:9; 1 Pet. 2:18–3:7), which begin to address this challenge by suggesting very concretely how Christians are to be faithful to the gospel in the midst of ongoing social responsibilities and by directing Christians to live within the social structures of the world and there to express love and obedience.

Others suspect that the author of Ephesians may be countering ascetic currents in early Christianity, perceiving a need to extol the institution of marriage in the face of its denigration, for Paul was not alone among early Christians in viewing celibacy as the Christian ideal and marriage as a second-best alternative. Indeed, the New Testament's household codes may have been, in part, "a conservative response to the empowerment of women through celibacy in Pauline churches."[24] Or perhaps a more defensive strategy was at work: the need to counter suspicion that the early church was socially disruptive by putting traditional family values on display.[25] Or maybe marriage was particularly well suited to serve the author's ecclesiological emphasis on Christian unity, providing the perfect example of the mutual submission required for harmony in the church as well as the home.[26]

We cannot know for sure. Nor do we know how the text related to the actual lives of those it first addressed, for Ephesians 5, like 1 Timothy 2, is prescriptive rather than descriptive in nature, which is to say that the author articulates his perception of an ideal that may not be realized, one perhaps with little correspondence to their lives. Among those addressed were surely persons who were married to non-Christians, divorced or widowed, and slaves, along with women who may not have been at all inclined toward gracious submission.

So what are desperate housewives and desperate preachers to do with such a text? Deal with it we must, for in many respects Ephesians 5 has had an even more tyrannical impact on the lives of Christian women than 1 Timothy 2. It is, after all, the most fully developed argument for gender hierarchy in the New Testament, making its case in consistently theological terms,[27] and we ought not to ignore or whitewash the problems it presents. Indeed, two prominent whitewashing strategies in particular are best avoided. I, for one, would not want to argue, as many have done, that the emphasis on mutual submission in verse 21 exonerates the text, either mitigating or critiquing everything that follows, for there is a decidedly lopsided development in the ensuing admonitions to subordination. Another avenue of speculation also is best avoided, here as in 1 Timothy 2: we should not assume that the New Testament household codes represent great advances for women over their supposedly miserable lot in Greco-Roman society or Judaism. As Sarah Tanzer has observed, interpreters are far too often inclined to exonerate difficult texts by drawing negative comparisons so that they "will be seen as less ugly (or perhaps even innovative) by contrast."[28] When in fact, as she notices, Ephesians 5 and other New Testament household codes reflect views of women that now appear to have been outmoded in their own time, already perceived as "dusty" and "reactionary."[29]

DIALOGUE WITH THE TEXT

So what do we do with Ephesians 5? My advice, once again, is to argue with the text (Recommendation 2), while striving not to throw the baby out with the bathwater (Recommendation 3), and to be instructed by both the dangers and insights it presents (Recommendation 4). In connection with Ephesians 5, Recommendation 3, "Don't throw the baby out with the bathwater," is perhaps the most challenging one—it is, at least, for me! So when faced with a tyrannical text, I find it a helpful exercise to ask myself and others, "Is there anything nice we can say about it?" It is so much easier to identify the problems, the things that outrage us. So let me try to say something nice, albeit through clenched teeth.

Speaking for myself, by no means do I find myself endeared to Ephesians 5, but I can now admit that it deserves at least a grudging measure of my respect. For one thing, I can appreciate the effort to discern how Christian faith shapes life at its most intimate and critical points, as well as its emphasis on using our relationship with the Lord as a means of discerning how we are to treat others. And I can acknowledge the author's genuine efforts to reframe marriage within the context of Christ's lordship. I appreciate the fact that Christian husbands, at least, who are on the receiving end of the bulk of the exhortations, are admonished, three times, to *love* rather than to dominate their wives: "*love her*" (v. 25), "*love her*" (v. 28), "*love her*" (v. 33). And they are to make no mistake about what that means. Love is more than that emotion extolled in Hallmark-speak as "the feeling you feel when you feel you're going to feel a feeling you've never felt before." Love, for the author of Ephesians, is defined by Jesus Christ and through the lens of the cross. Thus husbands are specifically directed to love their wives, "*as Christ loved the church and gave himself up for her*" (v. 25), which is to say that the husband must spare nothing, not even his own life if need be, in concern and care for his wife. Moreover, I can appreciate that the author urges Christian husbands not to stand on their secular prerogatives but to join their wives in mutual submission one to the other out of reverence for Christ (v. 21). Finally, no more elevated, positive description of marriage is found in all of Christian literature than at the end of Ephesians 5, where the author, grasping at metaphors, suggests that the mystery at the heart of marriage is profound—even mirroring the very mystery of the love that exists between Christ and the church. It is an improvement over Paul's take on marriage in 1 Corinthians as a means of sexual containment: "better to marry than to burn" (1 Cor. 7:9 KJV), hardly a ringing endorsement. Ephesians, by contrast, provides a joyful affirmation of marriage; indeed, a qualitatively new perception of it as a union that participates in, and reflects, the reality of grace.[30]

Nevertheless, let me hasten to assure you that Ephesians 5 was not read at my wedding! Yes, it does now command a grudging measure of my respect, but not my affection. How could it, when it continues to provide countless people with theological legitimation for a first-century patriarchal pattern of wifely subordination? After all, it cannot be said that the relation between Christ and the church, which the author uses to provide a parallel to marriage, is a relationship between equals. As the church is subordinate to Christ, so (according to the author) is the wife called to be subordinate to her husband—"*in every-thing*" (v. 24). Neither can it be said that the text addresses the husband and wife as equals, for while the Christian husband is addressed in terms of love, the Christian wife is addressed in terms of respect (lit., fear, *phobeō*) and submission. The author, to be sure, endeavors to reframe marriage within the context of Christian faith, but the first-century cultural pattern remains reflected in the text, combined now with a theology of Christ and the church and thereby theologically legitimated.

Moreover, Ephesians 5, perhaps more than any other text in the Bible, has proved to be hazardous to women's health. Those who minister among battered persons bear witness that it is "a very difficult passage for abused women struggling to find self-respect and some control over their lives."[31] When the author advised Christian women to be subject to their husbands, he was by no means exhorting their subjection to physical violence. But the marriage metaphor for the divine-human relationship, wherever it appears in Scripture, has proved to have enormous potential for abuse, lending itself to divinization of men and justifying male impunity in the face of female fallibility. This text in particular has been widely interpreted in ways that have made many Christian women more susceptible to violence, and it has heightened the likelihood that battered women will remain in abusive relationships longer than they should. In addition, the text has wreaked cross-cultural havoc, for Christian women around the globe attest how often it has been used to reinforce existing patterns of subjection and domination.

For all of these reasons, it behooves us to stay engaged with this text, to wrestle with it publicly, and to be part of the conversations it evokes rather than relinquish our opportunity—and our responsibility, I think—to make a contribution to it. A lot of people out there *are* talking about this text, rather loudly, and if we dismiss it, if we are not engaging it seriously, we are not likely to be heard or to make any impact on conversation about a text that continues to circumscribe the lives of women to this day. Writing out of her experience of Bible study with battered women, Susan Thistlethwaite contends that for those who care about violence committed against women and children in their own homes, there really is no substitute for learning and teaching alternative interpretations of Ephesians 5 and similar texts. Because for many women (especially those who self-describe as conservative or evangelical), "no authority *except* that of the Bible itself can challenge the image contained in these texts of woman as silent, subordinate, . . . and subject to the absolute authority of her husband." They need opportunities, she says, to "learn that the scriptures are much more on their side than they dared hope."[32] Virginia Mollenkott, recalling her own years as a fundamentalist wife in a dysfunctional marriage, says, "I was not able to trust anyone who told me to flout Scripture."[33] She says what *would* have been helpful, though, was encouragement "to notice the limitations placed on the metaphor of husband-as-Christ (that the husband is compared to Christ *only in Christ's self-giving, self-humbling capacity*)." What *would* have been helpful was assurance that "a domineering and abusive husband had already violated Ephesians 5"—that the demands of such a husband were inconsistent with Christ's lordship.[34]

But wouldn't it be helpful if all the folks in our pews, not only the battered ones, had opportunities to hear preachers and teachers wrestle publicly with tyrannical texts, with both the dangers and insights they present—and invitations to do the same, assured that wrestling with Scripture, even arguing with it, is an act of commitment to this holy book—indeed, an act of faithfulness? And there is plenty to argue with in Ephesians 5. I, for one, would want to argue that verse 21, "Be subject to one another, out of reverence for Christ," is a stunning ideal, an audacious claim, for the whole community of faith, but one that is not applied to its full potential, for only wives are singled out for address with explicit language of submission in the ensuing marital admonitions.

I would also want to question Ephesians's construal of Christ's lordship in hierarchical terms,[35] inviting interpretation of Scripture by Scripture, for did not Jesus, in the Gospels, tell his own disciples, in no uncertain terms, that they were *not* to model their relations of authority on those of the world at large—on rulers of the world who "lord it over" others and "are tyrants over them"? "It is not so among you," he said, "but whoever wishes to become great among you must be your servant, and whoever wishes to be first among you must be slave of all. For the Son of Man came not to be served but to serve, and to give his life a ransom for many" (Mark 10:42–45). Moreover, Jesus does not seem to have regarded love as a guy-thing and submission as a woman-thing,[36] for when he washed their feet on the night before his death (John 13), did he not demonstrate that love and subordination go hand in hand?

Most important of all, I want to consider interpreting Ephesians by Ephesians, for elsewhere in this epistle it appears that practices of subordination and love are binding on all members of Christ's body, male and female (4:1–3, 5, 15–16; 5:1–2). And then, of course, there is the greatest irony of all, nailed so compellingly by Sarah Tanzer: in eloquent terms the early chapters of Ephesians celebrate a new kind of equality, through Christ, of Jew and Gentile believers, proclaiming Christ as "our peace," who has "broken down the dividing wall, . . . the hostility between us." But the exhortations that follow in Ephesians 5–6 are clearly not about equals but about hierarchy—exhortations, as Tanzer recognizes, that do not break down dividing walls but rather establish them and teach one to live within them in the name of Christian unity.[37] This tension, this ironic inconsistency, like marriage, is a great mystery worth pondering! Indeed, could one not conclude, with Ian McFarland, that in important respects "Ephesians 5 can be read as testimony to the author's failure to interpret the lordship of Christ aright"[38]?

If so, we can surely be instructed by both the dangers and the insights that Ephesians 5 presents, for we too must discern what Christ's lordship means for the way we live in our time and place. That is why I now maintain that Ephesians 5 has a place in the canon and in fact a word for us today—whether we are single or married, male or female, straight or gay. For wherever we live and work, whatever our circumstances might be, Ephesians 5 reminds us that Christ's lordship does impact the structures of our lives. Many of us, for example, have families, whether we live under the same roof with them or not, and sometimes we share the sentiment of the cynic who said, "God gives us our relatives—thank God we can choose our friends." We all know that life together in families is not always easy, for there are no perfect parents, no perfect partners, no perfect children, no perfect in-laws. I must say, though, that I did find the perfect greeting card to send my mother this past Mother's Day: "I was hungry, and you gave me food; I was naked, and you gave me clothing; I was sick, and you took care of me; . . . I was a real jerk, and you didn't knocketh my block off." Who would deny it: life together in families stretches and strains us, and it is one of the best chances God gives us to grow out of ourselves and into something more nearly like that which we were meant to be. So, like the first generation of Christians, we too try to discern the ways in which Christian faith shapes and transforms our lives at this most intimate and critical point—how within our relationships with our partners, our parents, our children, and our siblings we can best love one another, forgive one another, and live in service to one another after the manner of Christ.

For believers, that discernment also includes life together in Christian congregations, which can be places where we realize that Jesus' commandment to *love one another*—to love those *within* the Christian community—is perhaps one of the most difficult things he asks us to do. Sometimes we empathize with the little girl who was asked by her Sunday school teacher if she wanted to go to heaven, and she replied, "Not if all these people are going to be there!" As Gail O'Day has astutely observed, "There are many circumstances in which it is easier to love one's *enemies* than it is to love those with whom we live, work, and worship day after day."[39] But sometimes, despite ourselves, are we not also reminded of the power of Jesus Christ to transform our life together in Christian community—as we are enabled to be gracious to each other, to forgive one another, to forebear with each other—to really listen and disagree in love, and to embrace our differences, our diversity, as a gift?

For all of these reasons, I urge you not to run for your scissors, and I have put away my own. To be sure, Ephesians 5 has had an unfortunate life and history of its own, and I still don't like it. But I trust that we can continue to be instructed by the underlying concerns and commitments it reveals. After all, as we come before this text, it *is* the new community that we see envisioned here, however imperfectly, engaged in acts of discernment that we continue in our time and place, also imperfectly.[40] We see faith being enacted in love and love seeking to effect its transforming power in the midst of this age. We see genuine, if halting, efforts to reform the structures of life together in the light of

Christ's all-inclusive love—inclusive efforts in which we too persevere as "a church reformed and always being reformed according to the Word of God" (though sometimes haltingly as well) as we continue on our way. This text reminds us that the God made known to us in Jesus Christ, through Scripture and the calling of the Spirit, continues to transform the structures before us, enabling discernment of ways in which we can serve one another in this time and place. Indeed, wrestling with and against this text is part of God's work in us, forming the mind of Jesus Christ in us. And for that mercy we may rejoice, knowing that neither sin, nor death, nor institutions, nor structures, nor any aspect of our lives together can escape the transforming power and riches of God's love for us in Christ.

QUESTIONS FOR DISCUSSION AND REFLECTION

What image would you use to describe the role Scripture plays in your own life? How would you articulate your own understanding of biblical authority?

What new insights or questions emerged from the discussion of biblical authority in this chapter?

What do you think of the contention that our formation by Scripture may require us to critique the biblical heritage at certain points?

What has been your prior experience with Ephesians 5:21–33? In what contexts have you encountered it? Has it impacted your experience? If so, how?

What strikes you most about Ephesians 5:21–33? What questions does it raise for you?

What new insights about Ephesians 5:21–33 have emerged from your engagement with this chapter, and why are they important to you? What questions linger?

What questions would you like to ask the author of Ephesians 5:21–33—or the women and men who were first addressed by these words?

What questions would you like to ask interpreters of Ephesians 5:21–33 who insist on "gracious submission" of wives to husbands? Clarice Martin has posed a perceptive question to her own black church tradition about interpretive inconsistency when it comes to biblical household codes, which promote the submission not only of women but also of slaves: "How can black male preachers and theologians use a liberated hermeneutic when preaching and theologizing about slavery, but a literalist herme-neutic with reference to women?"[41] Is this question relevant to the life of your own church tradition or others with which you are familiar? What accounts for interpretive inconsistency in readings of household codes, in your view?

Would you be inclined to preach or teach on Ephesians 5:21–33? Why, or why not? Would you recommend the reading of it at a wedding? Why, or why not?

3

Women and Worship Wars (I)

1 Corinthians 11:2–16

The apostle Paul is rightly celebrated for his theological profundity and rhetorical skill, but evidently he had days when he was off his game. The vexing text before us in this chapter represents one such moment, for its logic is routinely described by commentators as "tortured," "cryptic," "convoluted," "contorted," "inarticulate," "inconsistent," "incoherent," and "incomprehensible." Indeed, as Jouette Bassler has declared, "Paul's comments in these verses are as obscure as any he makes."[1] Nonetheless, as one of the lengthiest discussions of gender in the New Testament, it has garnered inordinate attention, and interpretations of it continue to have significant repercussions, shaping understandings of gender distinctions and roles within both church and home in ways that circumscribe the lives of many women to this day. Thus, avoidance and dismissal are irresponsible options when faced with such a text. It demands engagement, and it requires of us a special measure of patience and charity—a willingness to contend with its considerable difficulties. Given its length and complexity, it will also require a considerably longer discussion than other texts featured in this volume. So gird up your loins and listen to what the Spirit is saying to the church!

1 CORINTHIANS 11:2–16[2]

[2]I commend you because you remember me in everything and maintain the traditions just as I handed them on to you. [3]But I want you to understand that Christ is the head of every man, and man is the head of woman, and God is the head of Christ. [4]Any man who prays or prophesies with something on his head disgraces his head, [5]but any woman who prays or prophesies with her head uncovered disgraces her head—it is one and the same thing as having her head shaved. [6]For if a woman will not cover her head, then she should cut off her hair; but if it is disgraceful for a woman to have her hair cut off or to be shaved, she should cover her head. [7]For a man ought not to cover his head, since he is the image and glory of God; but woman is the glory of man. [8]Indeed, man was not made from woman, but woman from man. [9]Neither was man created for the sake of woman, but woman for the sake of man. [10]For this reason a woman ought to have authority over her head, because of the angels. [11]Nevertheless, in the Lord woman is not independent of man or man independent of woman. [12]For just as woman came from man, so man comes through woman; but all things come from God. [13]Judge for yourselves: is it proper for a woman to pray to God with her head uncovered? [14]Does not nature itself teach you that if a man wears long hair, it is degrading to him, [15]but if a woman has long hair, it is her glory? For her hair is given to her for a covering. [16]But if anyone is disposed to be contentious—we have no such custom, nor do the churches of God.

As you no doubt surmise, wrestling with this particular text entails engagement with daunting interpretive problems; but it also provides opportunities once again to eavesdrop on a fascinating family argument among our forebears in the faith. And as we listen to it, Paul's is not the only voice we hear. His is, to be sure, the predominant, canonical voice to which we have direct access, but there is no doubt that he is in the midst of a conversation—indeed, lively and ongoing correspondence. There was a great deal of letter traffic between Paul and the church he founded in Corinth. Although the New Testament epistles of 1 and 2 Corinthians are all that survives of it, they reflect a sequence of written and oral reports, visits, and delegations, back and forth, between Paul and this congregation (cf. 1 Cor. 1:11; 4:17; 5:1, 9; 11:18; 16:10–11; 2 Cor. 1:23–2:4; 7:5–11; 13:1). In fact, 1 Corinthians is the most dialogical of all Paul's letters, structured around answering questions the Corinthians posed to him (cf. 7:1, 25; 8:1; 12:1; 16:1, 5, 10). So if we listen closely, we can discern echoes of the voices, questions, and concerns of Corinthian Christians, engaged with Paul and each other in earnest debate—in the case of 1 Corinthians 11:2–16, over ecclesial attire. We ought not to trivialize this concern, given the social and symbolic significance that clothing bears in all times and places (not to mention the inordinate amount of time, attention, and expense sartorial concerns occupy in our own culture and lives). But after engaging 1 Timothy 2 (with its elaborate dress code, detailing expectations regarding female apparel, coiffure, and jewelry) and Ephesians 5 (with its attention to cosmetic ablutions required to ensure a spotless, unwrinkled, and unblemished bride of Christ), we are entitled to exasperation that questions and concerns regarding appearance and fashion, in both the biblical world and the contemporary one, bear disproportionately on the lives of women!

In Corinth, these concerns emerged after Paul's departure and centered on expectations related to a particular item of apparel, in the context of a particular role and a particular setting: head coverings worn by women (and, ostensibly, men) exercising leadership during worship assemblies. A striking feature of the conversation about this matter should not escape our attention: the entire discussion is predicated on the assumption, shared by Paul and the Corinthian Christians, that women *do* in fact exercise leadership in worship, engaging in ministries of prayer and prophecy—along with men. Both prayer and prophecy were modes of Spirit-inspired speech within the worshiping assembly. Prayer entailed articulating the community's speech to God, while prophecy entailed articulating God's will for the community, to meet needs within it for edification, encouragement, consolation, learning, guidance, and direction (1 Cor. 14:3, 31). (As in the Old Testament, prophecy was not simply a matter of predicting the future but rather of declaring God's will, speaking on behalf of God to a particular situation of need in the present.)[3] Corinthian women clearly exercised both leadership roles in worship, speaking to and from God on behalf of the congregation. The question that emerged had to do with whether or not their heads needed to be covered when they did so.

In recent years, scholars have debated whether hairstyles, rather than headwear, might be in view, since the language of the text is not entirely clear on this point. Ancient commentators understood Paul to be referring to head coverings,[4] as do most contemporary ones; but some now maintain that hairstyles, explicitly referenced near the end of the text in 11:13–15, may be the issue in earlier verses too. In those latter verses, a woman's hair is described as a "covering" or "wrapper" (*peribolaiou* in Greek), which might suggest that the bone of contention in Corinth had to do with whether women wore their hair hanging loose or bound up, that is, braided and otherwise wrapped around their heads.[5] Of course, the headwear and hairstyle options are not mutually exclusive if head coverings helped to keep the hair in order.[6]

Whatever the specific bone of contention, scholars have also puzzled over what evoked debate about this matter in the first place, and interpretive honesty demands acknowledgment that on neither question can we be certain of the answer. However, Richard Hays reflects a widespread view that has emerged, imagining the kind of inquiry that might have come Paul's way:

> Dear Paul,
>
> We remember you fondly and wish that we could see you again. Some of us are trying hard to maintain the traditions you taught us, such as the tradition we learned at our baptism that in Christ there is no longer any distinction between male and female [cf. Gal. 3:27–28]. You would be glad to know that, when we come together for worship, the women in our community continue to play a role equal to the men, praying and prophesying freely in the assembly under the inspiration of the Spirit, just as they did when you were here with us. But a dispute has now arisen on one point: some of the women, acting in the freedom and power of the Spirit, have begun to remove their head coverings and loose their hair when they prophesy, a sign of their freedom in Christ. Some of the more timid and conservative members of the community have objected to this, thinking it unseemly and disgraceful for women to let their hair down in public. Most of us believe, however, that you would surely approve of this practice, for it is an outward and visible sign of the truth of the tradition we received from you. We would be grateful if you could comment directly on this matter in order to dispel any doubt about this point. We remain
>
> Your devoted followers,
> The church in Corinth[7]

Like Hays, many scholars think it likely that Paul's own teaching about freedom in Christ occasioned the dispute that arose about ecclesial headdress. The early Christian baptismal formula found in

Galatians 3:27–28 is routinely adduced in connection with 1 Corinthians 11:2–16 as a probable example of the kind of instruction Paul delivered on this matter: "*As many of you as were baptized into Christ have clothed yourselves with Christ. There is no longer Jew or Greek, there is no longer slave or free, there is no longer male and female; for all of you are one in Christ Jesus.*" So perhaps Corinthian women were putting this teaching into practice, removing their head coverings (and/or loosening their hair) as a visible sign of this freedom—a ritual embodiment of Paul's emphatic conviction that "*if anyone is in Christ, there is a new creation: everything old has passed away; see, everything has become new!*" (2 Cor. 5:17).

Paul's response in 1 Corinthians 11:2–16 therefore may have surprised them, for it conveys strong disapproval of this practice. He is of the decided opinion that women should keep their heads covered (or hair bound up) when exercising leadership in worship. Some have argued that male headdress was also a matter of debate in Corinth, since Paul shares opinions about both, but the focus of his angst is rather clearly the state of female heads rather than male ones, given his far more explicit and elaborate attention to the latter.[8] As we attempt to wrap our own heads around the complicated argument that Paul constructs, it is important to bear in mind Recommendation 1: "The difficult text is worthy of charity from its interpreters!"[9]

LISTENING TO THE TEXT

The fledgling church at Corinth was a contentious assembly, plagued by factions; so Paul opened the letter with a call for unity, sounding his central theme: "Now I appeal to you, brothers and sisters, by the name of our Lord Jesus Christ, that all of you be in agreement and that there be no divisions among you, but that you be united in the same mind and the same purpose" (1:10). Throughout the letter he addresses various manifestations of this problem in the life of the community, and in 11:2–14:40 he turns his attention to expressions of it within corporate worship. Thus the discussion in 11:2–16 marks a new turn in the letter, introducing an extended discussion of several divisive aspects of the Corinthians' worship practice that have come to Paul's attention, all in need of immediate corrective action, in his view: the matter of head coverings or hairstyles (11:2–16), serious abuses at the Lord's Supper (11:17–34), and problems related to glossolalia (speaking in tongues) in the worship assembly (12:1–14:40). Throughout this section of the letter, Paul aims to persuade the fractious congregation to be united rather than divided in their common worship.[10]

Surprisingly, Paul's discussion of the first problem, the one that concerns us, begins with a word of praise: "I commend you because you remember me in everything and maintain the traditions just as I handed them on to you" (v. 2). It is the only point in the letter where Paul specifically praises this obstreperous church that apparently misunderstood most of what he taught them.[11] One wonders if Paul is speaking ironically or sarcastically, or perhaps placating them so that the corrective medicine that follows will be easier to swallow! But these words may also acknowledge that his own teaching occasioned the dispute that has arisen, in which case he moves quickly to expand upon (and correct misappropriations of) his initial instruction: "But I want you to understand . . ." (v. 3). In the labored (some would say "tortured") argument that follows, Paul marshals one argument after another, piling on an array of rationales to persuade the Corinthians that the women among them must cease what he considers an imprudent practice and take charge of their heads in traditional fashion. As J. Paul Sampley observes, "The underlying force of logic seems to be that if all these indicators or signs point in the same direction, who would presume to go against them?"[12]

First, before taking up the matter of literal heads, Paul speaks of metaphorical ones, laying down a theological framework for the corrective guidance to follow: "But I want you to understand that Christ is the head of every man, and man is the head of woman, and God is the head of Christ" (v. 3). If as their point of departure Corinthian women had taken the baptismal affirmation of freedom in Christ, in whom "there is no longer male and female" (Gal. 3:28), Paul articulates an alternative viewpoint, emphasizing distinctions between male and female, who have different metaphorical "heads." Interestingly, this theological perspective is not argued, justified, or explained, but simply presumed. At only two points in the New Testament is "headship" language used to describe the relationship between male and female: here (where it appears nine times in the space of fifteen verses) and in the Ephesians household code (Eph. 5:21–33), a disputed Pauline epistle. Thus 1 Corinthians 11 is the only point at which such language appears in Paul's undisputed letters, which makes it difficult to discern what, exactly, Paul is suggesting by introducing the "headship" metaphor.

What does it mean to say that "man is the head of woman," in the same way that "Christ is the head of every man" and "God is the head of Christ"? This matter, endlessly debated, is one of the serious interpretive difficulties the text presents, for "headship" language has a range of connotations, and scholars are not at all agreed on the sense it bears here. Two primary possibilities present themselves: (1) "Head" can connote the authority of one who rules over another (the traditional view). But (2) "head" can also denote origin or source (as in the word "headwaters"), in which case the man is the source or point of origin for the woman, from whose rib she was fashioned, according to Genesis 2. This creation narrative is referenced in 11:8, which asserts, "Man was not made from woman, but woman from man." So on contextual grounds, many find "source" or "origin" the most likely sense of the headship language, and happily, one that is less starkly hierarchical in its construal of the relationship between man and woman. However, these two possibilities are not mutually exclusive, for "head" as "source" could justify "head" as "ruler."[13] And it is hard to escape hierarchical implications completely when "headship" language is in view, for at the very least the man occupies a position closer to the Godhead, and the woman is "head" of no one. It would have been helpful if Paul had provided some explanation of, or justification for, the theological framework he establishes in 11:3, given the outsized impact it has had on understandings of the relationship between male and female throughout Christian history. But as David Garland reminds us, Paul's "purpose is not to write a theology of gender but to correct an unbefitting practice in worship"[14]—a point often overlooked in the history of the text's interpretation, which has placed far more emphasis on the former (theologically sanctioned hierarchy) than the latter (ecclesial headdress) and thus on the "means" by which Paul addresses the problem at hand (albeit presumed, not explained) rather than the "end." As E. Elizabeth Johnson points out, 1 Corinthians 11:2–16 contains the only assertion of gender hierarchy found in Paul's undisputed letters,[15] but it is regarded by many people as a quite definitive statement. Indeed, 11:3 in particular has been "one of the principal scriptural bases for the subordination of women in Christian culture."[16]

After Paul with this framework has established a distinction between male and female, the stage is set for separate instructions for each as he moves from a discussion of respective metaphorical heads to management of literal ones in 11:4–6:

> [4]Any man who prays or prophesies with something on his head dis-
> graces his head, [5]but any woman who prays or prophesies with her
> head uncovered disgraces her head—it is one and the same thing as
> having her head shaved. [6]For if a woman will not cover her head,
> then she should cut off her hair; but if it is disgraceful for a woman
> to have her hair cut off or to be shaved, she should cover her head.

The point has been made that everyone has a "head," and what one
does with one's physical head in worship apparently reflects upon one's
metaphorical head: upon Christ in the case of man, and upon man in
the case of woman. For reasons that are not entirely clear to us, men
with covered heads in worship are said to dishonor Christ, and women
with uncovered heads are said to dishonor men.

To understand this point, we need more cultural information
than we have in hand, for the evidence available is ambiguous and
complicated by varied cultural currents that need to be taken into
account—Greek, Roman, and Jewish. There is little evidence that men
in antiquity, in any of these cultures, typically covered their heads (the
practice of head covering by Jewish men, with which we are familiar in
our day, was not commanded in the Torah and evolved later), though
there is some statuary evidence that Roman men may have covered
their heads with the hood of their togas when presenting a sacrifice to
a pagan deity; so perhaps Paul seeks to distance Corinthian men and
Christian religious rites from idolatrous worship practices.[17] Some
contend that the same end may be served if women's hairstyles are in
view: maybe Paul wanted to distinguish Christian worship practices
from those associated with the cults of Isis, Dionysus, and Cybele (all
present in Corinth), where disheveled, unbound hair was characteristic
of women in states of prophetic frenzy.[18] About all we can say with
any measure of confidence is that head coverings and/or bound-up
hair apparently constituted an important mark of gender distinction,
in Paul's view, and conveyed an appropriate sense of modesty, avert-
ing "disgrace." It is much too much to claim (as many scholars do,
quite confidently) that women with uncovered heads were prostitutes,
advertising sexual "availability," or that women with unbound
hair were confessing to adultery.[19] As N. T. Wright points out, "Paul
doesn't say exactly this, and we run the risk of 'explaining' him in
terms that might (perhaps) make sense to us while ignoring what he
himself says."[20] In fact, studies of Greco-Roman portraiture suggest
that "bareheadedness in itself was not a sign of a socially disapproved

lifestyle."[21] Covering one's head, or not, was apparently a choice for women, not a requirement—something Paul himself seems to acknowledge in verses 6 and 10.[22] In short, we cannot claim certainty about cultural expectations relating to headdress in the first-century world of Corinth and how they might inform our reading of Paul's instructions on this matter. As Wright honestly observes, "We can only guess at the dynamics of the situation—which is of course what historians always do. It's just that here we are feeling our way in the dark more than usual."[23]

Whatever the expectations regarding headdress in first-century Corinth may have been, it is worth noting that in verses 4–6 Paul shifts into a different mode of argumentation. The notion of divinely patterned hierarchical headship (the focus of inordinate attention in the history of interpretation) drops out of view[24] as Paul begins to make his case primarily on the basis of cultural norms rather than theological ones—in particular, in terms of honor and shame. Honor, widely recognized as the pivotal value in the first-century world, entailed a person's (or group's) claim to status, along with the acknowledgment of that status by others in the community, the loss of which incurred its opposite, shame. Moreover, honor entailed clearly defined (and separate) gender identities and roles, the blurring of which crossed the line, bringing shame upon one's self, one's family, and one's community. In honor-and-shame cultures, what other people think—about you and those with whom you associate—matters profoundly. For first-century persons of all ethnicities in the Mediterranean world, honor was "the greatest social value, to be preferred over wealth and even life itself," for as Carolyn Osiek explains, without a good reputation, life had no meaning.[25] Honor was thus a powerful incentive and shame a powerful disincentive, and Paul employs both to full advantage as his argument unfolds, leaving theological notions of "headship" behind.

In fact, it is worth noting that the vocabulary of honor and shame pervades the text from beginning to end, assuming rhetorical prominence: language of *praise* or *commendation* (v. 2), *glory* (vv. 7, 15), *shame* (v. 6), *disgrace* (vv. 4, 5, 6), *propriety* (v. 13), *dishonor* or *degradation* (v. 14). Paul declares that men bring "disgrace" upon Christ and the community with covered heads, but the real focus of his angst is the disgrace occasioned by uncovered female heads, given his far more elaborate commentary upon them. Indeed, resorting to hyperbole, he equates an uncovered female head with the shocking image of a shaved head. Perhaps the point is that, if you are going to remove things from your head, why not go the whole nine yards and remove everything—cut all your hair off! (An echo, perhaps, of Paul's sarcastic wish for the proponents of circumcision in Galatia? "I wish those who unsettle you would castrate themselves!" [Gal. 5:12].) Paul presumes that a shaved head entails extreme disgrace and that his readers share this presumption. (We cannot be sure what a shaved head implied for them, though likely some form of humiliation.) Paul thus presents the Corinthian women with a "choice" between appropriate headdress (which honors both their metaphorical and literal heads) and the humiliating disgrace of shaved heads, and he hopes the persuasiveness of his rhetoric will move them to "choose" correctly!

Paul is clearly intent on maintaining gender differentiation during worship through appropriate management of female heads—differentiation to which considerable importance was (and still is) attached in cultures pervaded by an honor-shame ethos. To bolster this point, he takes a new turn in verses 7–9, providing a scriptural warrant for gender differentiation that grounds it in the very orders of creation. Appealing to the creation narratives in Genesis 1–2, he argues in midrashic fashion (vv. 7–9):

> [7]For a man ought not to cover his head, since he is the image and glory of God; but woman is the glory of man. [8]Indeed, man was not made from woman, but woman from man. [9]Neither was man created for the sake of woman, but woman for the sake of man.

It is a puzzling biblical warrant for gender differentiation. For one thing (and most obviously), the first creation story in Genesis 1 claims that *both* man and woman were created in the image of God: "God created humankind in his image, in the image of God he created them; male and female he created them" (1:27). Paul does not deny that woman, too, is created in the divine image, but he is silent on this point, instead identifying her as man's "glory"—a word that does not appear in either Genesis 1 or 2. In what sense is woman man's "glory"? Does this refer, perhaps, to the affirmation of the second creation account, "It is not good that the man should be alone" (Gen. 2:18), and to the joy he experiences upon beholding a suitable partner who finally makes him complete: "This at last is bone of my bones and flesh of my flesh!" (Gen. 2:23)?[26] The second creation account is quite clearly in view in 1 Corinthians 11:8–9, which alludes to the fashioning of this suitable female partner for the man from his own rib. Though man is the source, or point of origin, for woman in Genesis 2—a relational rather than hierarchical notion—Paul's midrash is not without problems, for by emphasizing the "priority" of man's creation, he implies that woman has secondary, derivative status. Moreover, unlike the man, she is created "for the sake of" or "on account of" another. (Creation "for the sake of" man would imply subordinate status; while "on account of" could imply "source," in line with 1 Cor. 11:8. Both translations are possible.)[27]

It appears, then, that Paul has harmonized the two separate creation accounts in Genesis 1 and Genesis 2, reading primarily through the lens of the second. It lands him, however, in what Richard Hays aptly describes as a "theological quagmire"—not to mention the fact that "Paul fails to explain how any of this is directly relevant to the issue of head coverings."[28] Thus, speculation abounds. Hays wonders if the point, perhaps, is that woman, as man's glory, needs to cover her head in worship, lest she deflect attention from the glory of God.[29] Alternatively, Ann Jervis speculates that this puzzling foray into the creation narratives is occasioned by Corinthian misunderstanding of new creation in Christ ("no longer male and female," Gal. 3:28) as restoration to an androgynous state, based on a misreading of the first creation story in Genesis 1, which claims that both man and woman reflect the image of God. She argues that Paul, therefore, "recontextualize[s] the first account of creation, which had formed the basis of their misunderstanding, with the second" in order to emphasize that "God intended there to be two distinct genders who would live in harmony in the Lord."[30] The point is that "the unity of man and woman in Christ does not obliterate the diversity of the sexes, but rather establishes it in all of its glory—and believers should not disguise this."[31] Appropriate headdress or hairstyle that clearly distinguishes female from male would celebrate this point. Whatever the case may be, the emphasis on "glory" in 1 Corinthians 11:7–9 is Paul's own—a concept he introduces into the creation midrash. It is linked with "honor" and stands as a positive counterpoint to the negative emphasis on dishonor and disgrace in verses 4–6. Perhaps, as Gordon Fee suggests, the point is simply that "she who was created to be man's 'glory' is behaving in a way that is causing shame."[32]

The verses that follow hardly clarify the point, for in verse 10, Paul abruptly provides yet another rationale for head covering—the most perplexing one of all: "For this reason a woman ought to have authority over her head, because of the angels." For what reason? The one that precedes (the creation midrash) or the one that follows (the angels)? In neither case does clarity emerge, for two other major interpretive problems also present themselves.

The first involves a consequential judgment call regarding translation. Should we read, with the NRSV (and many other English translations), "For this reason a woman ought to have *a symbol of* authority on her head"? The words in italics ("a symbol of," or "a sign of" in some translations) do not actually appear in the Greek text but are supplied by translators attempting to make some sense of it. Alternatively, we could read with the updated NIV (2011): "It is for this reason that a woman ought to have authority over her own head, because of the angels." This straightforward translation, which adds no missing phrases and tweaks a multivalent Greek preposition (*epi*, which can mean "on" or "over," among other things), ascribes more agency and choice to the woman, conveying that she should take charge of her head (or hair) in an appropriate manner. Increasingly, scholars incline toward this latter rendering, for there is no evidence that the word "authority" (*exousia* in Greek) is ever used to convey a sign or symbol of someone else's authority. Such use is unattested elsewhere in Paul's letters or in contemporaneous literature. Paul's use of the word always conveys the right or freedom to act held by the subject. In 1 Corinthians 8–9, for example, Paul addresses controversy in Corinth over the question of eating meat from animals used in pagan sacrifices and argues that Christians have the authority—the right or freedom or power—to eat whatever they want, though he urges them to renounce their rights for the sake of the greater good (cf. 8:9; 9:4–6, 12, 18). Some think that Paul may be trying to persuade Corinthian women to renounce their rights (regarding headdress) for the sake of the greater good too, though Paul does not explicitly argue on the basis of community benefit here.[33] But given the active rather than passive sense of *exousia*, Paul *is* most likely acknowledging the authority or right of the Corinthian woman to do what she wants with her head while at the same time exerting considerable pressure upon her to manage it in traditional fashion, maintaining appropriate gender distinctions. (In other words, "You have a choice—but here is the choice you should make!") In many respects, this abrupt acknowledgment of the woman's authority to do what she wants with her head would appear to reverse the arguments for head covering that have preceded it! However, Margaret Mitchell provides a perspective also worth pondering: perhaps

Paul is arguing both sides of the debate that is taking place in Corinth, urging disputing parties toward conciliation.[34]

The second major interpretive problem—and the most baffling conundrum in the text as a whole—is what to make of the intriguing reference to angels, which is presented as a decisive argument in favor of head covering. Paul and the Corinthian Christians apparently presumed angelic presence and participation in communal worship and shared an unstated understanding of their relevance to the matter at hand. We are left in the dark, though wild and wonderful speculation abounds! Given the preceding midrash on the Genesis narrative, are the angels in view perhaps those present at creation, guardians of the created order, interested in maintaining distinctions between male and female grounded in the divine creative work? Or are they rather, as at Qumran, guardians of liturgical order, purity, and propriety, along the lines suggested in the Dead Sea Scrolls?[35] Are they thus good angels, or perhaps renegade angels, like those in Genesis 6:1–4 and *1 Enoch* 6–7 (a popular Jewish apocalyptic text), sexual predators who might be tempted to mate with women who sport bare heads or cascading hair? Is it the angels who need to be protected, from offense or seduction—or the women, from supernatural rapists, angelic sexual attack?[36] Because the Greek word for angel (*angelos*) is also the word for "messenger," some even argue that Paul speaks of human messengers, rather than supernatural ones. He worries about impressions made on visitors in Corinthian communal worship in 14:23, and perhaps here, too, guests, envoys from other churches who might be scandalized by liturgical disorder, are in view. Paul may introduce angels out of the blue in 1 Corinthians 11 because they played an important role in the self-understanding of Corinthian Christians who believed, perhaps, that they spoke "in the tongues of angels" (13:1), likening themselves to angels in speech or in knowledge. All of these possibilities and more have been presented as explanations for the enigmatic appearance of angels in 1 Corinthians 11. What should we conclude? To be perfectly honest, that we haven't a clue! As Gordon Fee contends, "We must forever be content to 'look through the glass darkly'" and admit how little we know.[37]

But then we should prepare for interpretive whiplash, for having presented an array of rationales for appropriate and distinctive female headdress—theological, cultural, scriptural, and supernatural—Paul suddenly reverses direction in verses 11–12: "Nevertheless, in the Lord woman is not independent of man or man independent of woman.

For just as woman came from man, so man comes through woman; but all things come from God." These words appear to undercut the argument Paul has been constructing, for instead of gender hierarchy, he now affirms the interdependence of man and woman "in the Lord." And the temporal priority of man at creation is now balanced by woman's priority in childbirth, for though Eve was fashioned from Adam's rib, ever since then every man has been born of a woman. Apparently Paul can read creation in two different ways: in both a patriarchal sense (vv. 7–9) and an egalitarian sense (vv. 11–12).[38] And though he has implied that man is closer to God as God's own image and glory (v. 7), now he affirms that all things (presumably including woman) come from God, the direct source of all existence. Is Paul contradicting or even correcting himself—aware, perhaps, that he has been running off the rails? How should we resolve the obvious tension between verses 11–12 and the preceding arguments? Some resolve it in favor of gender hierarchy and some in favor of gender equality, but Judith Gundry advises, wisely I think, that the tension cannot be dispensed with easily, nor should it be.

In Gundry's view, this tension reflects the fact that Paul has two contrasting social contexts in mind that merge in worship: "the Corinthians' wider social context in which shame and honor depended on the preservation of distinct gender identities and roles, and the cultic context of Corinthian worship in which gender boundaries were crossed and hierarchy transcended."[39] As she explains, the church's worship "does not take place in a cultural vacuum,"[40] and so, in a sense, Corinthian Christians (both male and female) "had to wear two 'hats' at once"—that of the first-century Mediterranean man or woman whose hat was either masculine or feminine and connoted traditional gender roles, and that of the believer baptized into Christ, in whom there is "no longer male and female."[41] Thus Gundry contends that "the Corinthians' worship became an occasion for maintaining social acceptability as well as for participating in the new social equality 'in the Lord.'"[42] In sum, *"Paul lets social roles 'in the world' and social roles 'in the Lord' clash right in the setting of worship."*[43]

However, is Paul "letting" them clash or discovering that they do? J. Paul Sampley's similar explanation of the tension views Paul's thinking on this matter as very much "in process," in the midst of working things through: "In the process of writing 11:2–16, Paul discovers that two of his own values are in conflict: On the one side, he wants women believers to accommodate to the culturally aligned practice of wearing head coverings; on the other side, he believes that in Christ the cultural differentiations between men and women are eschatologically challenged by the gospel."[44] Both Gundry and Sampley do justice to the varied perspectives woven through Paul's complex discourse—as well as to the complex, overlapping contexts that Christians, both then and now, negotiate. But Margaret Mitchell's rhetorical insight could also account for the tensions in Paul's argument and is worth considering. Perhaps, as she suggests, the two-sidedness of Paul's argumentation is "deliberate (though annoying!)": "Paul's vacillating approach is part of his overall strategy of mediation in 1 Corinthians, by which he seeks to unite a divided church by ending 'contentiousness' (11:16)."[45] If this is the case, we may be hearing both sides of the debate at Corinth and Paul's acknowledgment that neither is without some logic or integrity.

However, having taken this detour to articulate divergent reflections, in the closing verses Paul resumes his course in the dogged direction of head coverings, invoking propriety, nature, and custom as final rationales for management of female heads in traditional fashion. As Jouette Bassler observes, "One senses conflicting views within Paul shutting down the rational process, and where reason fails, emotion and tradition take over."[46] Despite the conflicting considerations he entertains, he clearly still wants women who pray and prophesy in communal worship to do so with their heads covered or hair under control. As his argument comes to a close, he appeals to the Corinthians' own judgment, posing two rhetorical questions, both of which presume agreement with his point of view. The questions are addressed to the whole church, not just to the women who have occasioned this debate, for the matter is one for communal deliberation (indicated by the fact that the pronoun "yourselves" is masculine and plural):

> [13]Judge for yourselves: is it proper for a woman to pray to God with her head uncovered? [14]Does not nature itself teach you that if a man wears long hair, it is degrading to him, [15]but if a woman has long hair, it is her glory? For her hair is given to her for a covering.

The first question appeals to "propriety," to "what is fitting" or "seemly"—that is, to conventionally accepted standards of behavior. The second appeals to "nature" (an unusual move for Paul) and is likely to strike contemporary Christians as peculiar. For one thing, male hair is not "naturally" short but rendered so by a haircut. This indicates that Paul is not referring to "nature" in terms of creation or "natural law," but in terms of social convention. He is appealing, as the NIV translation of verse 14 puts it, "to the very nature of things," that is, "to the culture's established beliefs about 'the way things are' and ought to be."[47] And in the first-century Greco-Roman world, it was customary for men to have short hair and for women to have long hair. One might also wonder why women, who already have glorious hair as a "covering" for their heads, need another! But Paul is arguing on the basis of analogy. "Nature" (that is, "the very nature of things") has seen fit to provide women's heads with an extra measure of covering, and the Corinthian women should follow suit. Both rhetorical questions emphasize social conventions and share deeply entrenched cultural assumptions about honor and shame, which entailed clearly defined (and separate) gender identities. Men need to look like men, and women like women, with no blurring of the lines between the two.[48] As Fee observes, "In the end, it is plain that Paul wants the woman to maintain the tradition (whatever it is) and to do so primarily for reasons of 'shame' and 'honor' in a culture where this is the primary sociological value."[49] While Paul has produced a string of varied arguments in support of coverings for female heads, culturally grounded considerations of "honor" and "shame" assume central prominence.

Apparently Paul had reason to believe that his labored, multi-pronged argument might fail to convince, for he concludes with acknowledgment of this possibility and one final justification for his position, aimed to shut down discussion: "But if anyone is disposed to be contentious—we have no such custom, nor do the churches of God" (11:16). As Sandra Hack Polaski notes, this final appeal to prevailing ecclesial practice insists, in short, "*We* don't do it that way!"[50] These closing words may not be entirely peevish. In the opening verses of this letter, Paul encouraged this fledgling community of believers in Corinth to see themselves as part of a larger network of churches stretching around the Mediterranean world rather than as "spiritual free agents"[51] (1:2), and here again could be said to appeal to this perspective. However, this appeal is also a final rhetorical power play, for the "we" includes Paul and other churches he founded or is familiar with and effectively excludes from the wider Christian communion those who disagree with him.[52] Given the eventual growth of the church well beyond the Mediterranean into every corner of the globe (which was, after all, Paul's wildest dream), incarnating the gospel in infinitely varied contexts and cultures, it is doubtful that such an appeal to ecclesial custom, sartorial or otherwise, would (or should) hold global persuasive power today![53] Even then Paul expected continued opposition. He anticipated that some would, in fact, be "disposed to be contentious" (11:16) or "victory-loving" (*philoneikos* in Greek). Margaret Mitchell reports that is one of the most common terms used in Greek literature to refer to party strife, indicating that Paul is concerned about the role of this particular debate in the overall divisiveness and factionalism plaguing the Corinthian community.[54] Maybe headdress or lack thereof was even "emblematic of one's 'party-affiliation' at Corinth."[55]

Perhaps we can appreciate Paul's larger concern for the unity of the church, even as we wrestle with problematic aspects of this text. But having made a genuine effort to listen carefully and patiently to the text, we, like some of the folk in ancient Corinth, may be inclined to argue with it. We should exercise our freedom to do so, along with the minds that God has given us, without hesitation, confident that arguing with Scripture is an act of faithfulness, of taking the text with the utmost seriousness. We will not want to throw the baby out with the bathwater, for we can surely learn from this text—from both insights and dangers it presents. And in all our engagement with it, we can anticipate encounter with the living God, whose Spirit is at work within us, striving to form in us the mind of Jesus Christ.

DIALOGUE WITH THE TEXT

To this point, we have been engaged in listening carefully, patiently to the text, trying to wrap our heads (no pun intended!) around it—to imagine what occasioned the debate in a first-century church and to grasp the many threads of the convoluted argument Paul constructs in response to it. However, as we have had occasion to recognize in previous chapters, listening is not all that is required of us. The Bible is a living word through which God continues to meet us and speak to us in our own particular historical moment, and so it must be newly interpreted for new historical situations. And interpretation is not simply reiteration of the text, repeating what was said before, but rather the hard work of bringing it into our time and place.

But why bother with such an obscure and cantankerous text? Why go to all this trouble? Many are inclined to avoid it or dismiss it as an antiquated relic that no longer need concern us. Indeed, some may be inclined to dismiss the apostle Paul altogether in the spirit of the musical *South Pacific*: "I'm gonna wash that man right outa my hair"! However, at least two important reasons to engage such a cantankerous text recommend themselves. For one thing, many people in our time and place are talking about 1 Corinthians 11, and we need to be part of that conversation—to address this text directly and publicly and set forth alternative readings of it. What is more important, we are related by baptism to Paul and to the believers in first-century Corinth, and the canonical witness to their conversation continues to be a means by which the church, through the ages, discerns God's will for it in new times and places. By the power of the Holy Spirit, the text continues to bring us into the living presence of God and to shape our vision of the world, in the light of God's plans and purposes—even when we find ourselves wrestling with, and sometimes against, its claims.

New Perspectives on "Paul and Women"

As we meditate on the interpretive problems and possibilities before us in 1 Corinthians 11, awareness of an important shift in recent study of "Paul and women" (as the topic has often been framed) can deepen and broaden our engagement with it. In a groundbreaking essay in 1984, Bernadette Brooten noted that most of the research on women in early Christianity has not focused primarily on women but rather on what men thought about women.[56] Indeed, attempts to discern "what Paul thought about women" have often dominated discussion of what texts such as 1 Corinthian 11 have to contribute to our understanding of early Christian women, featuring dichotomous debates over whether he was a "misogynist" or a "liberationist," even a feminist—a friend or an enemy of women. Brooten proposed that a shift of focus was required—one that placed women in the center of the frame: "To write women's history, to place women at the center, is to say that men are not at the center of reality, that what men do and are is not more important than what women do and are."[57] Subsequently, important developments in feminist study of Paul's letters have unfolded, with the result that Paul's "attitudes" (to the extent that we can discern them) are no longer the sole focus of attention. Increasingly, as the basic social reality behind the epistles has been taken seriously, glimpses of the women themselves who were players in the early missionary movement have come into view. So as we grapple with the text, it is important to reframe our perspectives on both Paul and the Corinthian women in several respects.

With respect to Paul, it is important to break out of the simplistic, dichotomous frameworks noted above that so often characterize discussion and debate about "Paul's attitude toward women," casting him as misogynist or liberationist, enemy or friend of women. Such frameworks fail to do justice to the complexity of the man, the genuine ambiguities reflected in his letters, and the struggles in which he and fledgling Christian communities were engaged as they worked out implications of the gospel for life together in Christ. We also need to acknowledge that Paul was a first-century male in the ancient Mediterranean world, a product of his own time, and try to understand him within his complex historical, social, cultural, political, and religious contexts.[58] Paul and the churches to whom he wrote were negotiating life in multiple, overlapping contexts, and that ongoing process was messy, challenging, rife with competing values and contradictions, and far from complete. As he speaks from the midst of this process, and often from the midst of ecclesial debate, his voice is a predominant, canonical one that demands our engagement, but does this mean that the opinions he articulates are always, or necessarily, definitive ones? Paul himself acknowledges that "for now we see in a mirror dimly" and that his own knowledge is imperfect: "I know only in part" (1 Cor. 13:12). He describes himself as a man very much in process of growth in Christ: "Not that I have already obtained this or have already reached the goal [been made perfect, *teteleiōmai* in Greek]; but I press on to make it my own, because Christ Jesus has made me his own" (Phil. 3:12). We will want to discern his thoughts on the relations between women and men (as on other matters) to the extent that we can, yet we should consider the possibility that his views may well be in flux. Indeed, Richard Hays has said of Paul's grappling with gender concerns in 1 Corinthians 11 that "perhaps on no other issue do we see Paul struggling so visibly to get it right."[59]

With respect to the Corinthian women, reframing of our perspective is needed as well. As we strain to hear their voices, perhaps we ought not presume that they are entirely misguided and in need of apostolic correction. Traditionally, throughout the history of interpretation, Paul's letters have been read with the dogmatic presumption that Paul is always right, and those with whom he finds himself in conflict are always wrong. But as Cynthia Briggs Kittredge has noted, one of the important contributions feminist biblical scholars have made to study of Paul's epistles has been to challenge us "to interpret his letters not simply as reflecting conflict between an orthodox Paul and heretical or heterodox opponents, but as rhetorical arguments that can be read with a method that makes audible different voices who participate in debates about early Christian beliefs and self-understandings."[60] Thus, as we eavesdrop on Paul's conversation with our forebears in the church at Corinth, we should consider the possibility that "serious arguments and strong rhetoric" are "flying both ways."[61] Here, too, we should avoid simplistic, dichotomous frameworks—casting the Corinthian women, for example, as budding feminists, pitted against a male apostle hopelessly entrenched in patriarchal cultural norms. Moreover, it is important to bear in mind that Corinthian Christians (both women and men) apparently were engaged in debate over ecclesial attire not just with Paul, but also (even primarily) with each other, and all may represent arguments with measures of logic and integrity worthy of consideration. As we take seriously the social reality embodied in Paul's letters and the dialogical character of them, perhaps we will come to see the struggles of early Christian communities known through them "as pluriform movements of women and men gifted by the Divine Spirit and engaged in an ongoing theological debate over equality, freedom, dignity, and full 'citizenship' in the *ekklēsia*."[62]

With these perspectives in mind, let us proceed, then, to genuine dialogue with the text, actively participating in the interpretive process of bringing an ancient text into our own time and place, with every expectation that we may encounter the living God in serious engagement with it. The recommendations for wrestling with cantankerous texts considered in preceding chapters can continue to guide our conversation.

Arguing with the Text

"The difficult text is worthy of charity from its interpreters" (Recommendation 1), but this does not mean that we relinquish our right to disagree with it or check our brains at the door.[63] Arguing with the text (Recommendation 2) is an act of faithfulness. As we have navigated our way through the complex argument that Paul constructs in 1 Corinthians 11:2–16, we have already noticed several aspects of it that stand in need of challenge: most especially, the notion of divinely patterned hierarchical headship articulated in verse 3, and the notion that man "is the image and glory of God; but woman is the glory of man" in verse 7 (elaborated upon with implicit statements of woman's secondary, derivative, and subordinate status in vv. 8–9). In the history of interpretation, these aspects of the text have received far more attention than Paul's central focus on headdress, with the result that the "means" of Paul's argument have had more momentous and adverse impact on the lives of women throughout Christian history than the original "end." In fact, as we have noted, the headship principle in particular, though presented in 11:3 without explanation or justification, has been "one of the principal scriptural bases for the subordination of women in Christian culture."[64]

There are several constructive ways to argue with integrity against such a claim for subordination. Several classic principles of biblical interpretation recommend themselves—principles enshrined in the confessions of the Reformed tradition as well as in those of many other Christian communions: time-honored principles such as *the interpretation of Scripture by Scripture, the centrality of Jesus Christ,* and *the rule of faith.* (A fourth principle, *the rule of love,* will be introduced in the following chapter.) These principles have been implicit in our engagement with tyrannical texts in preceding chapters. We now raise them to explicit visibility as constructive principles of interpretation.

The historic practice of *interpreting Scripture by Scripture,* which we have exercised in preceding chapters, holds that the entire biblical canon is the context for understanding the fullness of Christian faith and life. Thus, it is important to struggle with challenging texts in the context of the whole of Scripture, interpreting the less clear in the light of the more clear, and bringing other biblical voices into conversation with them. Many, for example, would want to return to the first creation story in Genesis 1 and argue vigorously with Paul's interpretation of it: "For a man ought not to cover his head, since he is the image and glory of God; but woman is the glory of man" (1 Cor. 11:7). Does not this claim misrepresent the first creation story, which states pointedly that male and female *together* reflect God's image and likeness? "So God created humankind in his image, in the image of God he created them; male and female he created them" (Gen. 1:27). Jouette Bassler describes Paul's argument as "a misreading of Genesis 1:27"—an observation with which I agree. Don't you agree too? As Bassler observes, he does not deny that women are created in God's image, "but Paul also does not affirm it, and this silence is significant."[65] Indeed, it obscures, and even distorts, the first and arguably most theological statement on record in the biblical canon on matters of gender. Clarity about what Genesis 1 is affirming is crucial to any evaluation of Paul's argument in 1 Corinthians 11.

It is also intriguing to bring other emphases in Paul's letters into conversation with 1 Corinthians 11:2–16, for statements he makes elsewhere stand in marked tension with it! The baptismal formula in Galatians 3:27–28 is most frequently adduced as a striking counterargument: *"As many of you as were baptized into Christ have clothed yourselves with Christ. There is no longer Jew or Greek, there is no longer slave or free, there is no longer male and female; for all of you are one in Christ Jesus."* In fact, as we have mentioned, this may represent the perspective of the Corinthian women, for many scholars think it likely that Paul's own teaching about freedom in Christ, reflected in Galatians 3, occasioned the dispute that arose about ecclesial headdress. Perhaps Corinthian women were putting this teaching into practice, removing their head coverings (and/or loosening their hair) as a visible sign of this freedom.[66] Many contemporary Christians also regard Galatians 3:27–28 as a defining Pauline theological insight—one he perhaps found difficult to sustain in practice.[67]

Other tensions between 1 Corinthians 11:2–16 and statements elsewhere in Paul's letters can be noted. For example, Paul's focus on head coverings for women is oddly out of sync with a declaration he makes in his Second Letter to the Corinthians (3:12–18) regarding "veiling":

> [12]Since, then, we have such a hope, we act with great boldness, [13]not like Moses, who put a veil over his face to keep the people of Israel from gazing at the end of the glory that was being set aside. [14]But their minds were hardened. Indeed, to this very day, when they hear the reading of the old covenant, that same veil is still there, since only in Christ is it set aside. [15]Indeed, to this very day whenever Moses is read, a veil lies over their minds; [16]but *when one turns to the Lord, the veil is removed.* [17]Now the Lord is the Spirit, and where the Spirit of the Lord is, there is freedom. [18]*And all of us, with unveiled faces, seeing the glory of the Lord as though reflected in a mirror, are being transformed into the same image from one degree of glory to another; for this comes from the Lord, the Spirit.*

We have no idea what kind of head covering Paul recommends in 1 Corinthians 11:2–16 (if head coverings rather than hairstyles are in view): is he advocating a cover for the top of the head only; for the entire head, neck, and shoulders; or even the face as well? However, if veils are unnecessary for "all" who believe in Christ, one wonders why head coverings of any sort are requisite for Corinthian women.

Interpretation of Scripture by Scripture—and in this case, even interpretation of Paul by Paul!—becomes even more interesting when we turn our attention to the whole of the letter in which 1 Corinthians 11:2–16 is embedded, for it is out of sync with major theological emphases sounded throughout 1 Corinthians itself. One thinks, for example, of the remarkably evenhanded, egalitarian discussion of celibacy, marriage, and sexual reciprocity within marriage throughout 1 Corinthians 7. And most notably, elsewhere in this epistle Paul argues vehemently against the replication of social hierarchies within the Corinthian church, insisting that this represents a denial of the gospel.[68] There should be no hierarchical distinctions, for example, among groups involved in disagreement over food offered to idols (1 Cor. 8). In fact, in the discussion that immediately follows 1 Corinthians 11:2–16, Paul addresses abuses at the Lord's Supper and clearly regards the manifestation of socioeconomic distinctions in Corinthian liturgical practice as a threat to the integrity of the gospel itself (1 Cor. 11:17–34). And in 1 Corinthians 12, Paul speaks eloquently of the equivalence of all "members" of the "body of Christ," even elevating those presumed to be "less honorable," "less respectable," "inferior" members (12:22–25). These convictions do not cohere with 1 Corinthians 11:2–16, where he affirms a hierarchy of heads and woman's secondary, derivative, subordinate status. Social, economic, and ethnic distinctions and hierarchies are ruled out of order, but in 1 Corinthians 11:2–16, gender distinction and hierarchy, to some extent, remain. Dale Martin summarizes this inconsistency bluntly, noting that Paul does not treat gender differences with the same hermeneutic applied to ethnic and social divisions between males: "Paul does not do for women in the church what he has, to some extent, attempted for slaves, Gentiles, and people of low economic status."[69] Given these striking incongruities, one cannot help but suspect that Paul's reflection on matters of gender is very much in process—that he is still struggling to work out the implications of the gospel for gendered life together in Christ, and doing so more slowly than on other fronts.[70]

In sum, the classic principle of interpreting Scripture by Scripture plays a crucial role in the practice of arguing with tyrannical texts. As Ellen Davis observes, "If we disagree with a certain text on a given point, then it must be in obedience to what we, in community with other Christians, discern to be the larger or more fundamental message of the Scriptures."[71]

Another classic principle of biblical interpretation that can also inform our wrestling with Scripture is *the centrality of Jesus Christ*. This historic principle affirms that "all of Scripture is to be interpreted in light of the centrality of Christ and in relation to the salvation provided through him." Thus "no understanding of what Scripture teaches us to believe and do can be correct that ignores or contradicts the central and primary revelation of God and God's will through Jesus Christ made known through the witness of Scripture."[72] In the case of 1 Corinthians 11:2–16, then, a question to ask is whether interpretations of it that promote a headship hierarchy with respect to gender are consistent with scriptural accounts of Jesus' own teaching and embodiment of the will of God.[73] At only two points in the New Testament is "headship" language used to describe the relationship between male and female: here and in the Ephesians household code (Eph. 5:21–33), considered in the preceding chapter. In both texts, Christ's lordship, construed in hierarchical terms, provides the template for hierarchical ordering of relationships between male and female. Thus a question raised in chapter 2 in connection with Ephesians 5 is pertinent here as well: Is this hierarchical model consistent with Jesus' own teaching about relationships of authority? Jesus urged his disciples *not* to "lord it over" others, reminding them, "It is not so among you; but whoever wishes to become great among you must be your servant, and whoever wishes to be first among you must be slave of all. For the Son of Man came not to be served but to serve, and to give his life a ransom for many" (Mark 10:42–45). In the preceding chapter, we recognized that in many respects "Ephesians 5 can be read as testimony to the author's failure to interpret the lordship of Christ aright."[74] Could not the same be said of some of Paul's construal of hierarchical headship in 1 Corinthians 11:2–16 and countless interpretations based upon it?

In this connection, we can also identify an uncharacteristic feature of Paul's argumentation in 1 Corinthians 11:2–16: he appeals to creation theology and primarily to cultural norms, to values of honor and shame, rather than to the person and work of Jesus Christ.[75] Christology, along with eschatology, both so integral to the gospel that Paul proclaims, receive remarkably little play in 1 Corinthians 11:2–16. After the opening declaration of divinely patterned hierarchical headship in verse 3, the only other point at which a christological consideration rears its head is in verses 11–12, when Paul backtracks to affirm the mutuality and interdependence of male and female "in the Lord."

One final classic principle of biblical interpretation is playing an intriguing role in current interpretive debate over 1 Corinthians 11:2–16 and is also worth pondering as we wrestle with notions of hierarchical headship: *the rule of faith*, which designates the basic theology of the church, past and present—the essential contours of its confession of faith. As J. Todd Billings puts it, "The rule of faith is a communal, received account of the central story of Scripture that helps identify the center and the boundaries of a Christian interpretation of Scripture."[76] It does not settle points of detail as we engage in biblical interpretation, but it provides the big picture—the "overarching story"[77] or "expansive context"[78] in which ecclesial reading of Scripture takes place. We have access to "the rule of faith" through classic statements of the Christian faith such as the Apostles' and Nicene Creeds and through the confessions and catechisms of our particular Christian communions, which give expression to the doctrinal consensus of the church, the basic contours of its confession. And in this connection, the question that has been raised in recent debate over 1 Corinthians 11:2–16 is whether the notion of hierarchical headship articulated in 11:3 coheres with a crucial aspect of historic Christian confession: the doctrine of the Trinity.

This question has emerged primarily in "evangelical" circles in heated gender wars between "complementarians" (or "traditionalists") on one hand and "egalitarians" ("evangelical feminists," or proponents of "complementarity without hierarchy") on the other hand.[79] Paul's emphasis on gender hierarchy and distinction in 1 Corinthians 11:2–16 plays an important role in complementarians' insistence on the continuing need for a male leadership role in church and family life. Egalitarians, who challenge this view, have appealed to the doctrine of the Trinity to gain the upper hand in this debate, associating notions of hierarchy within the Godhead with the ancient heresy of "subordinationism," which holds that the Son and the Holy Spirit are subordinate to God the Father in nature and being—a lesser form of divinity. The doctrine of the Trinity, which did not receive classic formulation until the Council of Nicaea adopted the Nicene Creed in 325 CE, rejected subordinationism, affirming that God the Father, Son, and Holy Spirit are coequal, coeternal, and consubstantial—one in essence, nature, power, action, and will. In other words, both the Son and the Holy Spirit participate fully in the Godhead.

It would be anachronistic to claim that Paul, who wrote two and a half centuries earlier, understood the relations between the members of the Godhead in this precise manner—to presume continuity between Scripture and the Nicene Creed on this point.[80] However, the understanding of mutuality between the members of the Godhead that eventually emerged and that represents the collective wisdom of the church is an intriguing perspective to bring into conversation with 1 Corinthians 11:3 and interpretations of it—a text that has so often been cited as grounds for the subordination of women in Christian culture. Richard Hays concurs: "The subsequently developed ortho-dox doctrine of the Trinity actually works against the subordinationist implications of Paul's argument about men and women; it presses us to rethink the way in which 'in the Lord' men and women participate together in a new identity that transcends notions of superiority and inferiority."[81] Thus there are valid theological reasons for questioning both Paul's presentation of hierarchical headship as an appropriate model for relations between male and female and interpretations of the text that would insist upon it.

In my own communion of faith (the Presbyterian Church [U.S.A.], which stands in the Reformed tradition), we also affirm our faith by reading and studying together other confessional statements articu-lated by Reformed Christians in different historical eras. Weekly in worship in my home congregation, we read together from the most recent of those confessions, titled "A Brief Statement of Faith" (1991), which includes these lines:

> In sovereign love God created the world good
> and makes everyone equally in God's image,
> male and female, of every race and people,
> to live as one community.[82]

Affirmations of faith of this sort can and should be brought into conversation with interpretations of 1 Corinthians 11:2–16 that would propose anything to the contrary. In so doing, we are calling upon "the rule of faith," the collective wisdom of the church, articulated in its creeds and confessions and catechisms, to be part of our discern-ment of the implications of 1 Corinthians 11:2–16 for life together in our own time and place. Those creeds, confessions, and catechisms are themselves explications, in different historical contexts, of the will and work of God revealed in Scripture. Affirmations they articulate emerged out of collective discernment of the witness of Scripture.[83] Thus, if we appeal to them to counter declarations Paul may make in 1 Corinthians 11:3 or 7, we can hardly be said to be ignoring or dismissing Scripture; we are rather appealing to the church's collective sense of what it has heard in its engagement with the whole of it.

Engagement with classic principles of biblical interpretation such as *the interpretation of Scripture by Scripture, the centrality of Jesus Christ,* and *the rule of faith* provide various means by which we can argue with problematic aspects of contentious texts with integrity. But as we do so, we should resist the temptation to throw the baby out with the bathwater (Recommendation 3), remembering that we can learn from both insights *and* dangers that the text presents (Recommendation 4)!

Discerning Insights and Dangers

Insights and dangers that emerge from engagement with 1 Corinthians 11:2–16 are perhaps best considered together, since they seem to me to be intertwined. When in conversation with the text and with others about it, as soon as an insight is discerned, the flip side of the coin—a potential danger—slips into view!

For instance, one of the most striking things about this text is the length to which it goes to engage a cultural convention and the grounding of its argument in considerations of custom, honor, shame, nature, and propriety. In fact, such considerations assume rhetorical prominence. Some of the most important food for thought provided by the text, then, surely has to do with the church's relationship to the culture in which it finds itself—in particular, with the church's continued negotiation of cultural norms of decorum as it gathers for worship; for then as now, we do not worship in a vacuum. We cannot ignore norms of propriety—the conventions of polite society—for the sake of our life together or our mission, and among them are expectations regarding appropriate appearance (with respect to attire and coiffure). Indeed, the flouting of such expectations (if deemed flagrant or scandalous in a particular culture or setting) can have both internal and external consequences. On the internal front, they can distract attention from God in worship and provoke communal conflict (as was apparently the case in Corinth), thereby contributing to the disunity of the church. On the external front, they can also hamper the church's mission if they lead to misunderstanding and distraction, and thus prove to be an obstacle to hearing the gospel. In 14:23–25, for example, as Paul addresses other disorderly aspects of Corinthian worship related to speaking in tongues, he stresses their impact on visitors who may be present—on "outsiders or unbelievers" who may enter the worshiping assembly: "Will they not say that you are out of your mind?" (14:23). Paul hopes, instead, that the secrets of their hearts will be disclosed by the hearing of the gospel, so "that person will bow down before God and worship him, declaring, 'God is really among you'" (14:25). Given the pervasive angst about honor, shame, and cultural propriety throughout the discussion in 1 Corinthians 11:2–16, we may surmise that Paul, and others in the Corinthian assembly as well, are genuinely concerned about public impressions in this instance too—about the public visibility of Christian worship. They may have reasonable evangelistic concerns about impressions made on outsiders by women exercising worship leadership without attire deemed appropriate, wanting to ensure a measure of social acceptability so that the primary impression visitors leave with, instead, will be that of the gospel.

Moreover, as we noticed in the discussion of 1 Timothy's elaborate dress code (chap. 1 above), sartorial considerations are not entirely irrelevant to Christian faith. What we wear and how we present ourselves do convey messages of various sorts about us. There is surely something to be said also for expressions of modesty (which is apparently among Paul's concerns with respect to female headdress) in a society such as ours that is desperately in need of this virtue. Paul's overriding concern in 1 Corinthians 11–14, that worship be conducted "decently and in order" (14:40), is one that we, like the Corinthians, cannot afford to ignore if our worship is to glorify God and draw people into the divine presence.

But as soon as such legitimate concerns are identified, a flip side of this coin needs to be considered, and perhaps would have been argued by the Corinthian women. Head coverings, in some cultures to this day, are especially symbolic and gendered articles of clothing. The Corinthian women prophets no doubt were fully aware of this and of the import of their public flouting of norms of propriety. Even as their action evoked conflict, they nevertheless deemed the statement it made to be an important one to convey, despite the cost. We wish we could say with more certainty what that statement may have been.

At the very least, we can presume that they chafed at expectations regarding headdress and rejected assumptions conveyed by it. Were they also giving expression to a misunderstanding of new creation in Christ ("no longer male and female," Gal. 3:28) as restoration to an androgynous state, as Ann Jervis proposes?[84] Or were they perhaps proclaiming to their honor-shame culture that they now had a new basis of honor within Jesus Christ, the image of God, whom they had "put on," as Antoinette Wire contends?[85] Many scholars suppose that their statement was, in some way or another, a significant theological one—a sign of their baptismal freedom and new creation in Christ, in whom there is *"no longer Jew or Greek, there is no longer slave or free, there is no longer male and female; for all of you are one in Christ Jesus"* (Gal. 3:28).

Since early Christians gathered for worship as "house churches," many have supposed that ambiguity about whether they were in private, domestic space or public space might have contributed to the contention reflected in 1 Corinthians 11:2–16 over appropriate norms of decorum. Increasingly, however, the social sciences have recognized ritual/sanctuary space as one distinct from both domestic and public spaces—one that plays a significant role in the development and reinforcement of worldview.[86] In the liturgical, ritual space of the church's worship—in word, sacrament, and various other ways—Christians to this day act out signs and symbols of their new life in Christ and of the life to come. In so doing, we give expression to our worldview and are continually reoriented to the baptismal truth about ourselves as God's beloved children and to a vision of the world in light of God's plans and purposes. This truth and this vision invariably represent challenges to cultural norms and values, as the Corinthian women prophets no doubt recognized (and as Paul himself eloquently argues throughout 1 Corinthians in relation to a variety of other matters, if not this one). Symbolic proclamations of this challenge may well evoke conflict, but they may also represent powerful articulations of the gospel that arrest attention and draw others to it. In fact, we should not suppose that all outsiders to Corinthian worship would have been scandalized by what they were observing. Perhaps some would have been drawn to the community of faith in which such a theological statement could be made. In short, evangelistic considerations cannot be claimed exclusively by Paul and/or other "traditionalists."

One thinks, for example, of Rosa Parks, a devout woman finally compelled to make a symbolic theological statement of her own in

1955 by refusing to vacate her seat for a white passenger when so ordered on a Montgomery bus. (Obviously, this act took place on a city bus, rather than in the context of worship—though it surely can be argued that her formation in worship nurtured the conviction of her full humanity that led to her challenge of convention.) Her action profoundly flouted long-standing cultural norms and expectations and evoked conflict, indeed, ongoing civil unrest; but it also arrested attention, galvanizing thousands into action and into a gospel-inspired movement that changed the course of American history. That conflict was also felt within the internal life of the church, as evidenced by the reaction of white clergy to the movement she evoked, when in correspondence with Martin Luther King Jr. they described it as "unwise and untimely."[87]

So what I'm wondering is this: Could the Corinthian women prophets' challenging of cultural conventions also have been viewed, perhaps, as *unwise* or *untimely*? Some interpretations of the text lend themselves to such a reading. In what sense might their conduct be considered unwise, for example?[88] Some read 1 Corinthians 11:2–16 in tandem with 1 Corinthians 8–9, where Paul addresses controversy over the question of eating meat from animals used in pagan sacrifices. He argues that Christians have the authority (*exousia*), the right or freedom or power, to eat whatever they want but considers this to be ill-advised participation in view of the sensitivities of fellow believers. Thus he urges them to follow his own example and renounce this right for the sake of the greater good (cf. 8:9; 9:4–6, 12, 18), for freedom in Christ is more than freedom from restraint: it is freedom to act on behalf of one's neighbor.

Paul's understanding of freedom in Christ is important, but is it in view in 1 Corinthians 11:2–16? Some think so, arguing that Paul is trying to persuade Corinthian women to renounce their rights (regarding headdress) for the sake of the greater good. Robert Allard, for example, takes this view: "Paul is telling the Christian women of Corinth . . . they need to understand that being set free for their neighbors takes precedence over being set free from a veil."[89] This argument would be more plausible if Paul had cast the argument in these explicit terms, as in 1 Corinthians 8–9, and even more explicitly in 1 Corinthians 14, where the "upbuilding" or "edification" of the church is referenced repeatedly. Instead, in 1 Corinthians 11:2–16, the argument is cast primarily in terms of honor and shame, propriety, and cultural convention.

But for the sake of argument, if it were Paul's intention to provide instruction on the proper use of Christian freedom with respect to headdress, urging restraint of the sort he himself exercises in relation to food, an important question emerges: Are the situations in which Paul and the Corinthian women find themselves entirely parallel? It is one thing for an entitled male to set aside his "right" (e.g., to eat anything he wants). But isn't it another for him to beseech those on lower rungs of the social ladder to follow his example, to renounce their rights too for the sake of communal harmony? Paul's social location is not entirely comparable to that occupied by Corinthian women prophets, and those on the "underside" may have a very different perspective on the wisdom, or lack thereof, of a particular challenge to social convention.

Could the conduct of Corinthian women prophets have been viewed, not only as unwise, but also as "untimely"? Paul's apocalyptic eschatology is relevant in this connection and is reflected in many readings of the text, for throughout this epistle he endeavors to help the Corinthians see that they are people "on whom the ends of the ages have come" (10:11; or "on whom the overlapping of the ages has arrived").[90] They are, in other words, people who live in a time that can be described as "already" but "not yet": "already," because the cross marked the end of the old age, and the power of the Spirit at work in the life of the community is a sign that the new age has begun; but "not yet," because they still await Christ's second coming and the consummation of God's new creation. In short, believers (then and now) live "between the times," straddling both the old age and the new. The action of the Corinthian women prophets in eradicating cultural signs of gender distinction and subordination thus could have been viewed as "untimely" or premature in the sense that it neglected this "in-between" nature of their existence, emphasizing the "already" to the exclusion of the "not yet." As Richard Hays puts it, "Paul's ethical stance is comprehensible only in light of his dialectical eschatology: already men and women enjoy equality in Christ; however, not yet can that equality sweep away all the constraints and distinctions of the fallen order."[91] He goes on to say:

The calling of Christians at the turn of the ages, according to Paul, is to live sacrificially within the structures of marriage and community, recognizing the freedom of the Spirit to transform institutions and roles but waiting on the coming of the Lord to set all things right. In

the meantime, apostle and community find themselves poised on a
tightrope, seeking to discern the will of God in circumstances where
old norms no longer hold.[92]

This is a plausible perspective and perhaps one we can appreciate given
the centrality of Paul's dialectical eschatological perspective throughout the letter and the fact that we, too, find ourselves between the
"already" and the "not yet" and thus walk the same tightrope, negotiating cultural conventions that require similar challenges of discernment.

However, we have been waiting a good bit longer for the final
consummation of God's new creation and have had much more time
to engage in discernment, under the guidance of the Holy Spirit, of
implications of the gospel for gendered life together in Christ. In
light of that extended discernment, faithfulness to the gospel on our
parts entails more than simply waiting on the coming of the Lord to
set things right. It also entails joining in at those points where God's
future may be struggling toward realization now. The church, after all,
exists in this world as an embodiment of Christ's lordship, an outpost
of the coming future and a witness to the reconciliation that God
intends for all (as Paul himself eloquently insists). It is our vocation
to bear corporate witness to the future that God has in mind for the
whole creation. Thus we may be even more inclined to challenge Paul's
counsel to the Corinthian women than they may have been—perhaps
especially on the grounds of consistency, for when it came to relations
between Jew and Gentile, Paul refused to tolerate any distinctions.
There was no "already" but "not yet" on that front—it could not
wait! That dividing wall of hostility had to come down now! And
could it not be argued that the dividing wall of gender hierarchy and
subordination is an equally urgent and evangelical matter in our own
day—one that also bears on the integrity of the gospel and affects half
the human race?

In fairness to Paul, he understood himself to be called by God to
a particular apostolic task and was intensely focused upon it: the task
of proclaiming Christ among the Gentiles. As Sandra Hack Polaski
observes, "The fact that he pays less attention to other issues, or seems
ambivalent about them, is the result of his single-minded commitment
to the task of breaking down the dividing wall between Jew and Gentile."[93] Paul is thus "a limited, human model, . . . as all human beings
are limited—by time and place, by historical and cultural blindness."

But as Polaski also goes on to state, "The biblical witness, including the letters of Paul, is that God uses human beings to achieve bits and pieces of the divine purpose"[94] and that "we take Paul's writings most seriously when we commit ourselves to our particular calling—say, to gender or racial equality—as resolutely as he did to his."[95]

What do you think about this? Could the Corinthian women prophets' flouting of cultural norms perhaps have been viewed as "unwise" and "untimely"? Of course, analogical invocation of larger-than-life figures like Rosa Parks and Martin Luther King Jr. runs the risk of exaggeration and heroization, and that is not my intention. My point, rather, is that the examples set by Parks and King remind us that challenging cultural conventions is in some instances a proclamation of the gospel and integral to its integrity. Indeed, Paul bears witness to the countercultural nature of the gospel at other points throughout this letter, if not here—for example, with respect to sexual morality, litigation, idolatry, and socioeconomic status (cf. 1 Cor. 5; 6; 8; 11:17–22). Moreover, the conflict occasioned by such challenge is not always a bad thing in the life of the church. It may well turn out to be the arena of God's guidance and work among us and can play an important role in the divine work of shaping within us the mind of Jesus Christ. Surely we can appreciate Paul's concern for the unity of the church and at the same time acknowledge the importance of occasions when full engagement with conflict can be a means of collective discernment of God's will for us. In fact, "unity" and "conflict" are not mutually exclusive concepts. Our willingness to stick together and engage the often-painful process of communal discernment—when it would be easier to pick up our toys and play elsewhere—is in many instances our most convincing witness to the truth and power of the gospel we proclaim, for it is a gospel that makes a difference in how we deal with those with whom we disagree. Paul himself speaks elsewhere of the importance of "testing the spirits" (see 1 Cor. 14:29; 1 Thess. 5:19–22) and exercising forbearance as we live together with differences and disagreements over what proper response to the gospel looks like (see Rom. 14–15; 1 Cor. 8–9).

Is it reaching to imagine the Corinthian women prophets from this perspective? We cannot reconstruct their thoughts and motivations with certainty, and so we cannot say for sure. Thus we ought not idealize them—or those who disagreed with them (including Paul). But can we not imagine that all our foremothers and forefathers in the faith

(Paul included) were complex, well-intentioned people, genuinely engaged amid the messy business of communal discernment, teasing out the implications of the gospel for their life together, and negotiating faith in a complex world of overlapping contexts? Can we not consider the possibility that "serious arguments and strong rhetoric" were "flying both ways"[96] as our forebears, guided by the Spirit, "engaged in an ongoing theological debate over equality, freedom, dignity, and full 'citizenship' in the *ekklēsia*"?[97] And could the text's authority be "conceived more broadly as that of the full range of voices that speak through it"?[98]

Negotiation of cultural conventions is an important part of that debate in all times and places. Because cultural norms, perspectives on social propriety and decorum, vary and are constantly changing in different times and places, this matter requires ongoing communal discernment. And in view of this constant change, there are two other respects in which we might be instructed by dangers that the text presents as we reflect on the church's relationship to the culture in which it finds itself. One of those dangers is that of uncritically baptizing our cultural norms, granting them theological legitimation. As Daniel Kirk astutely observes, texts such as this can serve as a warning to us that "we are ever susceptible of wrongly baptizing society's standards into the name of Christ without recognizing that baptism into Christ always brings with it death to the old and resurrection to the new."[99] Paul clearly veers in this direction in 11:3 and 7–9 when he provides over-the-top theological and scriptural rationales to influence a matter of sartorial discretion. Also consider a more recent and blatant example: Many Western missionaries likewise veered in this direction as they first moved into Asian, African, and Latin American countries, imposing Western cultural norms (with respect to clothing, liturgy, and music, among other things) as integral to the gospel. Happily, contemporary efforts to "indigenize," "enculturate," or "incarnate" the gospel in the varied contexts around the globe in which the gospel has taken root are now celebrated, engaged with integrity and passion, and acknowledged as a gift to the life of universal church. As David Rhoads has observed,

> Diversity gives the church durability and adaptability. Diversity enables the church to meet the needs of many different people, to address and embrace the cultural distinctiveness of various ethnic groups, to adapt to changing times and circumstances, to ensure

that Christian life remains fresh and vital, and to enable us to be more imaginative in the church's mission to the world. God created such religious diversity, and we will surely need it to carry out our ministry in the world.[100]

In view of all this, Paul's concluding argument, "We have no such custom, nor do the churches of God" (11:16), is one he could scarcely make today.

Indeed, given the flourishing of Christianity today in every corner of the globe, in varied contexts and cultures, we are now aware, more than ever, of the danger of elevating a cultural norm to relevance in all times and places: this would be another danger to which the text bears witness. As Gordon Fee observes, "The 'customary' nature of the problem" Paul is addressing "in a monolithic cultural environment makes it impossible to transfer to multifaceted cultures in which the church finds itself today. In each culture there are modes of dress that are appropriate and those that are not."[101] In some communions to this day, women are still required to wear head coverings in worship and elsewhere on the basis of 1 Corinthians 11:2–16, to continue an ancient cultural practice. However, in contexts with a different set of cultural "givens," imposition of such a norm from the first-century world would hardly promote evangelism, but would have precisely the opposite effect, proving to be deeply offensive to many modern women and thus an impediment to reception of the gospel.[102] Ironically, any evangelistic concern Paul had in mind in addressing headwear in the first place would thereby be turned on its head.

Finally, one last matter that evokes reflection on both insights and dangers is also worth consideration in connection with 1 Corinthians 11:2–16 and the history of its interpretation: the eroticization of women. In fact, Pauline scholar Francis Watson has provided an intriguing reading of the text from this perspective, arguing that the erotic attraction of men to women is precisely what Paul is working against. In Watson's view, the item of apparel under discussion is not just a head covering, but rather a full-face veil[103] that makes it possible for a woman to speak authoritatively in worship in that it "intercepts and prohibits the male gaze that would convert her into an object and prevent her recognition as a speaking subject."[104] Her voice must be heard, for with the dawn of new creation, the Spirit is poured out on all flesh. For this to happen, agape, rather than eros, "must rule in the public sphere of the congregation, and for that reason the veil is interposed as the condition of woman's speech and of man's listening to woman's speech."[105] It "signifies the necessary distinction between eros and agape, excluding the one so as to preserve the space of the other."[106] On this reading, then, the veil is not a sign of subordination but of the woman's authority to speak to and from God on behalf of the congregation. Indeed, it is an affirmation that "in the Lord" women and men belong together.

Thankfully, Watson acknowledges the asymmetrical construal of eros (the desire of an active male subject for a passive female object) as a deeply problematic and decidedly androcentric aspect of Paul's argument. Female erotic attraction to male worship leaders is not considered in 1 Corinthians 11:2–16 (or else men, too, might need to veil their handsome faces in order to be heard)! Moreover, as Watson recognizes, the custom Paul proposes "grossly exaggerates the potential of the look to hinder reception of the word"; "insults women by compelling them to reckon with the male look as a fundamental problem of their existence, even within the sphere of the Christian congregation"; "insults men by stereotyping them as the helpless victims of eros"; and "undermines the familial dimension of the Christian community, within which the fellow-Christian is addressed as 'brother' or 'sister.'"[107] Neither does he overlook the fact that the veil, an ambiguous and easily misunderstood symbol, renders women invisible, which could lead toward silencing and exclusion from church leadership, contrary to Paul's intention.[108]

Nevertheless, Watson cautions us not to throw this problematic baby out with the bathwater: "Clumsy and ill-conceived though it surely is, this passage is not simply to be rejected. . . . The Pauline veil may be taken to represent not a viable practical proposal but as an invitation to think through the difference between eros and agape, on the assumption that genuine concerns of individual and corporate Christian existence may indeed be bound up with this distinction."[109] There may be no doubt about the fact that "the human attraction to the glory of the other is real enough, and the congregation will have to accommodate it and will not wish simply to deny it."[110] For this reason, we should "persist in the attempt to hear what Paul is saying, from behind the veil of his questionable theological arguments," for "the Pauline veil invites theological reflection not on the problem of a 'hierarchical' ordering of the sexes and the possibility of an 'egalitarian' alternative, but on the difference between agape and eros as the basis for the togetherness of man and woman in Christ."[111]

There is something compelling about Watson's argument. Not all will find it convincing, for the text speaks specifically (and repeatedly) of "head" coverings rather than "face" coverings, and it does not mention eros. The leading consideration appears, instead, to be "shame." Moreover, by reinterpreting the text in a way that makes it appear less harmful to women, some will suspect that it has been whitewashed.[112] However, Watson's reading represents a decided improvement over those of other interpreters who propose erotic construals of the problem being addressed in 1 Corinthians 11:2–16 (arguing, for example, that men can be distracted by glorious female creatures, that beautiful hair can be a sexual enticement, indeed, a "come-on," or that an uncovered head conveys "availability")[113]—though without Watson's recognition of the problematic nature of such observations. Without such recognition, they risk reinscribing the male gaze and sexualizing women in our own time and place through their preaching and teaching of 1 Corinthians 11:2–16, with the result that women are led to believe that their appearance and sexuality are problematic, dangerous, threatening realities in the life of the Christian community and so must be kept under wraps.

Perhaps 1 Corinthians 11:2–16 and Watson's reading of it can prompt our reflection on such matters, for sadly, the male gaze does continue to be a problem of female existence in our overly sexualized culture, pervaded by erotic and pornographic imagery that objectifies women, and it is one with which women in worship leadership roles still, to some extent, contend. In fact, maybe it can also prompt reflection on a continuing matter of very practical concern in the life of the worshiping community raised by Paul's discussion: that of clerical garb! In my own tradition, women and men exercising liturgical leadership typically "robe" for worship, precisely so that the congregation's focus will not be on their clothing or physical appearance but on the word of God they proclaim. Still, more clergywomen than one might imagine can attest to the exasperating commentary and critique to which they are sometimes subjected—not just on their sermons or prayers, but also on their hairstyles, footwear, accessories, or uncovered legs—as well as to inordinate interest in what they are wearing under their robes! (Clergymen are not as frequently subjected to this sort of inspection and curiosity.) If this text, along with others we have examined in this volume, prompts us to recognize and reflect on ways in which the eroticization of women and overemphasis on female appearance, so prevalent in our culture, can find expression even within the community of faith, then even exasperating aspects of the text may have a role to play in forming the mind of Jesus Christ in us!

In sum, there are both insights and dangers aplenty in 1 Corinthians 11:2–16 that provide rich food for thought as we negotiate the complex relationship between church and culture in our own time and place. And aren't we better off with, rather than without, this biblical snapshot of such a messy, conflicted moment in the life of the early church, even if we find our forebears negotiating the relationship in faltering fashion, imperfectly? Indeed, would we not be impoverished, in important respects, without it, despite the interpretive problems it presents? Early on in my relationship with the Bible (and with the apostle Paul in particular), I was inclined to discard a text like 1 Corinthians 11:2–16, but I no longer advocate doing so. It was not, after all, the practice of the biblical authors and scribes who bequeathed to us the living tradition of Scripture. As Ellen Davis notes, their preference for retention of problematic traditions likely reflects their understanding "that simply throwing away old ideas, even bad ones, is not the most effective way of handling them." As she goes on to explain, a living (and thus messy) tradition such as Scripture (in contrast to a pristine ideology) is distinguished by a sense of history: "A tradition earns its authority through long rumination on the past. A living tradition is a potentially courageous form of shared consciousness, because a tradition, in contrast to an ideology, presents (in some form) our mistakes and atrocities as well as our insights and moral victories." There is, to be sure, a price to be paid by those of us "who are (from a biblical perspective) privileged to live within a tradition": it requires "accepting a high degree of inherent tension." However, as Davis says, the possibility open to us, "which is not open to committed ideologues, is repentance, the kind of radical reorientation of thinking that the New Testament writers term *metanoia*, literally, 'a change of mind.'"[114] This is among the important reasons why wrestling with (and against) tyrannical texts has a role to play in God's own work in us, forming the mind of Jesus Christ in us.

CONCLUDING THOUGHTS

Since Scripture is a living tradition, the dialogue in which Paul and the Corinthians were engaged invites our participation. In many respects, concerns they were negotiating continue to bear on the life of

Christian communities in our own day. Thus, as a final exercise, I find myself compelled to continue the conversation by writing a few letters of my own—and I invite you to do the same!

Dear Paul,

Grace and peace to you from God our Father and the Lord Jesus Christ. If you have had a chance to read the manuscript enclosed with this letter, you will have gathered that I have been wrestling mightily with your counsel to the Corinthian women prophets regarding appropriate liturgical headdress, trying to wrap my own head (not altogether successfully) around it. Thus, in case you are wondering, I want you to know that I do give thanks to God for you, aware that your apostolic labors made it possible for those of us who are Gentiles, outsiders, strangers to the covenants of promise to be embraced in God's gracious, saving purposes for the whole world in Jesus Christ. If it were not for your passionate commitment to your vocation, I would not even be reading your mail as my own. I also (truly!) give thanks to God for the depth and enduring quality of your letters, which centuries later continue to evoke rich reflection on the meaning of Christ's lordship for our lives and to inspire the church to live as an outpost of the coming future and a witness to the reconciliation that God intends for us all. I even have a special appreciation for your correspondence with the Corinthian church, given the way in which it helps us think theologically about a remarkable range of practical concerns in light of the lordship of Jesus Christ.

However, I have to admit that despite all my exegetical effort I am still puzzled by your counsel to the church at Corinth in 1 Corinthians 11:2–16, and I find it one of the most obscure passages you wrote. I cannot pretend to have resolved the interpretive problems it presents. Indeed, it raises more questions than I can find satisfactory answers for. Even so, I want to commend you for raising to visibility a number of significant matters and prompting reflection on them. For one thing, I appreciate your underlying concern that worship should be conducted "decently and in order" (14:40) if it is to glorify God and draw people into the divine presence. (In fact, those of us who are card-carrying Presbyterians have made this a hallmark of our worship and polity. Perhaps you would appreciate the slogan featured on some of our T-shirts and bumper stickers, borrowed from you: "Presbyterians do it decently and in order!")

I also appreciate your witness to the careful and ongoing discernment required as the church negotiates its relationship to the culture and overlapping contexts in which it finds itself, for the sake of its fellowship and its mission. This text in particular provides a realistic snapshot of such a moment of discernment in the life of the early church—a moment in process, in all its messy, confusing, combative, visceral, and emotionally charged ambiguity. I have found it instructive, in both positive and negative ways, to eavesdrop as you think your way through it out loud. You see, we too (in the Protestant mainline at least—I can only speak for my own context) find ourselves mired in a somewhat analogous moment in our own time and place as we dispute the role of gay and lesbian Christians in the life and leadership (including worship leadership) of the church. For many, the notion of gay clergy represents a scandalous flouting of biblical and cultural norms and an impediment to the integrity of the church's witness in the world. For many others, however, the full inclusion of gay and lesbian persons in the life of the church, including its leadership, is integral to the integrity of both the church's witness and the gospel itself. Evangelistic concerns are present on both sides of the conflict, for some (inside and outside the church) are scandalized by the ordination of gay and lesbian persons, and others (inside and outside the church) are equally scandalized by exclusion. In the midst of our own heated moment of discernment, as in the one at Corinth, appeals to creation theology, custom, propriety, shame, Scripture, and nature are flying from all quarters and in all directions. God is no doubt at work in the midst of our current conflict as we struggle to discern together the shape of faithfulness to Jesus Christ. But clear ways forward are not always immediately at hand as we wrestle with varied considerations and competing values, and perhaps only in retrospect can we say whether accommodation or countercultural witness with respect to a particular cultural norm was the wisest course of action and in the best service of the gospel.

That said, I have to admit to regret that you erred on the side of accommodation with respect to women's liturgical attire in your counsel to the church at Corinth—especially given the decidedly countercultural thrust of your counsel in 1 Corinthians on so many other practical matters. I do recognize that crucial considerations of honor and shame endemic to your culture and concern about the public visibility of the church's worship had a great deal of influence on your thinking about this matter. However, shouldn't the church's worship provide a ritual space where we proclaim, embody, and are constantly reoriented to the truth of our baptismal identity in Christ—in contrast to all the false messages about who we are that inundate us daily?

I also have to confess that I think you were a bit heavy-handed. Indeed, some of your arguments are questionable and way over the top for a matter of sartorial discretion! And unfortunately, the regrettable theological "means" by which you argued your case (e.g., hierarchical headship and your problematic reading of the Genesis creation narratives) have received far too much attention by those who promote a divinely ordained, hierarchical vision of appropriate relations between women and men—to the neglect of the actual "end" you had in view with respect to headdress. Neglected also is your presumption that women in Corinth, along with men, were to continue exercising ministries of prayer and prophecy, speaking both to and from God on behalf of the gathered congregation. I like to think that you, too, would be dismayed that your words in 1 Corinthians 11:2–16 provide one of the principal scriptural bases for the subordination of women in Christian culture and circumscribe the lives of many women around the world to this day.

Centuries later, we continue to care a great deal about what you think and what we can learn from you about our life together in Christ, and thus scholars will no doubt continue to debate your theology of gender. Some argue that you may well have believed that women are, in some sense, ontologically inferior to men—that otherwise, the text does not make sense.[115] There may be something to that, for you were, after all, a first-century male, informed by ancient Greco-Roman gender discourse, and perhaps could not have thought otherwise. However, I do not think this perspective does full justice to your stunning vision of eschatological life "in Christ," which changes everything. Indeed, a glimmer of the equality and interdependence of women and men in Christ surfaces (in vv. 11–12) even in the midst of your otherwise convoluted argument! I'm also inclined to cut you a break, for whatever your ontological views, your whole discussion clearly presumes the functional equivalence of women and men in the life of the church: it presumes that women have, in fact, been gifted by the Holy Spirit for essential ministries that build up the body of Christ. The only issue is appropriate attire or coiffure when they do so! However, a word to the wise: don't mess with women's hair! It is best to let them exercise authority over their own heads, in ways they see fit (a point you acknowledge in v. 10, if fleetingly).

In sum, to be honest, I'm inclined to think you dropped the ball in this particular moment of discernment in the life of the church at Corinth, but not to worry. We'll pick it up and carry it further as we continue to discern the implications of the gospel for life together in our own time and place. Perhaps, as Sandra Hack Polaski has suggested, "The biblical witness" (your own letters included) "is that God uses human beings to achieve bits and pieces of the divine purpose"[116] and that we take your writings "most seriously when we commit ourselves to our particular calling—say, to gender or racial equality—as resolutely" as you did to your calling to proclaim Christ to the Gentiles.[117] I'm grateful for that insight, for your life's work and witness, and for your encouragement to bring every single aspect of our lives under the lordship of Jesus Christ. It is a challenging calling, as it was in your own day, for now, as then, we see in a mirror dimly—we, too, know only in part; but I will look forward to the time when we can continue this conversation face-to-face. Until then, may the grace of the Lord Jesus be with you . . .

FTG

Dear Corinthian women prophets,

Grace to you and peace from God our Father and the Lord Jesus Christ. I have been reading your mail (you may be surprised to learn that centuries later the church universal continues to treasure it as its own) and spending a great deal of time wrestling with the apostle Paul's counsel regarding appropriate liturgical headdress in 1 Corinthians 11:2–16. It is a text I find puzzling and exasperating in many respects. (I'm suspecting you may have found it thus as well! To be honest, there have been moments when I wanted to tear my own hair out while trying to wrap my head around why he was so concerned about yours.) But I also find it intriguing and inspiring in that it provides an extraordinary glimpse of you, foremothers in the faith! Indeed, one of the most striking things about the conflict reflected in the text is that it clearly presumes (on the part of all parties to it) that, by the power of the Spirit, you were in fact exercising ministries of prophesying and praying in your church—providing leadership in the worship assembly by speaking to and from God on behalf of the congregation. It is one of the earliest glimpses that we have of foremothers in the faith, confirming that you were there, participating actively, and highly significant in Christian history from its first moments. You are part of our history, part of our story, and I've come to appreciate Ann Lane's observation that "if we try to understand the past and leave women out, we have learned only a partial history,"[118] a partial story. It is one of the reasons I give thanks for a cantankerous text like 1 Corinthians 11:2–16, despite the interpretive problems it presents!

We wish we could hear your voices more directly, for we have only half of the conversation. We have to read between the lines of Paul's counsel to you, inferring your theology and practice as best we can from his labored effort to correct them. It is "mirror reading," and we find ourselves peering through it dimly. As Elisabeth Schüssler Fiorenza has put it, we see the tip of an iceberg,[119] leaving us to wonder: What is submerged?

Indeed, I'm left pondering many questions I wish I had your answers to! For instance, I'm wondering what, precisely, praying and prophesying in the worship assembly with uncovered heads meant to you. Are we correct in inferring that it was in some way an expression of the baptismal freedom you experienced "in Christ," a ritual embodiment of Paul's emphatic conviction that "if anyone is in Christ, there is a new creation: everything old has passed away; see, everything has become new!" (2 Cor. 5:17)? I gather that this practice was deliberate on your part and significant enough to you to warrant persisting in it, despite the conflict it evoked. (And apparently a great deal of cultural baggage must have been riding on this custom, given Paul's extended response to it!)[120] What, exactly, did head covering convey in your cultural context, and how did it limit what you understood to be your calling? Were you perhaps proclaiming to your honor-shame culture that you now had a new basis of honor within Jesus Christ, the image of God, whom you had "put on"?[121] You may be interested to know that head coverings for women—and the question of veiling in particular—is still a matter of considerable contention in our contemporary culture wars and religious conflicts, unjustly connoting inferiority, subordination, and sexuality in the view of some but appropriate modesty, privacy, and morality in the view of others (primarily of Islamic faith).

Inquiring minds also want to know: What was your response to Paul's counsel, and who won this argument in the end? Interestingly, Paul does not refer to this matter again in the later letter to Corinth that we also have in our possession (one we call 2 Corinthians), nor do the later disputed Pauline letters (2 Thessalonians, Colossians, Ephesians, and the Pastoral Epistles—not even the elaborate dress code for women in 1 Tim. 2) speak of any head-covering requirements, which makes me suspect that you may have prevailed in your own time and place. (Paul clearly expected that his word might not be the last one on this matter!) Sadly, however, this text that preserves the site of your argument eventually spawned restrictive interpretations and practices. As Jouette Bassler has noted, "It was not the uncontested assumption of functional equality that prevailed in the later church, but the message of secondary, deriva-tive status conveyed by firmly reimposed veils."[122]

There are many other matters I would like to discuss, perhaps face-to-face if Christ should return soon. In the meantime, know that feminist biblical scholars will continue to be hard at work, endeavoring to retrieve the voices of women in early Christianity, including your own. Also, for whatever it is worth, know that many churchwomen today share what must have been your exasperation, as well as your struggle, with overattention to matters of female attire and appearance in both church and culture! We take courage from your example and your ministry as we continue the struggle to live more fully into God's new creation in Christ, looking forward to the day when, with respect to sartorial concerns, surely our bap-tismal garments—putting on Jesus Christ—will suffice! Maranatha! Our Lord, come!

FTG

QUESTIONS FOR DISCUSSION
AND REFLECTION

For group study, this lengthy chapter can be divided into two manage-able sections under the headings "Listening to the Text" and "Dialogue with the Text."

What has been your prior experience with 1 Corinthians 11:2–16? In what contexts have you encountered it? Has it impacted your experience? If so, how?

What strikes you most about 1 Corinthians 11:2–16? What ques-tions does it raise for you? What new insights about 1 Corin-thians 11:2–16 have emerged from your engagement with this chapter? Why are they important to you? What questions linger?

Paul places a great deal of emphasis on maintaining appropri-ate "distinctions" between male and female appearance. Some commentators highlight this emphasis as a relevant insight that emerges from the text. Would you? Why, or why not?

The discussion in this chapter highlighted classic principles of biblical interpretation—such as "the interpretation of Scripture by Scripture," "the centrality of Jesus Christ," and "the rule of faith"—in its argument with 1 Corinthians 11:2–16. What do you think of these principles as means by which to wrestle with contentious texts with integrity? What insights emerged from engagement with them?

What do you think of the contention that Paul's reflection on matters of gender is still very much in process—that in 1 Corinthians 11:2–16 we see him struggling visibly to work out the implications of the gospel for gendered life together in Christ? What do you think of Sandra Hack Polaski's suggestion that "we take Paul's writings most seriously when we commit ourselves to our particular calling—say, to gender or racial equality—as resolutely as he did to his"?[123] What would you identify as your own particular calling?

Could the Corinthian women prophets' challenging of cultural conventions have been viewed, perhaps, as "unwise" or "untimely"? What do you think?

What would you say you learn from this text about the church's negotiation of the relationship to the culture in which it finds itself? What does it contribute to your reflection on the church's negotiation of this relationship in our time and place?

What insights do you glean from this text that bear on the worship life of your own congregation? What are the norms of decorum regarding "clerical garb" in your faith community?

Would you be inclined to preach or teach on 1 Corinthians 11:2–16? Why, or why not?

If you were to write a letter to Paul or to the Corinthian women, what would *you* want to say?

4

Women and Worship Wars (II)

1 Corinthians 14:33b–36

My first venture into the pulpit was not a happy experience, and the text before us in this chapter is largely responsible. I was a first-year seminarian enrolled in an introductory preaching course. The professor, for reasons that were not altogether clear, felt it important that we inflict one of our very first sermons on a local congregation; so my classmates and I were farmed out to churches within driving distance of the seminary. I was assigned to a small rural church in a neighboring county that was not entirely pleased to hear the news of my impending arrival. They were not unaccustomed to receiving preachers-in-training from the seminary but had never hosted one of the female persuasion. The governing body of the congregation met to discuss the grave crisis that the seminary had foisted upon them and in the end agreed (reluctantly) that I could come, on one condition: *I had to preach from Paul.* There was no need to stipulate the reason, for it was altogether clear, both to them and to me. Paul spoke a clear, uncompromising word against female speech in worshiping assemblies, and this would put me in my place.

1 CORINTHIANS 14:33b–36

[33b](As in all the churches of the saints, [34]women should be silent in the churches. For they are not permitted to speak, but should be

subordinate, as the law also says. [35]If there is anything they desire to know, let them ask their husbands at home. For it is shameful for a woman to speak in church. [36]Or did the word of God originate with you? Or are you the only ones it has reached?)

For the record, I went, I refused to preach from Paul, and we all managed to survive the ordeal. (In fact, I am happy to report that in the decades since then, they have called and installed female pastors.) But my experience was not unusual, for most women who have ever ventured into a pulpit have faced similar objections and have found themselves required to respond in some fashion or forum to 1 Corinthians 14:33b–36 and the apostle Paul's presumed opposition to women's religious leadership. Indeed, throughout Christian history 1 Corinthians 14:33b–36 has exercised formidable influence on ecclesial polity, barring women from preaching, teaching, and leadership roles, and to this day it continues to limit their full participation in many Christian communities.

Since that initial venture into the pulpit, I have made peace with Paul (for admittedly, the experience did nothing to endear him to me). Moreover, I no longer avoid engagement, in preaching or teaching, with contentious texts—even one as downright ornery and tyrannical as 1 Corinthians 14:33b–36! Indeed, throughout this volume I have contended that it is incumbent upon us to wrestle with them—directly, publicly, and with evident measures of integrity. Our ethical responsibilities as interpreters of Scripture require it, in view of their malefic influence; but opportunities present themselves as well—opportunities to learn more of our ecclesial family history, to be engaged by the living God in our encounter with Scripture, and to grow more fully into the mind of Jesus Christ. Thus blessings may be anticipated as we wrestle with both the problems and possibilities the text presents.

This overwrought text, like the previous three we have considered, is decidedly prescriptive in nature, and so we should not assume that it is descriptive of Christian women's religious experience in Corinth, that they were silent and subordinate in liturgical demeanor. Indeed, we can deduce from it that they were anything but, for prescriptive material is often the best historical evidence we have that the *opposite* is happening. As Deborah Krause has observed, "You don't tell women to shut up, unless they are talking."[1] This text reflects a rather strenuous effort to squelch customary practices. In fact, one of the most puzzling things about it is what to make of its apparent contradiction of the text we engaged in the preceding chapter, 1 Corinthians 11:2–16. There, as we have seen, the entire discussion is predicated on the assumption—shared by Paul and the Corinthian Christians—that women do speak publicly in worship, exercising leadership in prayer and prophecy. The issue at stake is what they are to wear on their heads (or how they are to arrange their hair) when they are speaking to and from God on behalf of the congregation. However, three chapters later, in 1 Corinthians 14:33b–36, all such speech appears to be prohibited in harsh, uncompromising fashion. Interestingly, these two texts bookend the discrete section of the letter that stretches across 1 Corinthians 11–14, in which Paul addresses divisive aspects of the Corinthians' worship practice that have come to his attention (the matter of head coverings or hairstyles in 11:2–16, abuses of the Lord's Supper in 11:17–34, and problems related to glossolalia or speaking in tongues in 12:1–14:40). This section both begins and ends with admonitions related to women's speech in worship, but antithetical ones, and the contradiction they represent is among the major interpretive puzzles with which we must grapple. Before doing so, however, let us attend closely to the language of the text and try to grasp its logic, bearing in mind Recommendation 1: "The difficult text is worthy of charity from its interpreters."[2]

LISTENING TO THE TEXT

As N. T. Wright has observed, "There are many churches today where there is so much order and peace that Paul might have wondered if everyone had gone to sleep." However, this was decidedly not the case in Corinth, where worship assemblies were "bordering on the chaotic."[3] Throughout 1 Corinthians 14, the apostle strives to restore liturgical "decency" and "order" (14:40), for "God is a God not of disorder but of peace" (14:33). The guiding principle he proposes as the measure of decency, order, and peace is the "edification," or mutual upbuilding, of the whole church: "Let all things be done for building up" (14:26). Edification ("building up") language surfaces repeatedly throughout the chapter (14:3, 4, 5, 12, 17, 26). In light of this principle, Paul strives to make a case that "prophecy" (intelligible speech that can be understood by all) is much to be preferred over "speaking in tongues" (unintelligible speech) unless an interpreter is present, for "those who speak in a tongue build up themselves, but those who prophesy build up the church" (14:4).

As the chapter comes to a close, he turns to the nuts and bolts of regulating speech within the worshiping assembly, providing very specific directives for three groups of people whose verbosity has been disruptive: glossolalists, prophets, and women (14:26–36). All three are admonished to be silent. Those who speak in tongues ("only two or at most three") are to be silent if there is no one to interpret their speech for others (14:27–29). In like manner, "two or three" prophets may speak, "one by one"; they are to "be silent" when other prophets are speaking (14:29–32). Finally, women too are silenced, but in far more categorical fashion: "Women should be silent in the churches. For they are not permitted to speak, but should be subordinate" (14:34). The silence that glossolalists and prophets are to observe is temporary in nature: glossolalists may speak (two or three of them at least, "in turn") if an interpreter is available; and prophets may speak (two or three of them at least) if no one else has the floor. By contrast, women are to observe an indefinite silence, presumably enduring in nature.

Dual commands convey this admonition in verse 34: women are to "be silent" and to "be subordinate." Why are silence and subordination required of this third disruptive group? Three reasons are given: (1) they do not have permission to speak; (2) the law requires it; and (3) considerations of honor and shame, core cultural values, demand it (indeed, "it is shameful for a woman to speak in church"). If 14:33b ("as in all the churches of the saints") serves as an introduction to this unit, rather than as a conclusion to the preceding verse (a debated matter), then a fourth consideration is appended: (4) universal observance of this admonition in "all" other churches, highlighting Corinthian deviation from a universal norm.

In important respects, these commands and rationales are ambiguous. To whom or to what, for example, are Corinthian women to be subordinate? Many interpreters presume that subordination to husbands or to men in general is in view, but this is not explicitly stated. Some contend that women are to be subordinate to the worship leadership, to the good of the worshiping assembly as a whole, or to authority in general—but these, too, are arguments from silence.

Neither is it clear to what "the law" refers, for oddly (and in contradistinction to standard Pauline practice), no specific legal precedent is cited. Many interpreters have filled in this blank, presuming that Genesis 3:16 is referenced ("Your desire shall be for your husband, and he shall rule over you"). But Genesis 3:16 says nothing about wifely speech or silence; it speaks more specifically of sexual dominance and desire, which will overrule reluctance a wife may have, given the dangers of childbirth and multiple pregnancies.[4] Others presume that "Jewish law" in general is in view, but the Old Testament contains no such prohibition of public female speech. Nor does Paul refer to rabbinic tradition in general as "law"; thus the "blame it on the Jews" strategy, to which Christian interpreters are all too frequently inclined, should be avoided. Interestingly, contemporaneous prohibitions of female speech come from Greco-Roman authors, rather than Jewish ones, and no doubt illumine the culturally acquired notions of honor and shame attached to public female speech that are explicitly noted in verse 35b ("*It is shameful for a woman to speak in church*"). For example, Plutarch, a Greek historian and philosopher (45–125 CE), provides a close parallel in his *Moralia*:

> [31][Theano said,] "It is necessary that not only the arm of the prudent (wife), but her voice too should be hidden. One should shun her voice as one would shun exposing her nakedness to view, and guard her against this when she is out of doors. For it is her speech that reveals her feelings, character, and attitude."[32]Phidias' representation of the Aphrodite of Elis with her foot on a tortoise symbolizes both the domestic character of woman and her silence. She must speak either to her husband or through her husband. . . . [33][As in the relationship between rich men and philosophers,] so too in the case of women when they submit to their husbands, they are praised, but when they wish to exercise domination, they act in a more indecorous manner than those subject to domination. Nevertheless, the husband should rule over his wife not like a despot, but as the soul rules over the body.[5]

Such opinions were in the cultural air but were not included among Roman legal statutes. In sum, it is not at all clear to whom or to what exactly women are to be subordinate; nor can we identify the "law" presumed to require it. But there may be no doubt about the fact that women are being pressured, rather forcefully and for a host of reasons (including lack of permission, legal decree, cultural considerations of honor and shame, and universal ecclesial practice) into silence.

A concession is granted, allowing for female speech in an altogether different context: "If there is anything they desire to know [learn], let them ask their husbands at home" (v. 35). Worship space is distinguished from domestic space, and female speech is restricted to the latter.[6] (A similar distinction between liturgical and domestic space can be observed in 1 Cor. 11:22, 34.) Such speech on the part of women is presumed to be interrogative in nature. Women may have questions they need to "ask" in order "to learn" (*mathein*); any such questions are to be directed to their menfolk. The marital relationship is not necessarily the only male-female relationship in view (as the NRSV translation implies, by specifying "husbands" as authoritative repositories of answers to questions). Daughters, widows, or slave women may also have questions, and these, too, are to be directed to male household residents, which (given the extended nature of the ancient household) could include other "menfolk" (e.g., brothers, sons, or other male relatives, in addition to husbands) who live under the same roof.[7] (The possibility that other women in the household might be able to address questions that arise is not considered!)

Having conveyed the dual command to silence and subordination, supporting rationales and a concession, the unit then concludes, oddly, with an exasperated outburst, conveyed by two sharply stated rhetorical questions: "Or did the word of God originate with you? Or are you the only ones it has reached?" (14:36). Shifting from third person (in vv. 33b–35) to second person, these sardonic questions are direct words of challenge, but to whom are they addressed? Many assume that the disruptive women are on the receiving end of them. However, grammar argues against this, for the second "you" (*hymas*) is modified by an adjective (*monous*, "only") that is masculine in form (*hymas monous*, "you only") rather than feminine (*hymas monas*), which suggests at the very least that a mixed-gender group is in view. In all likelihood the whole community is upbraided for indulging women's disruptive, prohibited, shameful speech. Whatever the case may be, the questions convey a stinging rebuke, challenging any arrogant presumption of special access to divine wisdom and knowledge. Moreover, they assert Paul's authority, for as the one who first preached the gospel to them, he is in a position to insist on adherence to norms that will restore decency and order to Corinthian worship. But they also indicate that he does not expect his admonitions to be accepted without protest.[8]

Many contemporary readers will be inclined to protest as well! Thus, once again it is important to remind ourselves that arguing with a text is not to be equated with rejection of biblical authority; indeed, arguing with a text is a faithful practice that honors the text by taking it with the utmost seriousness. However, let us first review the vigorous, ongoing debate about this text and consider various ways in which scholars have construed its historical context and resolved the central interpretive problem it presents, to see if they provide food for thought that might inform our own wrestling with it.

MAKING SENSE OF A PERPLEXING TEXT: THE SCHOLARLY DEBATE

The central interpretive dilemma facing interpreters of 1 Corinthians 14:33b–36 is what to make of its apparent contradiction of 1 Corinthians 11:2–16 (which takes for granted that women speak publicly) and other undisputed Pauline texts in which women are presented as full partners in Paul's ministry. Jouette Bassler summarizes the dilemma:

> How can women exercise their acknowledged right to pray and prophesy (1 Cor. 11) if they must keep absolute silence? How can women like Euodia and Syntyche (Phil. 4:2–3), Prisca (Rom. 16:3; 1 Cor. 16:19), Mary (Rom. 16:6), Junia (Rom. 16:7), and Try-phaena and Tryphosa (Rom. 16:12) function as coworkers in the churches if they cannot speak in those churches? How can Phoebe fulfill the role of deacon (Rom. 16:1–2) if she cannot speak out in the assembly? Something is seriously amiss here.[9]

No kidding! The admonitions to silence in 1 Corinthians 14:33b–36 stick out like a sore thumb among Paul's undisputed letters, and interpreters must somehow account for the discordance. Various proposals have been set forth, but each has drawbacks, and none are altogether conclusive. The possibilities can be clustered under three umbrellas for consideration.

It's not as bad as it sounds!

A number of proposals limit the scope of the admonitions to silence, thereby mitigating their severity. Some contend that the admonitions are not addressed to all women, but to a subgroup of them, and/or that a particular kind of speech (rather than all speech) is prohibited. The Greek word *gynē*, for example, can denote a "woman" or a "wife," and thus some argue that only married women are silenced. So perhaps different groups of women are addressed in 1 Corinthians 11:2–16 and 14:33b–36: prophesying and praying virgins, widows, or celibates in the former; and married women in the latter, in which case the two texts would not be contradictory after all.[10] In the same vein, some contend that 1 Corinthians 11:2–16 is addressed to worship leaders and 14:33b–36 to nonofficiants (those in the pews, so to speak).[11]

A number of scholars also limit the scope of the speech in view to disruptive "chatter." Thus the Greek word *lalein* (to speak), which appears twice in verses 34–35, conveys that women (or even more specifically, wives) "are not permitted to *chat.* . . . For it is shameful for a wife to *chat* in church."[12] Women's inspired speech (such as the prayer and prophecy noted in 1 Cor. 11:2–16) is allowed; only "unspiritual and uninspired" speech is prohibited.[13] Paul objects not to female exercise of liturgical leadership but rather to "outburst[s] of feminine loquacity,"[14] unlearned speech, or "extracurricular chatter."[15]

Other scholars limit the scope of prohibited speech in a different manner, directing attention to Paul's earlier admonition that when prophets speak, others are to "weigh what is said" (14:29). Reading 14:33b–36 in conjunction with 14:29, they propose that married women are not to participate in the communal scrutiny of prophecies uttered by their husbands. A wife should refrain from publicly questioning, challenging, correcting, and otherwise evaluating her husband's prophetic authority, for to do so would shame him, give the appearance (especially to outsiders) of marital insubordination, and thereby undermine the good order of the household.[16] Any questions they have about a husband's prophecy should be addressed to him privately, at home (v. 35).

All of these proposals mitigate the severity of a troublesome text, making it somewhat easier to swallow and reducing its tension with 1 Corinthians 11:2–16. We are given to understand that it is not quite as bad as it sounds! However, none of these proposals are entirely convincing, for a number of reasons. For one thing, if Paul were speaking of different groups of women in 1 Corinthians 11 and 14, he could have done so more clearly, as he does in 1 Corinthians 7. There he uses distinctive language to differentiate women who are unmarried and celibate (*hē gynē hē agamos*), betrothed virgins (*parthenos*), married (using forms of the verb *gameō*), and widows (*chēra*; see, for example, 1 Cor. 7:8, 34). And if he were prohibiting a particular kind of female speech, rather than female speech in general, would not this, too, be more evident? Limiting the meaning of the Greek word *lalein* (to speak) to idle "chatter" or "prattling" of some sort would seem to be ruled out by the use of this word throughout 1 Corinthians 14 in connection with both prophetic speech and glossolalia (cf. 14:2, 3, 4, 5, 6,

9, 11, 13, 18, 19, 21, 23, 27, 28, 29).[17] It may also reflect the imposition of gender stereotypes upon the text, for the liturgical disorder in Corinth would appear to have more to do with "an over-abundance of *inspired* speech"[18] than with "feminine loquacity." Neither can *lalein* be limited to the "weighing" or "judging" of prophecies. The language Paul uses in 14:29 for communal scrutiny or discernment of spirits is *diakrinein*, but 1 Corinthians 14:35 features the language of "asking" (*eperōtaō*) for the sake of "learning" (*mathein*) rather than language of discernment or scrutiny (*diakrinein*). Moreover, 14:29 and 14:33b–36 are separated by several verses, so a connection between them is not self-evident. In short, as much as contemporary Christians might wish that the text were not quite as bad as it sounds, these proposals are inconclusive.

If the severity of the text cannot be mitigated, there is one other tactic to consider: perhaps one can limit its application and thereby mitigate its damage. Thus, some contend that the admonitions of 1 Corinthians 14:33b–36, addressed to a specific problem in a different time and place (that is, to a particular group of disruptive, garrulous Corinthian women), should not be construed and applied more broadly as enduring ecclesial policy. However, the text's appeal to the universal practice of "all the churches of the saints" in verse 33b and also to "the law" argues against this—and has throughout the history of the text's interpretation.

It is as bad as it sounds, but these are not Paul's words!

Many other scholars, attending to the plain sense of the text, suspect that it *is* as bad as it sounds but that the admonitions to silence are not Paul's own words. Two very different proposals find a place under this second umbrella. One is a quotation theory and the other an interpolation theory.

According to the first, in verses 34–35, Paul is actually quoting the words of others—a slogan, perhaps, of certain Corinthian men bent on silencing women in worship—to which he then emphatically objects in verse 36: "*What?!* Did the word of God originate with you? Or are you the only ones it has reached?" This would correspond to Paul's mode of argumentation earlier in the letter, where he quotes from a letter he has received from the Corinthians, identifying queries they have raised in it before responding in a way that challenges or qualifies their concerns. In 7:1, for example, he writes, "Now concerning the matters about which you wrote: 'It is well for a man not to touch a woman.'" In the NRSV, the NIV, and other recent translations, these words appear in quotation marks because most scholars now believe that they represent a Corinthian slogan that Paul begins to counter in 7:2 ("But . . ."). This same pattern of referencing a query raised by the Corinthians before responding can be observed in 7:25; 8:1, 4; and 10:23. In the last three examples, Corinthian slogans to which Paul is believed to be responding are now placed in quotation marks in the NRSV and NIV, as in 7:1. So according to this theory, 14:34–35 should be enclosed in quotation marks too, to convey that Paul is quoting the words of others rather than stating his own opinion. This proposal accounts for the odd outburst and shift in tone in verse 36 and gives the opening Greek particle (*ē*) its "full force" as a disjunctive conjunction—that is, a word that introduces an alternative, refutation, or protest.[19] It also makes sense of the masculine adjective (*monous*) attached to the "you" (*hymas*) addressed ("you only," *hymas monous*). Verse 36 has long been regarded as Paul's rebuke of garrulous Corinthian women, but according to this theory, domineering Corinthian men ("you men") find themselves addressed! This theory also resolves the dissonance between 1 Corinthians 11 and 14, for if the sentiments articulated in 14:34–35 are not Paul's own, then there is no contradiction! As Sandra Hack Polaski observes, "If this reading is correct, the church's tradition of reading this text would be a sad irony, putting in Paul's own mouth a view he vigorously rejects."[20]

As appealing as this theory may be, many regard it as wishful thinking. For one thing, there is no clear signal that Paul is quoting a Corinthian point of view, as in 7:1, for example, where he begins with "Now concerning the matters about which you wrote . . ." (see also 7:25; 8:1). Moreover, earlier citations of Corinthian points of view in 1 Corinthians 7–10 are brief and to the point—on the order of "slogans," in contradistinction to the elaborate admonitions in 14:34–35.[21] It can also be observed that Paul's purported response in 14:36 fails to counter them effectively. But perhaps the most telling argument against the quotation theory is that the letter provides no other evidence that Corinthian men held any such viewpoint.

The second possibility under this umbrella has gained much more traction. The scholarly debate is far from over, but proponents of the interpolation theory currently represent the majority point of view.[22] According to this theory, the admonitions in 14:34–35 (perhaps even the whole of 14:33b–36) were written by someone other than Paul and inserted into 1 Corinthians 14 at some point in the process of scribal transmission. This is not an inconceivable possibility. For centuries, before the invention of movable type and the printing press, biblical texts were copied and recopied painstakingly by hand, and scribes sometimes inadvertently incorporated marginal notes into the text they were copying, thereby altering the original reading. Altered texts were then transmitted by subsequent copiers. Thus proponents of this theory believe the sentiments expressed particularly in verses 34–35 are those of a later interpreter who felt compelled to qualify Paul's instructions and left note of this in the margin, perhaps to bring 1 Corinthians more in line with the more restrictive admonitions of later New Testament epistles such as 1 Timothy (cf. 1 Tim. 2:11–15). Eventually the marginal note was incorporated into the text itself.

A number of compelling arguments have been marshaled in support of the interpolation theory. Chief among them is the dissonance between 1 Corinthians 11 and 14. Indeed, apart from 1 Corinthians 14:33b–36, no other passage in the six undisputed Pauline letters conveys any such restrictions on women's participation in the life of Paul's churches. The admonitions to silence also contradict his contention throughout 1 Corinthians 12–14 that the Spirit bestows gifts on all members of the church for the edification of the whole community, that "each" has a gift to share in worship, and "all" can participate. In 14:26, for example, Paul advises, "When you come together, *each one* has a hymn, a lesson, a revelation, a tongue, or an interpretation." In 14:31, he affirms that all may prophesy but should do so in turn: "For you can *all* prophesy one by one, so that all may learn and all be encouraged." And no gender restrictions are mentioned in this remarkable word of encouragement, apparently to all: "So, my friends, be eager to prophesy, and do not forbid speaking in tongues; but all things should be done decently and in order" (14:39–40; see also 14:23–24).

Further aspects of 1 Corinthians 14:33b–36 strike many scholars as decidedly uncharacteristic of Paul, perhaps none more so than the appeal to "the law" in verse 35—an unspecified law at that—in support of an ethical admonition.[23] Neither does Paul typically use language such as "[it is] not permitted" (v. 34). Indeed, the language of permission, subordination, and silence is far more characteristic of 1 Timothy (e.g., 1 Tim. 2:11–15), and such is deemed reflective of ecclesial concerns of a later generation, a time when women's leadership was increasingly contested.[24] The admonition that women should be silent "in the churches" (plural) is also odd, for Paul is not given to generalized instruction for churches at large. In 1 Corinthians, he deploys the epistolary genre in his customary fashion to address specific problems in a particular local congregation. In addition, the "concession" granted in 14:35, instructing women to direct any questions to their husbands at home, is oddly out of sync with the "fundamental reciprocity" that characterizes Paul's discussion of the marriage relationship in 1 Corinthians 7.[25]

In short, 1 Corinthians 14:33b–36 just doesn't sound like Paul! Moreover, verses 34–35 are said to disrupt the flow of Paul's argument on prophecy—you can skip from verse 33 to verse 37 (or even to verse 36) without missing a beat. The fact that 14:33b–36 now appears in parentheses in the NRSV reflects a sense on the part of its editors that it is disruptive, as well as their uncertainty as to whether or not these verses originally appeared in 1 Corinthians 14.

All of these arguments in favor of the interpolation theory constitute what biblical scholars call "internal evidence"—that is, evidence based on the likelihood of a reading going back to the original author (taking characteristic style, language, and theology into account) or to an error introduced by a scribe. In the case of 1 Corinthians 14:34–35, a strong argument for interpolation has been made on the basis of such considerations. However, in rendering a text-critical decision (a decision regarding the original wording of a text), scholars must also take into account "external evidence"—that is, consideration of whether or not the manuscript evidence at our disposal would also support such a reading, and it is on this point that the interpolation theory is inconclusive. Indeed, though widely championed, it has one major drawback: *none* of the ancient Greek manuscripts (and we have access to thousands of them) omit verses 34–35! So if these verses were inserted into the text, they were added at a *very* early stage in the manuscript tradition. Interestingly, in a handful of Greek-Latin bilingual manuscripts, verses 34–35 appear at a different point in 1 Corinthians 14—at the conclusion of the chapter, after verse 40. Some scholars point to this dislocation as evidence of uncertainty on the part of the ancient scribes about these verses. In recent years, attention has also been drawn to distinctive markings ("umlaut sigla") next to verses 34–35 in Codex Vaticanus, one of the earliest and best Greek manuscript witnesses to the text of the New Testament, dating from the fourth century. The markings appear to have been left by the original scribe throughout the manuscript to identify passages with textual problems.[26] Still, there is no getting around the fact that we do not have even one reliable ancient manuscript of the Greek New Testament in which verses 34–35 are omitted—a not insignificant consideration. Thus, even though the interpolation theory has garnered wide support, proponents of it cannot claim to have made a conclusive argument. In fact, a third possibility needs to be considered.

These are Paul's words, and it is as bad as it sounds!

Some scholars have had to conclude that this troublesome text was in fact authored by Paul and that it is as bad as it sounds; among them are notable feminist scholars who might wish that it were otherwise. They are not convinced by arguments that 1 Corinthians 14:33b–36 is "disruptive" in its context, that it sticks out like a sore thumb, lacking coherence with other aspects of the argument Paul has been making, for rhetorical analysis establishes clear points of connection. As we have noted, as 1 Corinthians 14 comes to a close, Paul provides specific directives for three groups of people whose verbosity has been disruptive—glossolalists, prophets, and women (14:26–36)—and the three sets of instructions bear similarities. Explicit linguistic connecting threads can be discerned, such as the language of "speaking" (*laleō*, 14:27, 28, 29, 34, 35), "being silent" (*sigaō*, 14:28, 30, 34), "subordination" (*hypotassō*, 14:32, 34), and "learning" (*manthanō*, 14:31, 35). The specific instructions for the three different groups also share a similar form: in each case, "a third-person imperative about a particular group is explained and then illustrated in the conditional form."[27] In short, 1 Corinthians 14:33b–36 is not an altogether bad fit in its immediate literary context.

Moreover, 1 Corinthians 11:2–16 and 14:33b–36 are not as entirely dissonant as they might appear at first glance. Both texts, for example, reference female subordination and include strong appeals to considerations of honor and shame as they address vexations related to female demeanor in worship. Both also cite written tradition (Genesis in 1 Cor. 11, and an unspecified legal mandate in 1 Cor. 14) and the practice of other churches in support of their arguments. And as Gillian Beattie has observed, "The means which Paul uses to achieve his ends in 1 Cor. 11.2–16 and 14.33b–40 are quite similar": "In both passages he prioritizes his sensibilities and concerns over those of the women whom he seeks to control; in both he demonstrates his power over all the Corinthians by assuming the right to determine their identity as Christians on the basis of their reaction to his commands" (see 14:37–38).[28] Perhaps it is of no little significance that the lengthy section of the letter addressing divisive aspects of Corinthian worship practice (1 Cor. 11–14) is bracketed on each end with admonitions related to women's speech.

Antoinette Wire calls attention to such considerations in her landmark study of women, gender, and 1 Corinthians (1990).[29] In her reading of this epistle, Paul throughout the letter contends with influential women prophets, wise and gifted women whose theology and spiritual authority in the Corinthian congregation compete with his own. Through close analysis of Paul's rhetoric, she infers their half of the conversation, sympathetically reconstructing their theological self-understanding as people who have been resurrected to new life in Christ and who thus share in a new humanity in which dominating relationships give way to abundant new life in the Spirit. They live by a new standard of honor and shame, directed to God alone, and do not share Paul's fear of disorder in worship, for they rejoice in the profusion of the Spirit's gifts and thrive on the vibrant confluence of voices in worship as believers become channels of the Spirit to one another. Mirror reading of Paul's sardonic questions in 14:36 reflects their confident claim to the gift of spiritual insight and the right to speak freely to and for God, as well as Paul's attempt to establish his own authority as the source of all they know and to expose their "strictly local impact in comparison to his active, worldwide role in bringing the gospel to Corinth and carrying it further."[30] In Wire's view, "Paul develops his argument as the letter proceeds, increasing restrictions on women's worship participation until he feels able to demand their silence."[31] So after "gaining an inch" in 1 Corinthians 11 with the preliminary restriction on their dress and behavior, he then "takes a mile" in 1 Corinthians 14 with more comprehensive restriction.[32] In Wire's reading of the letter, then, the silencing of these women in 14:33b–36 is hardly "a parenthetical matter," as it appears in the NRSV. Instead, it is "the apex of the argument," the "turning point in his argument concerning the spiritual. Once he has called for their silence, he has done all he needs to do."[33]

Not all are persuaded that women prophets play as prominent a role throughout Paul's argument in 1 Corinthians as Wire contends or agree with all aspects of her reconstruction (which is far more elaborate and sophisticated in methodology than this brief summary allows).[34]

Still, her reading prompts us to listen closely for other voices in the text and to imagine alternative points of view—and also to reflect on Paul's genuine humanity and feet of clay. Once again we are reminded of the social reality embodied in Paul's letters and the dialogical character of them, and we are asked to consider the possibility that the early Christian communities known through them were "pluriform movements of women and men gifted by the Divine Spirit and engaged in an ongoing theological debate over equality, freedom, dignity, and full 'citizenship' in the *ekklēsia*."[35]

Wire is not the only prominent feminist scholar who has argued at length for the authenticity of 1 Corinthians 14:33b–36. In a meticulous rhetorical analysis of 1 Corinthians (1991), Margaret Mitchell contends that "the patriarchal conservatism of these verses, though in seeming contradiction to 11:5, is fully at home in an argument for unity and concord such as we find in this chapter (14:33) and throughout 1 Corinthians."[36] The whole of the letter reflects a strategy of reconciliation, urging unity on a divided church, and the call for Christian unity above all else entails an inherent conservatism, as group concord results from concession and submission. A significant interdisciplinary study by Jorunn Økland (2004) takes a very different tack but also supports Paul's authorship of 1 Corinthians 14:33b–36, arguing that there was no fixed understanding of "woman" in Paul's complex Greco-Roman cultural context; therefore, we should not expect him to speak in a unified manner on the subject. Instead, there was an "unsettled" mix of different models or "discourses" of gender in the broader cultural air (e.g., woman as helper, receptacle, chaos, and deficient male) that informed Paul's thought and in which he participated. Økland contends, moreover, that space was gendered in antiquity and that "ritual/sanctuary space" (distinct from both public and private space, and the framework for 1 Corinthians 11–14) was gendered male (as in 1 Cor. 12, where Paul speaks of the church as the "body of Christ"). Thus, as Paul navigates concerns related to women's unsettled place in this sacred setting, he "veers" between "different discourses, different ways of structuring gender in the space of the *ekklēsia*."[37] As a result, his directives do not always hang together in a logical manner, to our way of thinking.

Significant feminist scholarship has staked out ground under all three of the umbrellas identified in this overview of the scholarly debate; hence there is no such thing as "the" feminist position, for feminist scholars disagree among themselves about 1 Corinthians

14:33b–36. They employ a range of methodologies and reach a variety of different conclusions, as demonstrated by the three quite different studies clustered under this final umbrella. But as we come to the close of this quick survey of the debate, this third possibility, too, is now on our radar: Paul may very well have authored 1 Corinthians 14:33b–36, and it may be as bad as it sounds!

ARTICULATING OUR OWN SENSE OF THE TEXT

Debate over 1 Corinthians 14:33b–36 is far from settled and will no doubt continue to be vigorous, given the dismay it evokes for many contemporary Christians and its invocation by many others as enduring ecclesial policy. It behooves us to participate in the debate, to articulate our own sense of the text, and to set forth alternative readings of it. We have a responsibility to do so if we claim to be "people of the book" who cling to the Bible as a foundational document that authors Christian identity and community. As Jean-Paul Sartre declared, "You are perfectly free to leave the book on the table. But if you open it, you assume responsibility for it."[38] Thus we must deal forthrightly with a text that Holly Hearon has aptly described as "a canonical embarrassment."[39]

The fact that it *is* canonical further compels our own wrestling with it. The authorship question has little bearing on the question of its authority, for whoever authored 1 Corinthians 14:33b–36, it is still in the biblical canon. Its authority stems not from its authorship, but from its canonical status. Thus it will not do to declare that Paul did not write it, or to pronounce it an antiquated relic that no longer need concern us and thereby summarily dismiss it.[40] As we have already noted, we are related by baptism to the believers in first-century Corinth and to the author of this text (whether Paul or another!), and the canonical witness to their conversation continues to be a means by which the church, through the ages, discerns God's will for it in new times and places. We are not just reading someone else's mail—we are reading our own, and by the power of the Holy Spirit, it continues to bring us into the living presence of God and to shape our vision of the world in light of God's plans and purposes—even when we find ourselves wrestling with its claims and sometimes against its claims. Thus, even a text like 1 Corinthians 14:33b–36 has a role to play in forming within us the mind of Jesus Christ.

The practice of listening carefully and patiently to the text and to the scholarly debate that continues to swirl around it has been the starting point for our engagement with it. As varied points of view have been considered, each of us has no doubt found some perspectives more compelling than others, though all have provided intriguing food for thought. Speaking for myself, I have long found "the interpolation theory" a largely (if not entirely) persuasive explanation for the text's puzzling lack of coherence with other aspects of Paul's theology and practice—for example, his fundamental insistence on the Spirit's generous bestowal of gifts on all members of the church for the edification of the whole community, with the result that "each" has a gift to share in worship and "all" can participate, as well as his evident full partnership with women in ministry and mission. On most days, I still find this theory somewhat compelling!

However, increasingly I find myself suspecting that the "dissonance" and "contradiction" I have perceived in 1 Corinthians 14:33b–36 may not be as "glaring" as I once thought—that it is not outside the realm of possibility that Paul wrote it, and if so, his thoughts were genuinely ambiguous as he engaged the challenging process of working out the implications of the gospel for gendered life together in Christ. As we noticed in the preceding chapter, Paul and his churches were negotiating life in multiple, overlapping contexts, and that ongoing process was messy, rife with competing values and contradictions, and far from complete. Moreover, Paul himself acknowledged that "for now we see in a mirror, dimly" and that his own knowledge was imperfect: "I know only in part" (1 Cor. 13:12). He described himself as a man very much in process of growth in Christ (Phil. 3:12). So increasingly I find myself reflecting on the complexity and genuine humanity of the man, who may be struggling more visibly with gender matters than with any others, here as in 1 Corinthians 11:2–16, as he thinks through the implications of the gospel.[41] Should we expect logical consistency from him on this front? Is it impossible to imagine that his reflections (and his mood) fluctuated between 1 Corinthians 11 and 14? His thoughts may well be in process and are clearly in conversation with those of others, whose voices we are only beginning to discern. Thus it would be well for us to consider the possibility, once again, that "serious arguments and strong rhetoric" are "flying both ways"[42]—that all the parties to this conversation may articulate arguments worthy of consideration.

DIALOGUE WITH THE TEXT

But listening—both to the text and to scholarly elucidations of it—is not all that is required of us. Making some sense of the text in its historical and literary context is important but not fully sufficient for our needs, since interpretation requires that we take a further crucial step, one not to be slighted—that of bringing the text into our own time and place. And interpretation, as we have insisted throughout this volume, entails much more than reiteration of the text, more than repeating what has been said before. It demands discernment of the text's significance for our own lives of discipleship in service to a living God and a resurrected Lord. So let us finally turn to reflection on this important matter, guided by practices that can facilitate this discernment: that of arguing with the text (Recommendation 2) while at the same time resisting the temptation to throw the baby out with the bathwater (Recommendation 3), for we can learn from both insights *and* dangers that the text presents (Recommendation 4)!

Arguing with the Text

So what are we to do with 1 Corinthians 14:33b–36? Once we have made a good-faith effort to listen carefully to the text with all the charity and patience we can muster, striving to grasp its historical and literary context as best we can, we must then argue with it, directly and publicly. Our ethical responsibilities as interpreters of Scripture demand it, for interpretations of this text continue to exercise tyrannical influence in the life of the church, circumscribing women's participation and leadership in many Christian communities to this day. More importantly, fidelity to the larger witness of Scripture demands it. Indeed, we argue with the text, not simply because we don't like it or we support equal rights for women—and certainly not because we are guided by "experience" or "culture" rather than by Scripture (as often alleged). Rather, we argue with the text primarily in order to be faithful to what we understand to be the fundamental witness of Scripture, discerned through communal engagement with it in worship, study, and prayer.[43]

For this reason, *the interpretation of Scripture by Scripture* is a guiding principle for engagement and argument with contentious texts, a principle summoned throughout this volume. First Corinthians 14:33b–36 is not the only text in the canon that bears on questions related to women's participation and leadership in the life of the Christian community, and scholarly discussion of the text has called attention to striking points of dissonance, even contradiction, with other emphases in Paul's own letters. Indeed, it is not insignificant that 1 Corinthians 14:33–36 is the lone note of restriction on women's participation and leadership in Paul's undisputed letters; it is greatly outweighed by a range of other Pauline texts that affirm an egalitarian vision (e.g., Gal. 3:28), presume that "all" have received gifts of the Spirit for liturgical leadership and edification of the community (e.g., 1 Cor. 11:2–16; 14:23–24, 26, 31, 39), and specify women as full partners in Paul's practice of ministry (e.g., Phoebe, Prisca, Junia, Euodia, and Syntyche, among others; see Rom. 16; Phil. 4:2–3).

Other biblical witnesses also can be brought into the conversation: an example in Acts is the witness to the formation of the church on Pentecost as fulfilling Joel's prophetic vision of the pouring out of God's Spirit upon all flesh, with the result that daughters as well as sons, women along with men, prophesy (Acts 2:14–18; Joel 2:28–32; see also Priscilla's authoritative teaching of Apollos in Acts 18:24–26). The biblical witnesses do not all speak with one voice. As Richard Hays states, "The unresolved discussion in the early church about the appropriate role of women as public witnesses to the gospel . . . has left its marks in the divided teaching of our canonical New Testament." So what are we to do? We are to exercise the minds that God has given us. As Hays suggests,

> Our hermeneutical responsibility is to recognize these tensions where they exist and to make *theologically informed* judgments about how the different texts speak to our situation. We must try to discern the fundamental themes of the New Testament's teaching and make decisions about contested matters in light of that discernment. . . . With respect to the issue of women's public leadership, there are good theological reasons to insist that we should be guided by Paul's vision of Christian worship in which the gifts of the Spirit are given to *all members of the church, men and women alike*, for the building up of the community. The few New Testament texts that seek to silence women (such as 1 Cor. 14:34–35, and 1 Tim. 2:11–15) should not be allowed to override this vision. As our congregations wrestle with the ongoing task of discerning God's will for our life together—a task to which 1 Corinthians repeatedly calls

us—we must be faithfully attentive to Paul's wider vision of men and women as full partners in the work of ministry.[44]

For most of Christian history this lone Pauline prohibition of women's speech in 1 Corinthians 14:33b–36, in concert with prohibition of women's teaching in 1 Timothy 2, has exercised sway over ecclesial polity, drowning out contravening biblical witnesses. To this day some Christians continue to attribute definitive authority to these two texts. As a result, in many Christian communions women are barred from religious leadership. However, the Bible has continued to shape and form Christian communities throughout history, and *on the very basis of that formation*, after long years of communal discernment, many Christian communions have come to believe that the church has been wrong about this, and they have formally amended their polity to remove any such restrictions. Denominations that have moved in this direction have not "rejected" Scripture and its authority but have rather determined to be faithful to what they have discerned to be the broader, more fundamental witness of Scripture. They have changed their practice with respect to women's ordination and exercise of leadership roles not *in spite* of Scripture, but *because* of Scripture.

In my own denomination, the Presbyterian Church (U.S.A.), this "change of mind" regarding what we believe God has called us through Scripture to be and do is now reflected in our confessional standards, as well as our polity. The Brief Statement of Faith (1991), the most recent addition to our Book of Confessions, contains two striking statements that reflect this communal discernment and would contest the way 1 Corinthians 14:33b–36 has been interpreted through much of church history. It affirms trust in the work of God the Holy Spirit, who *"calls women and men to all ministries of the Church"* and who, *"in a broken and fearful world, . . . gives us courage . . . to hear the voices of peoples long silenced, and to work with others for justice, freedom, and peace"* (lines 64, 70–71).[45] Affirmations of faith of this sort can and should be brought into conversation with interpretations of 1 Corinthians 14:33b–36 that would propose anything to the contrary. In so doing, we are calling upon *"the rule of faith,"* the collective wisdom of the church, articulated in its creeds and confessions and catechisms, to be part of our discernment of the implications of 1 Corinthians 14:33b–36 for life together in our own time and place. Creeds, confessions, and catechisms are themselves explications, in different historical contexts, of the will and work of God revealed in Scripture.

Affirmations they articulate emerged out of collective discernment of the witness of Scripture. Thus, when we appeal to them to counter interpretations of 1 Corinthians 14:33–36b (or any other text with which we may find ourselves arguing), we are hardly ignoring or dismissing Scripture; instead, we are appealing to the church's collective sense of what it has heard in its engagement with the whole of it.

In addition to *the interpretation of Scripture by Scripture* and *the rule of faith*, other classic principles of biblical interpretation can inform argument with 1 Corinthians 14:33b–36, such as *the centrality of Jesus Christ* and another we have not yet explored: *the rule of love*. As mentioned in the last chapter, attention to *the centrality of Jesus Christ* prompts our reflection on the coherence of the text with Jesus' teaching and embodiment of God's will, for "no understanding of what Scripture teaches us to believe and do can be correct that ignores or contradicts the central and primary revelation of God and God's will through Jesus Christ made known through the witness of Scripture."[46] In the case of 1 Corinthians 14:33b–36, serious questions can be raised as to whether categorical silencing of any portion of the community meets this standard. Both women and children in Jesus' day, as often in our own, were socialized to be "seen and not heard," but Jesus rebuked his disciples when they sought to prevent children from coming to him (Mark 10:13–16); and he refused to let the woman who claimed healing by touching the hem of his garment remain invisible. To the consternation of his disciples, he stopped and demanded to know who touched him, insisted on personal contact with her, and summoned her speech (Mark 5:25–34).

One thinks also of the feisty Canaanite woman, endowed with liturgical and theological speech and activity, as Matthew tells the story of her encounter with Jesus. She addresses him by using christological titles such as "Lord" and "Son of David" and in the language of prayer ("Lord, have mercy"), repeatedly and rather loudly. She assumes the liturgical posture of "kneeling" before him and makes explicit reference to the "masters' table" or "lords' table" and her right to be fed there, calling to mind the central table in the worship of the church (Matt. 15:21–28). The evangelist Matthew's careful attention to such details suggests that his community may have struggled with the role of women within the liturgical and theological life of the community and that he deemed Jesus' recognition of her "great faith" a word the community needed to hear—one that affirmed women's significant participation within the church.[47]

One final classic principle of biblical interpretation, *the rule of love*, can also inform our wrestling with contentious texts and is relevant to engagement with 1 Corinthians 14:33b–36. According to this historic principle, articulated centuries ago by St. Augustine, "the fundamental expression of God's will is the two-fold commandment to love God and neighbor, and all interpretations are to be judged by the question whether they offer and support the love given and commanded by God. When interpretations do not meet this criterion, it must be asked whether the text has been used correctly in the light of the whole Scripture and its subject."[48] In short, the validity of any interpretation of Scripture that promotes contempt for God or neighbor needs to be questioned. An argument can surely be made that categorical silencing of any portion of the Christian community, much less half the human race, is a violation of this standard.

Discerning Insights and Dangers

Throughout this volume, I have contended that arguing with Scripture and with others about our interpretations of it is an act of faithfulness—of taking the text with the utmost seriousness (Recommendation 2). As we do so, however, I have also urged us to resist the temptation to throw the baby out with the bathwater, for there is much we can learn from both dangers and insights that contentious texts may present (Recommendations 3 and 4). What insights and dangers emerge from engagement with 1 Corinthians 14:33b–36? Among them would surely be reflections on the role of speaking and silence in the life of the church, and in congregational worship in particular.

On the one hand, as Ann Jervis suggests, there is something to be said for the "spiritual value" of silence in worship, since it entails more than suppression of speech; it also allows "stillness, repose, peace, and receptivity."[49] (Indeed, some yearn for more silence and less verbosity in their worship experience!) Moreover, there is something to be said for Paul's concern that worship be conducted "decently and in order" (14:40) if it is to glorify the God of peace (14:33), create space in which the many gifts of the Spirit can find expression, and thereby edify the life of the Christian community. Our practice of worship may not border on chaos, as it apparently did in ancient Corinth (though some may yearn for livelier worship experience). Still, when more than one person speaks at a time, it is difficult for members of the congregation to honor speakers by listening carefully to the word that they share. Silence is requisite if we are to be receptive to, and reflect carefully upon, what another is saying in worship. Thus self-restraint is called for "so that all may learn and all be encouraged" (14:31)—ourselves included! Moreover, in Paul's view, such self-restraint is an expression of the love that is to govern the exercise of all spiritual gifts in the life of the community, according to 1 Corinthians 13—the love he has described as "patient" and "kind," *not* "envious or boastful or arrogant or rude. It does *not* insist on its own way" (13:4–6). Such love finds expression when we relinquish our right to speak and yield the floor to others—a cruciform disposition apparently not much in evidence in Corinthian worship, in Paul's view.[50] And when self-restraint is not observed, making it impossible for others to speak or to learn, those who disrupt the community's worship may well be in need of admonition to silence. Most of us probably can appreciate the perspicacity of the anonymous commentator on human foibles who observed, "There are only two kinds of speakers—those who have something to say, and those who have to say something." And with respect to the latter, on occasion we may find ourselves grateful for admonitions to silence! Although there is a world of difference between the voluntary silence of self-restraint and the silence that someone imposes on another, both have a role to play in the life and worship of the Christian community.

But on the other hand, injunctions to silence also bear dangers and can serve oppressive ends, especially when urged by those in dominant positions on those in subordinate or marginal positions in relation to them. As we have noted, in 1 Corinthians 14:26–40, three disruptive groups find themselves on the receiving end of exhortations to silence: glossolalists, prophets, and women. The silence enjoined upon the first two groups is explicitly temporary in nature; glossolalists and prophets are to speak "in turn" (14:27), "one by one" (14:31). However, the silence urged upon women is indefinite in nature and throughout Christian history has far too often been construed as a comprehensive prohibition of women's ecclesial speech. Only in the case of this third group has the admonition to silence been enshrined as an enduring policy dictate, muzzling half the human race. Pauline scholar F. F. Bruce once observed, "I think Paul would roll over in his grave if he knew we were turning his letters into torah."[51] I suspect the apostle would agree with Bruce on this point, especially with regard to 1 Corinthians 14:33b–36. Whatever the case may be, this text surely can help us reflect on the dangers of admonitions to silence, on "selective" readings of Scripture, and on the use of Scripture to endorse oppressive ends. Perhaps it can also serve as a reminder that resort to such measures may tempt us especially when in pursuit of Christian unity above all else—when silencing voices of dissent may seem to be a means by which to restore communal harmony and reestablish the status quo.

Responsibility for the historical silencing of women cannot be laid entirely at the church's or the Bible's feet; we are now more aware than ever that women's voices throughout human history and in every arena of human endeavor have been ignored, silenced, and left out of the public record. But the church has been complicit with culture in this suppression, and 1 Corinthians 14:33b–36 and its unfortunate history of interpretation can prompt open and honest reflection on the church's sins in this regard—the owning of our dirty laundry—and inspire repentance. And the fruits of repentance can include commitment to countering and healing the continuing impact of this history on the lives of girls and women. In its ministries of Christian education and formation with children, youth, and adults; and in its preaching and pastoral care, biblical and theological reflection, and social outreach—in all these the church can contribute in significant ways to the flourishing of life, to the fullness and abundance of life that is God's will for all in Christ, female and male (John 10:10). This surely entails nurturing in all its members a strong sense of their baptismal identity as one of God's own, created in God's own image, as well as hearing them into speech.

Ministries informed by such a commitment are vital, for gender socialization in our culture continues to deform the minds and spirits of girls and women, many of whom still grow up learning that they are to be "seen and not heard" and still shrink from raising their voices. Psychologists and educators, for example, have documented that schoolgirls and young women in our culture often think of themselves as far less entitled than their male classmates to take up airspace with their speech. This socialization starts early, for beginning at about age eleven "girls learn to internalize the gender expectations of the dominant culture, dismissing their own emerging sense of themselves."[52] Hearing the silence of women's voices in college classrooms, Carol Gilligan has suggested that a woman's later education may hinge on the retrieval of her "twelve-year-old self—a journey linked with the recovery of voice and therefore with psychological survival."[53] I recognize this as an apt description of my own socialization and educational journey and that of many women (young and old) who now sit in my classroom. During every single semester over the course of almost thirty years of teaching, at least one or two female students have at some point pulled me aside to ask anxiously, "Am I talking too much?" (Only rarely have male students asked me that question—and frankly, more of them should have been concerned about this!) For very good reasons, the concept of "voice" has been central in feminist thought and practice since the beginning of the "women's movement" in the 1960s, as it is closely related to empowerment and development of a sense of self. And if engagement with 1 Corinthians 14:33b–36 can help us remember and acknowledge our ecclesial sins, call us to repentance, and inspire us for ministries that counter the deformation of women's minds and spirits, then the text has a role to play in forming the mind of Jesus Christ in us.

However, women are by no means the only members of the church who have experienced unjust imposition of silence. The voices of others, too, have been suppressed, and perhaps this text can prompt reflection on the costs of imposed silence, whenever it takes place. New Testament scholar Holly Hearon, for example, has perceptively recognized that the text can raise provocative questions for gay and lesbian Christians: "What happens when we silence a portion of the community? What does such an action say about the community and what is lost from the life of the community when such an action is undertaken? Is such an action ever justified? As people who have been routinely silenced, GLBTI communities may find it helpful to retain the painful witness represented by these verses so that these important questions might be raised."[54] Indeed, these are important questions for us all.

However, there is also a sense in which all who have suffered from ecclesial imposition of silence can take courage from a text like 1 Corinthians 14:33b–36. It preserves the site of an important argument in the early church regarding who has a voice and authority to speak—an argument that is far from over and that summons our participation. Without it, we would lose important pieces of our family history, for it discloses the presence and struggles of foremothers in the faith and their resistance to suppression of their voices. As Deborah Krause has perceptively declared, texts such as 1 Corinthians 14:33b–36, as well as others we have engaged in this volume,

> are witnesses to the struggle that women and men have engaged to define the nature of the church's leadership, the shape of human

community within the church, and the intersection between religious experience and the authority to speak of it. We can see from
the Pauline tradition that these challenges were far from settled
within the early church. We know from contemporary practices
of Christian rhetoric in all its diversity that these challenges are far
from settled today. In this new vein the letters of the Pauline tradition and the rhetoric of the contemporary church are witnesses to
an enduring struggle within which women and men who hope for
a more humane, inclusive, and just church will not necessarily take
comfort but through which they might take courage.[55]

Indeed, engagement with such texts can be a means by which the
Spirit, "in a broken and fearful world, . . . gives us courage . . . to hear
the voices of peoples long silenced, and to work with others for justice,
freedom, and peace" (Brief Statement of Faith).[56]

QUESTIONS FOR DISCUSSION
AND REFLECTION

How would you describe your prior experience with 1 Corinthians
14:33b–36? In what contexts have you encountered it?

What strikes you most about 1 Corinthians 14:33b–36? What questions does it raise for you? Has your view of this text changed in
any way as a result of your engagement with it in this chapter?
If so, how?

In your view, which of the following explanations makes the best
sense of 1 Corinthians 14:33b–36? (1) "It's not as bad as it
sounds!" (2) "It is as bad as it sounds, but these are not Paul's
words!" Or (3) "These are Paul's words, and it is as bad as it
sounds!" Why do you find your choice most persuasive?

How would you resolve the apparent tension between 1 Corinthians 11:2–16 and 14:33b–36? Of the varied scholarly explanations
of the dissonance, which do you find most compelling, and why?

What questions would you like to ask the Corinthian women, or
Paul, about this text? What questions would you like to ask those
who interpret it differently than do you?

As the author of Ecclesiastes observed, "For everything there is a sea-
son, and a time for every matter under heaven," and this includes
"a time to keep silence, and a time to speak" (Eccl. 3:1–8). What

has your engagement with 1 Corinthians 14:33b–36 contributed to your reflection on speech and silence in the life of the worshiping assembly and your own life of faith?

In addition to *the interpretation of Scripture by Scripture, the centrality of Jesus Christ,* and *the rule of faith,* a fourth classic principle of biblical interpretation was introduced in this chapter: *the rule of love,* which holds that valid interpretations of Scripture must offer and support love for God and for neighbor. What do you think of this principle as a guide to interpretation? Do you consider 1 Corinthians 14:33b–36 a violation of it? Why, or why not?

Why do you think women and girls in our culture continue to view themselves as less entitled to take up airspace with their speech than men? Has this reality impacted your own socialization and journey? In your experience, what role has the church or the Bible played in this socialization—or in your liberation from it? What are some of the concrete ways in which the life and ministries of a local congregation can counter the deformation of mind and spirit suffered by many women and girls? How can a congregation empower them and hear them into speech?

Articulate your response to the important questions raised by Holly Hearon: "What happens when we silence a portion of the community? What does such an action say about the community and what is lost from the life of the community when such an action is undertaken? Is such an action ever justified?"[57] Who would you identify as groups within the life of the church today who experience "silencing"?

Is 1 Corinthians 14:33b–36 a text from which you can take courage? If so, how? If not, why not? Would you be inclined to preach or teach on 1 Corinthians 14:33b–36? Why, or why not?

5

Reining In Rambunctious Widows

1 Timothy 5:3–16

In this chapter we return to the intriguing little letter of 1 Timothy, which provides more specific commentary on women and exhibits more anxiety about controlling their behavior than any other book in the New Testament! This makes it a fascinating resource for anyone interested in piecing together the history of women's lives and ministries in the early church. The text we will engage is not as well known as the four we have considered in previous chapters. It is rarely invoked in ongoing debates over women's roles in church, family, and society, though it has a great deal to say about these matters. But like the others, it can surely be described as "tyrannical" and "contentious," even "ornery" in nature; so it, too, presents interpretive challenges and prompts reflection on the way in which it exercises "authority" in our lives as Scripture.

The identification, care, and comportment of "widows" are the foci of the text's sustained reflection. First Timothy 5:3–16 represents, in fact, the longest discussion of widows in the New Testament; but the widows themselves are not addressed directly. The text is presented as "man-to-man" conversation in which the senior apostle Paul counsels Timothy, his younger associate in ministry, on how to exercise oversight of a variety of problems that have emerged in connection with the widows. Most scholars, for very good reasons, think that Paul was not actually the author of this letter—that 1 Timothy is pseudonymous, written in the apostle's name by someone attempting to interpret his legacy for a church within the Pauline orbit at a later time (the late first or early second century), when Christians found themselves constrained to think about the organizational shape of the church's ongoing life. The letter is no less "authoritative" on this count, for its authority derives not from its authorship but from its canonical status. Moreover, the concrete reality addressed is by no means fictitious. As Elsa Tamez emphasizes, there may be no doubt about the fact that a community existed and presented the problems and conflicts that are reflected in the letter of 1 Timothy—problems and conflicts that were quite real to those who faced them.[1] And interestingly, none evoke more extended and complex instruction than those presented by "widows" within the congregation; apparently problems related to this particular group were deemed to be of special urgency and scope. The author's response to them is decidedly "prescriptive" in nature, reflecting a desire to redefine and rein in a group judged to be out of control in several respects. As we listen to the text, we need to bear in mind that the widows themselves undoubtedly perceived things quite differently!

1 TIMOTHY 5:3–16

[3]Honor widows who are really widows. [4]If a widow has children or grandchildren, they should first learn their religious duty to their own family and make some repayment to their parents; for this is pleasing in God's sight. [5]The real widow, left alone, has set her hope on God and continues in supplications and prayers night and day; [6]but the widow who lives for pleasure is dead even while she lives. [7]Give these commands as well, so that they may be above reproach. [8]And whoever does not provide for relatives, and especially for family members, has denied the faith and is worse than an unbeliever.

[9]Let a widow be put on the list if she is not less than sixty years old and has been married only once; [10]she must be well attested for her good works, as one who has brought up children, shown hospitality, washed the saints' feet, helped the afflicted, and devoted herself to doing good in every way. [11]But refuse to put younger widows on the list; for when their sensual desires alienate them from Christ, they want to marry, [12]and so they incur condemnation for having violated their first pledge. [13]Besides that, they learn to be idle, gadding about from house to house; and they are not merely idle, but also gossips and busybodies, saying what they should not say. [14]So I would have younger widows marry, bear children, and manage their

households, so as to give the adversary no occasion to revile us. [15]For some have already turned away to follow Satan. [16]If any believing woman has relatives who are really widows, let her assist them; let the church not be burdened, so that it can assist those who are real widows.

A basic and apparently controversial matter with which the text grapples is the question of who could even be identified as a bona fide, card-carrying widow. In our own time and place, the term "widow" designates a woman who has lost her husband by death and not remarried. While the term bore this common meaning in the early Christian centuries as well, it expanded to include other women living without husbands—women who were divorced, separated, or abandoned. In some places, celibate women who chose not to marry were also referred to as widows. Bishop Ignatius of Antioch, for example, greets "the virgins who are called widows" in his letter to Christians in Smyrna, dated around 110 CE.[2] This may explain why 1 Timothy 5:11 and 5:14 speak of young widows "marrying" rather than "remarrying": celibate women, rather than bereaved women, may be in view. Further complicating matters (both for the first recipients of this letter and for our own grasp of what they were contending with), a distinct ministerial "order" of widows emerged within the early centuries of the church—a recognized ecclesial office for women devoted to ministries of prayer, charitable endeavor, hospitality, and instruction; early stages of this development appear to be reflected in 1 Timothy 5. As Joanna Dewey notes, "There is thus confusion in the Pastorals between 'widow' as a Christian minister and 'widow' as a welfare recipient."[3] Bear these definitional bones of contention in mind: they may shed light on some of the perplexing features of the text before us.

What other circumstances evoked the tensions reflected in 1 Timothy 5:3–16 and may illumine our reading of it? As we consider this matter, let us endeavor to do so, once again, with a spirit of "generosity and patience toward the text," for *the difficult text is worthy of charity from its interpreters*" (Recommendation 1)![4]

LISTENING TO THE TEXT

The text is complex due not only to the definitional issues noted above, but also to the range of concerns addressed and intertwined within it. Some of those concerns are practical, organizational ones; others appear to be political and theological; and all bear implications for ecclesial public relations that deeply unsettle the author. Unraveling varied strands of concern reflected in the text may help us begin to wrap our heads around it. At least four distinct problems appear to be addressed.

Problem 1: charitable assistance for widows

The text both opens (5:3) and closes (5:16) with attention to a practical, organizational concern: the church's provision of aid for truly destitute widows. In the Old Testament, care for widows (and orphans) was a standard criterion of Israel's covenant faithfulness (Exod. 22:22; Deut. 10:18, 24:17; Ps. 68:5; Isa. 1:17). As the most vulnerable members of society, they were special objects of God's concern and of the covenant community's responsibility. At points throughout the New Testament, it is evident that the early church continued this practice of providing charitable support for its widows (see Acts 6:1–6; 9:36–42; Jas. 1:27), and 1 Timothy 5:3–16 (like Acts 6:1–6) bears witness to the strain this placed on the community's resources. Timothy is exhorted to ensure that the community "honors" widows who are "really widows" (5:3). "Honor," a central value in ancient Mediterranean culture, surely entailed the extension to them of recognition and respect; it also bore material, financial implications (as the use of this same "honor" language in 1 Tim. 5:17–18, in relation to financial remuneration for "elders," suggests). The problem at hand was apparently twofold, in the author's opinion: there were far too many recipients of such aid (freeloaders among them), and the church was bearing more than its fair share of the financial burden.

He addresses the first problem by distinguishing between "true widows" deserving of support ("widows who are really widows," that is, truly destitute, without family connections, and thus utterly dependent upon God) and (implicitly) "faux widows"[5] (self-indulgent widows who are not truly destitute and take advantage of the church's generosity). "True widows" not only receive aid but also reciprocate, serving the church through a constant ministry of prayer ("night and day"), in contrast to self-indulgent "faux widows" who live only for themselves ("for pleasure") and are as good as dead. It is a harsh critique!

The author addresses the second problem by insisting that others shoulder their fair share of the support owed widows, thereby lessening the church's "burden" (5:16). Chief among those shirking responsibilities are family members (e.g., children and grandchildren) who are not living up to their filial obligations, leaving care of their widows to the church. Verse 4 seeks to motivate all such slackers in positive fashion, insisting that care for family members is a serious religious obligation and mark of authentic piety. Verse 8 then takes a negative tack, condemning and shaming them in the strongest possible terms as persons who have "denied the faith" and are "worse than unbelievers."

The closing verse of the text also addresses the "believing woman" who (translating literally) "has widows" (5:16, *echei chēras*), exhorting her, too, to provide assistance for "real widows." The expansive NRSV translation ("If any believing woman has *relatives* who are really widows") infers that the widows referred to are female relatives, but another possibility presents itself. This verse may provide an intriguing glimpse of a living arrangement in early Christian communities that presented an alternative to the traditional patriarchal household: groups of celibate Christian women living together in communal homes, sheltered by a woman of financial means. Tabitha (in Acts 9:36–42) was perhaps such a benefactress of widows, providing material support and shelter for them. This practice is well known in the third and fourth centuries, but 1 Timothy 5:16 may bear witness to its emergence at an even earlier date. By urging families and believing women of means to step up to the plate (assume responsibility), the author seeks, in a sense, to "privatize"[6] care of widows, to integrate them into existing households and thereby reduce the church's financial burden so that it can devote its energies and resources to those most in need of them. The fact that the text begins and ends on this note, with explicit reference to lessening the "burden" of the church (5:16), indicates that this is among the author's primary concerns.

Problem 2: the list

Another administrative concern emerges in 5:9–15 as the author turns to the matter of official enrollment of widows, specifically denoting prerequisite qualifications for placement on "the list" (5:9). It is not altogether clear whether these verses continue the discussion in 5:3–8, thereby referring to a list or roster of "real widows" (destitute widows who are truly alone in this world and thus deserving of charitable assistance from the church), or whether the author now turns his attention to a ministerial "order" of widows (one that might include "real widows" but would not be limited to them). Early Christian writings (including those of church fathers such as Ignatius, Polycarp, and Tertullian, and ancient church orders such as the *Didascalia*) attest the existence of a distinct ministerial order of widows from the second through the fifth centuries—a "recognized service organization"[7] devoted to works of prayer, charitable endeavor, hospitality, and instruction; the question is whether 1 Timothy 5:9–15 reflects embryonic stages of this office. There is considerable scholarly debate about this matter, but there are good reasons to believe that an emerging office, or recognized "circle"[8] of some sort, is in view. For one thing, context suggests as much, for the letter of 1 Timothy reflects the early church's transition from movement to organization,[9] devoting a great deal of attention to matters pertaining to other emerging church offices: bishop/overseer (3:1–7), deacon (3:8–13), and elder (5:17–22). Moreover, qualifications for enrollment are enumerated, some of which parallel those specified for bishops and deacons (e.g., widows, like bishops and deacons, are to have been "married only once" and to have excelled in carrying out household responsibilities [5:9–10]). Specific "duties" for widows are not specified, but neither are duties for deacons. The author could presume familiarity with them on the part of his readers and focuses instead on requisite personal characteristics of those who serve. Reference to a "pledge" or vow of some sort in 5:12 further supports the likelihood that an office or recognized circle of some sort, rather than a roster of charity recipients, is in view. Since young widows who desire to marry are described as "violating" this vow ("their first pledge") and alienating themselves from Christ (5:12), it likely entailed public commitment to celibacy and single-minded devotion to serving Christ and his church, on the analogy of marriage.

The author's evident concern about enrolled widows is more than practical and administrative; the fact that he severely circumscribes membership in this group suggests that his motives are political too. He is not establishing a new order but endeavoring to restrict the size of an existing group that has become far too large and unwieldy, and presumably influential, in his view. An enrolled widow must be "not less than sixty years old" (a decidedly advanced age in the New Testament world) and "married only once"[10]—prerequisites that would disqualify young widows (indeed, anyone under sixty!) and any who married per the author's instructions in 5:14 (and as Roman legal

incentives also pressured women under fifty to do). That the qualifications include not only service to the community of faith but also
domestic accomplishments (such as rearing children) would eliminate
also all women who, like Paul, had chosen a life of celibacy. The result
of such explicit prerequisite qualifications would be a very short list of
rostered widows! As Sandra Hack Polaski observes, the author "seeks
to keep their numbers, and thus their influence, as small as possible,
and to limit their ranks to those who had already demonstrated their
allegiance to life in the patriarchal household."[11]

Problem 3: young widows

An unusual feature of the Pastoral Epistles, in contrast to the undisputed letters of Paul, is the manner in which they separate the congregation into groups according to age, gender, and social status (slave or
free). In this particular text, it is also worth noting the manner in which
widows, too, are divided into dichotomous groups:[12] "real widows" are
distinguished from "not real"/"faux" widows, old widows from young
widows, destitute widows from those with apparent means who "live
for pleasure," and widows with children or other relatives from those
who are "left alone." And of these subgroups, it is altogether clear
that "young widows" in particular are the focus of the author's most
intense angst and ire, and thus his most derisive rhetoric. In his view,
they are guilty of three major transgressions that disrupt the internal
and external life of the church and consequently should not be put on
"the list" (5:11).

First, young widows are not to be "put on the list" because they
are unable to sustain the celibate life of the enrolled widow.[13] Their
"sensual desires" (or "sexual itch," as some commentators describe
it) distract them from dedicated service to Christ and his church, to
which they have apparently pledged themselves with a vow, and thus
they want to marry. Interestingly, they are described as wanting "to
marry" rather than "to remarry," which may indicate that some have
never been married and are what Ignatius referred to as "virgins called
widows." It is also striking that their desire is "to marry" rather than
"to be married"—the active voice perhaps suggesting initiative on their
parts that flouts social convention (5:11). It is odd to hear the author
deprecate a desire to marry; he has, after all, declared childbearing to
be a woman's means of salvation (1 Tim. 2:15) and expressly urges

marriage upon young widows several verses later, in 5:14. But the young widows' failure to follow through on a public commitment to their vocation as "enrolled" widows, to which they pledged themselves with a vow, apparently has brought disrepute upon the church, incurring "condemnation" (whether from God or from outsiders is not altogether clear, but the opinions that outsiders have of the church are a major focus of attention throughout the letter, so the latter is surely of concern, and perhaps both are in view). The author's anxiety about the sexual vigor and disruptive power of young widows is quite evident. In fact, as Deborah Krause explains, the imperative (*paraiteomai*), which the NRSV translates with the language of "refusal" ("But refuse to put younger widows on the list," 5:11), is strong language that can also convey "avoidance," even "exclusion": "Keep away from younger widows," or even drive them out from the church—nuances this language conveys elsewhere in the Pastoral Epistles when referencing false teachers (e.g., 1 Tim. 4:7; 2 Tim. 2:23; Titus 3:10).[14]

Indeed, the second transgression, and the heart of the author's concern, is the association of young widows with false teachers within the congregation. As we had occasion to note in chapter 1 in the discussion of 1 Timothy 2, the author of the Pastoral Epistles is mightily distressed about false teachers, whom he believed to be distorting Christian faith and endangering the well-being of the church (see chap. 1 under "Strategies for Engagement"). The clues that present themselves (1 Tim. 1:4; 4:3; 6:20; 2 Tim. 2:18) suggest that they were of proto-gnostic stripe and that their teaching of rigorous asceticism and celibate piety found a hearing especially among women. We see this in 2 Timothy 3, where the author says this about his opponents (vv. 5–7): "Avoid them! For among them are those who make their way into households and captivate silly women, overwhelmed by their sins and swayed by all kinds of desires, who are always being instructed and can never arrive at a knowledge of the truth."

Women are the only members of the church explicitly identified in connection with the false teachers. And in 1 Timothy 5:3–16, young widows in particular are described in ways that intimate association with false teachers. The language of "learning," for instance, is used to describe their misbehavior: "They learn to be idle" (5:13). As Marianne Kartzow observes, this is a strange thing to learn, usually not requiring much education![15] In all likelihood, the problem is not that they are without pursuits but rather that the ones in which they are engaged are deemed inappropriate. In fact, Gail Streete points out that another translation is possible: "Being idle, they learn."[16] From the author's perspective, they have way too much time on their hands and should not be indulging intellectual curiosity. Moreover, like the roving false teachers "who make their way into households and captivate silly women" with questionable instruction, young widows are described as itinerant, as "gadding about from house to house" and as "gossips and busybodies, saying what they should not say" (1 Tim. 5:13). The content of their speech is of real concern and does not have the author's seal of approval: "there is good reason to believe that the young widows were not merely gossiping about the weather, but promoting a version and interpretation of Christian faith that the author finds objectionable and heretical. Only this adequately explains the strong terms in which their activity is censured."[17] Indeed, the author reserves his harshest and most problematic rhetoric for young widows, sexualizing (5:11), trivializing (5:13), and even demonizing them (5:15) with stereotypical notions of feminine vice disseminated by moral philosophers of the day, with whom he shared a pejorative view of unsequestered women. Given this stereotyped, polemical invective, we need to bear in mind that the young widows themselves surely would have described their peripatetic activity quite differently—perhaps as an active ministry of teaching and learning, proclaiming the faith, and pastoral visitation. Maybe, as the apostle Paul recommended, they eschewed marriage in order to render "unhindered devotion" to "the affairs of the Lord" (1 Cor. 7:32–35). Whatever the case may be, the author aims to put an end to their freedom of movement and the spread of false teaching and ensure that they will stay put under the roof of the patriarchal household: "I would have younger widows marry, bear children, and manage their households, so as to give the adversary no occasion to revile us" (1 Tim. 5:14).

As 5:14 indicates, the third transgression of which young widows are guilty is in the realm of public opinion. The gadabout, gossipy young women are themselves gossiped about.[18] In a world in which marriage was the norm, in which the patriarchal household was viewed as the very foundation of social order and stability, in which men outnumbered women, and in which legal incentives discouraged any inclination to remain unmarried and childless[19]—in such a world abstention from marriage or remarriage, by young women in particular, was unconventional behavior that attracted negative public attention, threatening the church's reputation. As Margaret MacDonald has demonstrated, critics of early Christian communities had a great deal to say about early Christian women. She makes a compelling case, in fact, that in the Pastoral Epistles, "what outsiders were saying about early Christian women is being internalized and transformed into a teaching about the behavior of women."[20]

Problem 4: public relations

The author's anxiety about public opinion is by no means limited to the comportment of young widows, though they present the major challenge on this front; the church's public image and reputation is a central focus of concern throughout the Pastoral Epistles and bears on all the matters addressed in 1 Timothy 5:3–16. Concern for the community's reputation is apparent, for example, in the author's rebuke of self-indulgent "faux" widows and negligent family members, whom Timothy is to exhort "so that they may be above reproach" (5:7). Moreover, relatives who have shirked responsibility for their widows, leaving their care to the church, are shamed into doing the right thing by moral comparison with outsiders: "Whoever does not provide for relatives, and especially for family members, has denied the faith and is worse than an unbeliever" (5:8). Even unregenerate persons know better; thus failure to live up to familial duties damages the church's public image. Public relations concerns also inform the radical downsizing of the office (or circle) of "enrolled" widows—of those who qualify for "the list." That marriage and childbearing are included among the prerequisites ensures that those eligible have led a life conforming to Greco-Roman social expectations.[21] And by raising the age limit to the advanced age of 60, the office is restricted to those who no longer would have been expected to remarry—to "celibate elderly women" who "would not have threatened cultural values and social expectations."[22]

Clearly the world is watching and suspicious of new religious movements, and the author is anxious for the church's "family values" to be on display. And once again, we need to try to appreciate that far more than the church's public image was at stake. Its mission was also in view. As Margaret MacDonald has explained, "Gossip is far more than a minor aggravation to an emerging religious community; it is an extremely important conveyer of public opinion" that could prompt suffering, hostility, or misunderstanding that "threatened to thwart the early church's hope of winning the world."[23] Nowhere in the New

Testament do we find so explicit a statement of God's desire to save all as in 1 Timothy 2:4, God's desire for "everyone to be saved and to come to the knowledge of the truth." In sum, the author's pervasive anxiety about social respectability is linked, in large measure, with his desire that the gospel receive as wide a hearing as possible and that no obstacles stand in the way. Perhaps we can appreciate this concern and empathize with real difficulties he faced in the midst of a complex historical moment, even as we regret choices he made as he articulated a response to them!

DIALOGUE WITH THE TEXT

Having made an effort, first, to listen carefully to the text with measures of charity and empathy (Recommendation 1), we further honor the text by engaging in honest dialogue with it and careful reflection upon it. In so doing, we begin to discern and articulate its significance for our own time and place. Once again, practices that can guide us include arguing with the text (Recommendation 2) while at the same time resisting the temptation to throw the baby out with the bathwater (Recommendation 3), for we can learn from both insights *and* dangers that the text presents (Recommendation 4)!

Arguing with the Text

All the passages we have examined in this volume thus far have been contentious texts that preserve sites of important arguments in the life of the early church. All have been decidedly prescriptive in nature, exerting considerable effort to control or suppress existing practices. So in each case, we have tried to discern echoes of the voices of other parties to the conflicts—to imagine the other side of the arguments. In the case of 1 Timothy 5:3–16, we have a bit more to work with, for other literary resources with evident points of connection to 1 Timothy provide insights that help us reconstruct, to some extent, the views of those with whom the author is contending—views that might inform our own practice of arguing with the text.

We have, for example, Paul's own letters—1 Corinthians in particular, which sheds light on matters of dispute in 1 Timothy 5, for in it we find the apostle's own (and only) discussion of widows. His comments appear in 1 Corinthians 7 (vv. 8–9, 39–40), in the midst of his extended discussion of sex and marriage:

> [8]To the unmarried and the widows I say that it is well for them to remain unmarried as I am. [9]But if they are not practicing self-control, they should marry. For it is better to marry than to be aflame with passion. . . .
> [39]A wife is bound as long as her husband lives. But if the husband dies, she is free to marry anyone she wishes, only in the Lord. [40]But in my judgment she is more blessed if she remains as she is. And I think that I too have the Spirit of God.

This counsel, with its express preference that widows remain unmarried, differs markedly from that offered in 1 Timothy 5. One suspects that the apostle himself might have objected to 1 Timothy's admonitions, for one of the striking things about Paul's discussion throughout 1 Corinthians 7 is that he "argues for options," contending that "there is more than one way to live a holy life."[24] Lives of faithful integrity can find expression in both marriage and celibacy. Paul clearly favors the latter; indeed, in his view celibacy has decided advantages, enabling one to devote oneself fully, without distraction, to "affairs of the Lord" (7:32–35). But he recognizes that all do not have the gift of celibacy, in which case marriage is advisable so that sexual desires can be appropriately channeled.

One can surmise, then, that women who lived within the Pauline mission field would have found sanction for a life without marriage, devoted fully to the service of God, within the apostle's own teaching and letters. However, as we have noted, marriage (and as the Augustan marriage laws would have it, remarriage for widows under fifty) was the norm in the Greco-Roman world; abstention from it was a decidedly countercultural practice that attracted increasing public scrutiny and thus greatly concerns the author of 1 Timothy. He does not eliminate celibacy as a viable Christian lifestyle but takes action to ensure that it is a limited, geriatric practice! Indeed, as Deborah Krause has observed, he finds himself in an incongruous position: "Ironically, the letter writer must use Paul's name and authority in order to combat a social reality that resulted from Paul's own teachings."[25]

A second-century extracanonical work, *The Acts of Paul and Thecla*, indicates that there were competing interpretations of the Pauline tradition within the early church. It has probable connections to the Pastoral Epistles that further illumine the conflict reflected in 1 Timothy

5. The heroine of this apocryphal story is a young woman named Thecla who is captivated by Paul's teaching of sexual asceticism and breaks her engagement to be married in order to follow him, inciting deadly opposition. Her own mother, dishonored by her daughter's rejection of marriage and family life, compels the governor to have her burned at the stake so that "all the women who have been taught by this man [Paul] will be afraid!"[26] It is but the first of several attempts on Thecla's life (others include confrontations with wild beasts), all of which she escapes by miraculous (even fantastic) means. In the course of itinerant adventures, she baptizes herself, zealously teaches and proclaims the word of God, and eventually wins Paul's validation of her ministry. Toward the end of the second century, the church father Tertullian denounced *The Acts of Paul and Thecla* in his protest against an unnamed woman who appealed to Thecla's example and Paul's authority as a warrant for her own teaching and baptizing ministry.[27] Other women no doubt did the same. Dennis MacDonald[28] has made a compelling case that the Pastorals were written to counter the image of Paul in popular legends such as *The Acts of Paul and Thecla*. If he is right about that, the Pastorals and *The Acts of Paul and Thecla* together provide a fascinating window onto controversy engaged by heirs of the Pauline tradition. The Pastoral Epistles could even be said to represent "the other side of Thecla's story."[29]

First Timothy may be referring to the kind of teaching one finds in *The Acts of Paul and Thecla* when it warns against the instruction of false teachers in 4:7: "Have nothing to do with profane myths and old wives' tales." And perhaps the "gossip" and objectionable speech attributed to young widows in 5:13 included stories such as Thecla's. Her portrait bears resemblance to 1 Timothy's young widows, for like them, she is described as moving frequently from house to house, and ironically, though celibate, she is dogged by suspicions of sexual immorality (even accosted on the street as a whore). She finds shelter and protection under the roof of a woman of means named Tryphaena—a reflection, perhaps, of the kind of alternative household arrangement referenced in 1 Timothy 5:16. She also receives support from other women (including interspecies support from female wild beasts)! Few would question that *The Acts of Paul and Thecla* is legendary in nature and thus of dubious historicity, but as Margaret MacDonald notes, it "mirrors the actual experiences of early Christian women in the second century who rejected marriage and who found themselves in violent confrontations with society."[30] Indeed, "it is not for Christianity that

Thecla was sentenced to death, but for her refusal to marry."[31] Abstention from marriage, though a lifestyle sanctioned by the apostle Paul,
increasingly came under public scrutiny as a subversive challenge to the
order of the patriarchal household—one that was perceived as under-
mining the basic building block of society and thus the empire itself.
In addressing the challenges and potential dangers of this historical
moment, the author of 1 Timothy radically curtails celibate options for
women and sets forth a hierarchically structured vision of the church
as the "household of God" (3:15).

We do not know the immediate outcome of the argument to which
1 Timothy 5 bears witness, though there is reason to believe that in the
short term its author was not entirely successful in squelching other
interpretations of the Pauline tradition.[32] *The Acts of Paul and Thecla*
retained its popularity for some time in Asia Minor, where a vibrant
Thecla cult survived well into the fifth century; yet in the long run it
was the Pastorals' interpretation of the Pauline heritage that obtained
canonical status and set the terms for subsequent discussion of church
structures and leadership conflicts. As for the widows, Francine Cardman has reported that "despite attempts to limit their influence, the
widows remained a difficult group to control, which prompted renewed
efforts to restrain them in the third and fourth centuries."[33] Virtually
all of the patristic writings that reference the ministry of widows are
concerned with "constraining, limiting, and maintaining male authority over this ministry" rather than affirming it.[34] Indeed, Carolyn Osiek
says this about the discussion of widows in ancient church orders, such
as the *Didascalia/Apostolic Constitutions* (a third-century document):

> The length of texts devoted to the subject and the vehemence
> expressed are exceptional . . . and seem to indicate a reaction to
> some real or imagined threatening situation. It is not difficult to
> formulate a few guesses as to what that threat may have been. The
> more hierarchically structured Christian churches of the second and
> third centuries often felt themselves to be in a state of siege because
> of the threat posed by the more "charismatic" or loosely structured
> communities that more often than not seemed to have allowed a
> great deal of freedom and responsibility to women, especially in
> the area of religious leadership. Gnostic, Montanist, and Marcion-
> ite communities existed down the street from the orthodox com-
> munities in eastern cities. . . . The attempt to restrict severely the
> activities of widows is, no doubt, part of the well-known reaction
> against the freedom exercised by women in rival Christian groups.

Or, more specifically, it could be a reaction against the very important role played by members of the order of widows in neighboring
churches.[35]

Whatever the reason, the order of widows clearly faced fierce opposition from church authorities, and in the long run it fades from view.

So what are we to make of all this? David Horrell points out that
readings of the text tend toward opposite extremes, "exhibiting either
sympathy for the author and suspicion of opponents, or sympathy
for the opponents and suspicion of the author": "For some, 'Paul'
is clearly right to restrict the activities of young widows and protect
the church from the heresy they embody and promote"; and for others, the author's strategy is "a regrettable attempt to use a position
of power to exclude and stigmatize those who represent a different
'take' on the Christian gospel—a different vision of what the church
should be like."[36] To be honest, most of us probably have decided
inclinations in one or the other direction! So as we eavesdrop on the
argument reflected in 1 Timothy 5 and wade into it ourselves, it is
well to remember that we are listening to a family quarrel and that we
are related by baptism to all the parties to it—to both the author and
to those he sought to restrain. And in the spirit of charity, perhaps we
should consider the possibility that all may have had concerns that
merit measures of our empathy, as well as the fact that all had feet of
clay. After all, proverbial wisdom holds that "there are three sides to
every argument: my side, your side, and the truth"!

So, upon reflection, though my own sympathies incline toward the
women who have been clobbered and denigrated by 1 Timothy 5's
admonitions (both then and since), I doubt that I would be able to
embrace, in their entirety, theological perspectives that some of the
widows inveighed against are likely to have held. If, for example, the
asceticism practiced by some was of an incipiently gnostic variety that
shunned the material world (as many scholars suspect), and for this
reason forbade marriage and demanded "abstinence from foods which
God created to be received with thanksgiving" (1 Tim. 4:3), I would
want to object. On this point I am grateful for 1 Timothy's robust theology of creation—its insistence, in the face of opinion to the contrary,
that everything that God created, including food, marriage, and the
bearing of children, is good. Moreover, the historical distance that separates my social location from that of 1 Timothy's widows accounts for
another difference in my perspective, stated succinctly by Sandra Hack

Polaski: "Feminist readers today may reject the model of an ascetic virgin for the ideal woman in ministry. In ancient times, however, sexuality was so inextricably intertwined with a hierarchical social order that a woman's freedom to travel and proclaim would logically have been connected with the repudiation of marriage and family life."[37] Thankfully, ministry and marriage are no longer mutually exclusive options in our own time and place!

However, on several other points, I am inclined to argue with the author of 1 Timothy and would join the widows in objections they surely had to his restrictive admonitions. A case in point: apparently he can envision only one suitable lifestyle for young widows (and presumably all women under sixty years of age):[38] "I would have younger widows marry, bear children, and manage their households" (5:14). Indeed, he aims to integrate widows into patriarchal households and ensure that celibacy is a very limited, geriatric practice. But as we have noticed, the apostle Paul himself (in whose name this author purports to write) "argues for options," contending that "there is more than one way to live a holy life."[39] The widows surely found in Paul's own teaching and writings sanction for a life without marriage. Interpreting Scripture by Scripture, I, too, would want to place Paul's discussion of this matter in 1 Corinthians 7 in conversation with 1 Timothy 5 and to argue, in concert with Paul, that lives of faithful integrity can find expression in both marriage and celibacy. The fact that Jesus, John the Baptist, and Paul all were celibate is not insignificant as we reflect on this matter. As Richard Hays has observed, "Scripture bears witness that lives of freedom, joy, and service are possible without sexual relations" (and, we would add, without marriage, the bearing of children, and management of patriarchal households). "Indeed," Hays goes on to say, "however odd it may seem to contemporary sensibilities, some New Testament passages (Matt. 19:10–12; 1 Cor. 7) clearly commend the celibate life as a way of faithfulness."[40]

I also want to argue with 1 Timothy 5's drastic restrictions on women's practice of ministry. If an emerging church office—a ministerial order of widows—is reflected in 1 Timothy 5 (and I am largely convinced that it is), the author seeks to ensure that the pool of applicants for such service will be very small by stipulating eligibility requirements that would eliminate the vast majority of women. One wonders, for example, why rostered widows must be "not less than sixty years old" (5:9; a far more advanced age in the first century than the twenty-first), since no such age restrictions are compulsory elsewhere in the letter in discussions of qualifications for bishops, elders, or deacons. And in light of Paul's commendation of celibate lifestyles, one wonders why eligibility also presumes marriage and requires the rearing of children.

In addition, one of the most troubling features of the text is its trivializing characterization of women's speech. In describing young widows as gadabout, gossipy busybodies who are "saying what they should not say" (5:13), the author clearly exploits conventional stereotypes, "downloading" from "his cultural encyclopedia the idea that gossip is feminine speech."[41] In fact, as Marianne Kartzow points out,

> Every time women and their speech are mentioned in the Pastoral Epistles, it is always formulated negatively: they shall *not* be slanderers, talebearers, gossipers, busybodies, or babblers. These epistles provide no instructions as to how they shall speak. The ideal woman shall exist in silence. . . . If she breaks the silence, what she says is most likely gossip. The underlying agenda in these epistles seems to be that she better not open her mouth at all.[42]

One suspects the women in view would have objected to the consistent devaluation of their speech, and we should as well, for as Kartzow suggests, the stereotypes to which the author resorts do "not tell the whole truth about their positions as contributors and shapers of early Christian history and theology. It may be that these female gossipers played an important role in keeping parts of the tradition alive, bringing to new generations the common memory of the early Christian communities."[43]

Of course, this is not the first time we have encountered censuring of women's speech or restrictions on their practice of ministry—regrettably, these have been all too consistent themes in most of the contentious texts featured in this volume! However, as we have had occasion to notice, Scripture does not speak with one voice on these matters, and the one who speaks in 1 Timothy 5 is in many respects out of sync with other biblical voices. So once again, it is important to bring other biblical witnesses into the conversation—to *interpret Scripture by Scripture*. Points at which the author of 1 Timothy, though writing in Paul's name, departs from emphases in Paul's own letters (e.g., celibacy) have been recognized above, and other significant Pauline counteraffirmations are worth noting: Pauline texts do affirm an egalitarian vision (e.g., Gal. 3:28), presume that "all" have received gifts of the Spirit for liturgical leadership and edification of the community (e.g., 1 Cor. 11:2–16; 14:23–24, 26, 31, 39), and specify women as full partners in Paul's practice of ministry (e.g., Phoebe, Prisca, Junia, Euodia, and Syntyche, among others; see Rom. 16; Phil. 4:2–3). Other biblical witnesses also can be brought into the conversation; for example, Acts gives witness to the formation of the church on Pentecost as the fulfillment of Joel's prophetic vision of the outpouring of God's Spirit upon all flesh, with the result that daughters as well as sons, women along with men, prophesy (Acts 2:14–18; Joel 2:28–32).

Another classic principle of biblical interpretation noted in previous chapters, Augustine's *rule of love*, is also relevant to engagement with 1 Timothy 5. According to this principle, valid interpretations of Scripture must offer and support love of God and love of neighbor: "*No interpretation of Scripture is correct that leads to or supports contempt for any individual or group of persons either within or outside of the church.*"[44] As the author of 1 Timothy 5 interprets Paul's legacy, bringing it to bear in a new time and place, he crosses this line when he resorts to trivializing, eroticizing, and demonizing rhetoric in his censure of early Christian women, thereby promoting contempt for them. Trivializing of their character and pursuits (and what may have been their ministry) is evident in his description of them as idle, gadabout, gossipy busybodies; eroticizing of young widows is evident in his anxiety over their purportedly uncontrollable sexual vigor; and demonizing is evident in his judgment that "some have already turned away to follow Satan" (5:15) and are affiliated with evil, with the devil himself. Conflict often drives parties to it toward rhetorical extremes, but observations such as these convey questionable, harmful, and persistent gender stereotypes and promote contempt for fellow members of the body of Christ (indeed, for half the human race)—whether articulated in the first-century church or reinscribed by contemporary interpreters of the text in their preaching and teaching of it in our own time and place.

These are by no means the only points at which one may find oneself inclined to argue with the text! It is full of tensions and contradictions, and other aspects of it surely merit scrutiny and objection. But I hope a central thesis of this volume is clear by now: that arguing with the text is a faithful practice—one that honors the text by taking it with the utmost seriousness. God has given us minds to think deeply, minds that are to be exercised in honest engagement with Scripture!

Discerning Insights and Dangers

We also honor the text by wrestling with it further—by resisting any inclination to throw the baby out with the bathwater (Recommendation 3), confident that our own lives of discipleship and the life of the church can be edified by learning from both insights and dangers the text presents (Recommendation 4). Sustained reflection on the text, and discernment and articulation of both positive and negative ways in which it can instruct us, further assures that our engagement with it has integrity and creates space for the Spirit of God to do the holy work of forming the mind of Jesus Christ in us.

So are there positive, constructive insights that emerge from engagement with 1 Timothy 5? As ornery as the text may be in many respects, is there anything nice one can say about it? There are several respects in which I can muster measures of appreciation for its presence in the canon. As one of the most extensive discussions of women in the New Testament, and the longest discussion of widows, it preserves important pieces of our ecclesial family history that would otherwise be lost to us and the site of an important conflict in the life of the early church. It is the "tip of an iceberg,"[45] enabling us to catch a glimpse of early Christian women and prompting research and reflection on what is submerged.

Moreover, 1 Timothy 5 bears enduring witness to significant aspects of Christian life and faith. In some cases the insights that emerge are quite positive; in others they are closely intertwined with potential dangers and in need of joint reflection; there are also ways in which the text instructs us by negative example. Among the positive things we can appreciate about the text (and 1 Timothy as a whole) is its assumption of a fundamental connection between beliefs and behavior. Our conduct gives embodied witness to the authenticity of our faith. Moreover, throughout 1 Timothy, the family is considered a primary arena of discipleship. Our relationships with our own family members—parents and grandparents, siblings, spouses, and children—also bear witness to the integrity of our faith. These emphases are reflected in 5:4, for example, which speaks of the care of widows incumbent on their children and grandchildren not simply as a familial or social obligation, but also as a religious duty—an expression of authentic piety that "is pleasing in God's sight." Given the fundamental connection between beliefs and behavior, failure to attend to the well-being of family members is described in the strongest possible terms as having "denied the faith" (5:8). This is a perennial aspect of faithful disciple-ship that the text continues to hold before us. In so doing, it stands in continuity with the Fifth Commandment: "Honor your father and your mother" (Exod. 20:12; Deut. 5:16).

The text also bears witness to the early church's depth of commit-ment to honor and support its most vulnerable members. We should not presume that all widows, then or now, are destitute. But in all times and places, elderly widows continue to be among those most likely to fall through whatever "safety nets" a society has in place to ensure the well-being of its most vulnerable citizens. And in our own day, faithful ministry to elderly members, male and female, will become ever more important as the baby boomers age and both church and society face an unprecedented explosion of the older generation.

As we engage this challenge, 1 Timothy 5 presents both insights and dangers for our consideration. On the one hand, it sets a high standard, reminding us that honoring and supporting our most vul-nerable members is an essential aspect of faithful life and ministry in God's covenant communities. It can also prompt discernment of other vulnerable persons and groups in our midst who may be in special need of support—perhaps single parents or infirm members of our communities.

On the other hand, the text also reflects an ever-potential danger on this front: casting those in need of support solely as objects, rather than as subjects, of ministry—failing to honor them as persons capable of giving as well as receiving, of making significant contributions to the life and ministry of our congregations. First Timothy 5 provides a nod in the right direction in 5:5, where it speaks of the "real" widow's constancy in intercessory prayer—a significant ministry in the life of any church. However, the discussion of "enrolled" widows drastically downsizes an office or circle devoted to service, eliminating the majority of women from consideration and conveying the decided impression that "the list" is to be restricted to recipients, rather than practitioners, of ministry; and the critique of young widows clearly aims to curb their "gadding about from house to house" (5:13), which may well have entailed their exercise of ministry. Moreover, 5:16 describes ministry to widows as a matter "burdening" the church. But in a recent book significantly titled *A Vision for the Aging Church: Renewing Ministry for and by Seniors*, James Houston and Michael Parker urge congrega-tions to confront "the common thinking that older persons are more of a burden to the church than a gift": "The ever-growing, aging church is no burden; instead, this burgeoning reservoir of accumulated experience and talent can provide a lasting legacy of God's love to the younger generations." Indeed, "their wisdom, testimony, and courage are needed in the church," and "younger people can benefit from vibrant, reciprocal relationships with older persons."[46] Thus, truly "honoring" those to whom the church extends support surely entails ensuring opportunities for the community as a whole to benefit from their gifts for ministry and the blessings of intergenerational fellowship.[47] And in connection with our reflection on widows in particular, it is well for us to bear in mind the wisdom of anthropologist Margaret Mead, who reportedly observed, "There is no more creative force in the world than the menopausal woman with zest"!

Nevertheless, there is no denying that challenging matters of discernment are entailed in any ministry to vulnerable persons in need of support. Financial resources must be allocated wisely, and in this connection, too, both insights and dangers are worth weighing. With respect to constructive insights, Luke Timothy Johnson observes the manner in which 1 Timothy 5 highlights "the classic problems confronting all welfare systems through the ages":

> What help should come from the community as such, and what help should be provided by private sources? And what sort of behavioral norms should be sought to determine who ought to receive community help? . . . there is not a simple or single answer for every case. Rather, discernment is necessary, above all because there is no limit to human need, but there are real limits to any community's disposable possessions.[48]

These are practical, realistic, unavoidable, and challenging considerations with which any congregation must contend. Communities cannot engage in effective endeavor without budgets and careful financial planning. Consideration of both the possibilities and constraints that budgets present is thus an inescapable reality of life and ministry in the real world, and 1 Timothy 5 prompts reflection on such matters.

Yet a note of suspicion also is warranted as we consider the author's discussion of practical, financial matters. No congregation has unlimited resources, but there is reason to believe that the community to which 1 Timothy was first addressed was relatively prosperous. After all, in 2:9 the author exhorts women to "dress themselves modestly and decently in suitable clothing, not with their hair braided, or with gold, pearls, or expensive clothes" (which apparently were sartorial options for some); some members owned slaves (1 Tim. 6:1–2; Titus 2:9–10); and the letter closes with a reminder that "the love of money is a root of all kinds of evil" (6:10) and exhortation to the rich: "As for those who in the present age are rich, command them not to be haughty, or to set their hopes on the uncertainty of riches, but rather on God who richly provides us with everything for our enjoyment. They are to do good, to be rich in good works, generous, and ready to share, thus storing up for themselves the treasure of a good foundation for the future, so that they may take hold of the life that really is life" (6:17–19). Moreover, in 1 Timothy 5:17–22, the text that immediately follows the discussion of widows in 5:3–16, the author considers the question of financial remuneration for elders, arguing that those who labor in preaching and teaching are worthy of "double honor"—that is, double remuneration. Deborah Krause calls attention to the striking difference between the treatment of the widows and the elders in this back-to-back discussion in 1 Timothy 5:3–22:

> Some commentators explain that the letter writer sharply curtails the number of legitimate widow positions within the community on financial grounds. The call for families to fulfill their financial obligations to their dependent women is taken as an indication of a shortfall within the letter writer's understanding of the financial resources of the community. . . . Times were tight. Cuts had to be made.
>
> This apology, however, soon runs into the contradictory evidence of 1 Timothy 5:17 where the letter writer exhorts that elders who "rule well" be afforded "double honour" (*diplēs timēs*), or extra financial compensation. One can hardly make a case that the finances of the community were stretched thin when such a merit raise is afforded to one group, while the rolls of the other office were being drastically cut. Clearly, an agenda other than economic scarcity is afoot for the letter writer.[49]

Indeed, Krause perceptively concludes, "If we examine . . . the uneven treatment of compensation and concern for finances regarding the two groups of widows and elders, the allocation of money becomes a raw statement of the distribution of power within the church. That distribution, under the close direction of the letter writer, is made along age and gender lines."[50]

This is not the only point at which notable "double standards" come into view in 1 Timothy. As we have observed, bishops, elders, and deacons apparently face no age restrictions like those imposed on rostered widows, who must be "not less than sixty years old" if they are to be "put on the list" (5:9). And while widows are caricatured in denigrating fashion (as wanton, idle, gossipy, etc.), the reputation of elders is carefully safeguarded against false accusation (5:19): "Widows apparently are subject to ad hoc character assassination, while elders merit balance, objectivity and fairness."[51] The text thus presents both constructive and cautionary food for thought as we reflect on the challenging matters of discernment entailed in allocation of the church's available resources in ministries of support to those in need. It also prompts attention to what our budgets (and our rhetoric) convey about power dynamics and differentials within our community of faith—about who and what we most value.

Both constructive and cautionary wisdom may also be gleaned on another front as we consider the text's evident concern about public relations, about impressions that outsiders may have of the community of faith. On the one hand, public opinion is never an inconsequential matter, and certainly it was not for a fledgling religious movement under public scrutiny and suspicion. Moreover, the author's pervasive anxiety about social respectability is linked, to a great extent, with his desire that the gospel receive as wide a hearing as possible and that no obstacles stand in the way. As Margaret MacDonald observes, "For a group intent on winning the world, public opinion simply could not be ignored"[52]—nor can it be ignored in our own time and place. There is something to be said about the integrity of the church's struggle to live in the world, rather than withdraw from it, and to stay in dialogue with culture for the sake of the gospel.

But on the other hand, 1 Timothy's public relations campaign proves costly, and women and slaves pay the price for it. As Jouette Bassler explains, "The author's instructions concerning slaves and women . . . reflect a serious problem, one faced by any religious group seeking to make converts: how to maintain the distinctive (but, to outsiders, sometimes offensive) theological and social features of the group while building enough bridges to the outside world to make conversations possible. The author of the Pastoral Letters consistently chooses a conservative social route."[53] Others describe the author's strategy more pointedly as one of cultural accommodation, at least with respect to women and slaves. He accommodates conventional expectations regarding their deportment within Greco-Roman patriarchal households, presenting his own hierarchically structured vision of the church as the "household of God" (3:15). The problematic result, as Frances Young observes, is that "the theology of the Pastorals presents us with a whole culture of subordination":[54]

> As scripture, the Pastorals have shaped a world in which women and others have been subordinated and devalued on the authority of God's Word. . . . The Pastorals encourage a hierarchical view of the way things are. Not only have they appeared to establish a clerical hierarchy, . . . but their actual text reinforced patriarchal hierarchy in family, society and church, apparently providing warrant for this from scripture. Such texts contained in a sacred authoritative canon cannot but become "texts of terror" in a democratic society which views the position of women, lay people, servants, slaves, etc. in a totally different light. Taken at face value they appear to perpetuate with the authority of God patterns of relationship which are no longer acceptable, and may be regarded as opposed to the fundamental outlook of the Christian tradition, even of Paul himself in his better moments (e.g. Gal. 3.28).[55]

Many will agree with Young's contention that 1 Timothy's "hierarchical view of the way things are" needs to be challenged by the broader witness of Scripture, not least by christological considerations and a cruciform vision of Christian life. Indeed, we should add this to the laundry list of matters worth arguing about in our engagement with the Pastoral Epistles. But like 1 Timothy, we too must engage the struggle to stay in dialogue with culture for the sake of the gospel; and like 1 Timothy, we too, no doubt, will negotiate the relationship imperfectly. Thus this epistle continues to bear witness both to the importance of this challenge for our mission and also to the costs it can exact, prompting reflection on who is bearing that cost—and at what price to their well-being, to that of the community as a whole, and to the integrity of our proclamation of the gospel.

There are also final respects in which we can learn from painfully imperfect efforts to embody the gospel reflected in 1 Timothy 5:3–16. Christian community needs structure and leadership, and the Pastoral Epistles grapple with these necessities, negotiating the shape of the church's ongoing life. But the author's own exercise of leadership can instruct us by way of negative example, for in accord with the "hierarchical view of the way things are," the letters are pervaded by "a truly authoritarian spirit."[56] As we have noticed, the author's injunctions for widows are not relayed to them directly, but in the guise of man-to-man counsel for a junior associate in ministry charged with keeping the widows in line. The text also reflects, sadly, the rhetoric of gender derision. The author is, to be sure, under duress, dealing with false teachers who present serious internal challenges to the church's theological integrity, and women are the only members of the community explicitly identified in association with them. But his strategy for dealing with both is one of caricature and dismissal,[57] and his derisive rhetoric surely violates Augustine's *rule of love* by promoting contempt (rather than love) for fellow believers. But thanks be to God: we can learn from such dangers, as well as from the insights, that biblical texts present. When recognized and named as they manifest themselves in both the ancient text and our own lives, they call us to repentance, and by the power of God's Spirit at work within us, to renewal, evoking discernment of ways in which we might more faithfully embody the gospel in our own time and place. For is not the cross at the heart of the gospel really God's promise that new life can emerge out of broken places?

QUESTIONS FOR DISCUSSION
AND REFLECTION

What has been your prior experience with 1 Timothy 5:3–16? In what contexts have you encountered this text? Has it impacted your experience? If so, how? What strikes you most about 1 Timothy 5:3–16? What questions does it raise for you?

As you eavesdrop on the site of an ancient argument in 1 Timothy 5:3–16, do you find yourself empathizing most with the author and the struggles he faced, or with the widows who are the focus of his angst? Why? Can you imagine that both might be entitled to measures of your empathy? Why, or why not? What would you most like to ask the author of this text—or the widows of whom he speaks?

Are you inclined to argue with the text? If so, what would you most want to argue about? And how might classic principles of biblical interpretation (e.g., *the interpretation of Scripture by Scripture, the centrality of Jesus Christ, the rule of love,* or *the rule of faith*) inform your wrestling with it?

Are you familiar with *The Acts of Paul and Thecla*? If you have not read this extracanonical work and would like to do so, you

can find it online: http://www.earlychristianwritings.com/text/
actspaul.html. What strikes you most about this legendary tale?
How does it inform your reading of 1 Timothy 5:3–16? What
do you think of the possibility that the Pastoral Epistles represent
"the other side of Thecla's story"?

Share your thoughts on the public relations concerns reflected
throughout 1 Timothy 5—the pervasive angst about social
respectability. In what ways do such concerns manifest themselves in the life of your congregation?

The text bears witness to the depth of commitment on the part of
the early church to honor and support its most vulnerable members. Who would you identify as vulnerable persons or groups in
your community of faith in special need of support? Do those
whom your church supports also have opportunities to give as
well as receive, to make contributions to the life and ministry of
your congregation?

What do you think of Deborah Krause's contention that the allocation of money can be "a raw statement of the distribution of
power within the church"?[58]

What role have intergenerational relationships played in your own
life of faith? What role does intergenerational fellowship play in
the life of your congregation?

Do you think 1 Timothy presents a "hierarchical view of the way
things are" and reflects "a truly authoritarian spirit"? Why, or
why not? Would you agree with the contention that the text
reflects derisive gender rhetoric—that it trivializes, eroticizes, and
demonizes early Christian women? Does this rhetoric constitute a
violation of *the rule of love* in your view? Why, or why not?

What constructive and/or cautionary insights have emerged from
your engagement with this text? Why are they important to you?
What questions linger? Would you be inclined to preach or teach
on 1 Timothy 5? Why, or why not? What connections do you
discern between this text and the life of your church?

6

Women in Ministry

Romans 16:1–16

I hope I have made a case for the practice of keeping company with tyrannical texts—texts that may raise our blood pressure, making the effort to read deeper, probe further, and perhaps find in them some word of edification for the church that we have failed to hear. And I hope you have found, as I have, that contentious texts can turn out to be places of encounter with the living God, who is present in all our wrestling with Scripture, whether with or against its claims. They can be media of God's own work within us, forming the mind of Jesus Christ in us. Still, as important as it is to engage tyrannical texts patiently, publicly, and with integrity (for a host of noted reasons), a steady diet of them is not conducive to mental and spiritual health! And fortunately, the Bible is filled with life-giving texts that require much less strenuous effort on our parts to wrestle a blessing from them.

So in closing, let me direct your attention to one such Pauline text that serves as an important counterpoint to all the texts we have considered in this volume. It has not had the outsized impact on ongoing debates about appropriate roles for women in church and society as ones we have engaged in the preceding chapters, though it should have. In fact, it has been largely overlooked, though there is no question that it comes directly from Paul's hand and is a gold mine of information about women's participation in early Christian ministry. It appears in Romans 16, the last chapter of the apostle Paul's longest, most substantial letter, "arguably the most influential letter ever written" and "certainly the most significant letter in the history of Christianity."[1] As the letter comes to a close, Paul provides a long list of personal greetings to the church at Rome, directly naming ten women as colleagues in ministry—women who exercised leadership in early Christian communities and actively contributed to the formation and expansion of the church. Consider Romans 16:1–16, and listen to what the Spirit is saying to the church!

ROMANS 16:1–16

[16:1]I commend to you our sister **Phoebe**, a deacon of the church at Cenchreae, [2]so that you may welcome her in the Lord as is fitting for the saints, and help her in whatever she may require from you, for she has been a benefactor of many and of myself as well.
[3]Greet **Prisca** and Aquila, who work with me in Christ Jesus, [4]and who risked their necks for my life, to whom not only I give thanks, but also all the churches of the Gentiles. [5]Greet also the church in their house. Greet my beloved Epaenetus, who was the first convert in Asia for Christ. [6]Greet **Mary**, who has worked very hard among you. [7]Greet Andronicus and **Junia**, my relatives who were in prison with me; they are prominent among the apostles, and they were in Christ before I was. [8]Greet Ampliatus, my beloved in the Lord. [9]Greet Urbanus, our co-worker in Christ, and my beloved Stachys. [10]Greet Apelles, who is approved in Christ. Greet those who belong to the family of Aristobulus. [11]Greet my relative Herodion. Greet those in the Lord who belong to the family of Narcissus. [12]Greet those workers in the Lord, **Tryphaena** and **Tryphosa**. Greet the beloved **Persis**, who has worked hard in the Lord. [13]Greet Rufus, chosen in the Lord; and greet **his mother**—a mother to me also. [14]Greet Asyncritus, Phlegon, Hermes, Patrobas, Hermas, and the brothers and sisters who are with them. [15]Greet Philologus, **Julia**, Nereus and **his sister**, and Olympas, and all the saints who are with them. [16]Greet one another with a holy kiss. All the churches of Christ greet you.

How does this text differ from those we have considered in preceding chapters? For one thing, it is not a "contentious" text: it does not preserve the site of an ancient argument. Neither is it overtly "prescriptive," aiming to change existing patterns of behavior. The ten women are mentioned in passing, in matter-of-fact fashion, clearly reflecting an assumption on Paul's part—one that did not need to be argued or defended—that they were valued colleagues in ministry.

Moreover, Romans 16 is unusual in the Pauline corpus as a whole, for while the letters typically conclude with greetings of some sort, an extraordinary number of people (totaling twenty-eight) are singled out here—more than in the rest of Paul's letters combined. No one questions the fact that the apostle Paul authored this text, but some have thought it unlikely that he would have known so many people in Rome. Romans is, after all, the only Pauline letter addressed to a church he did not found and had never visited. Thus, in years past, some scholars have argued that this chapter was perhaps originally addressed to the church at Ephesus, where Paul spent a substantial amount of time, and appended to Romans at a later time when the letter circulated there.

However, scholars are now largely unanimous in their opinion that Romans 16 was originally part of Romans and that it is integral to the letter as a whole. Indeed, the extraordinary number of greetings makes far more sense in a letter addressed to a church Paul had never visited! Why? For one thing, it would surely be impolitic to single out so many, but not all, for greeting in a church where all were well known—which probably explains why Paul singles out only a few people for individual greetings in letters to churches he founded. More importantly, Paul is at a transition point in his ministry and plans to visit Rome in the near horizon. He has completed his missionary labor in the east, having preached the gospel "from Jerusalem and as far around as Illyricum" (15:19). He now anticipates a new venture in mission in the west, on the heels of a visit to Rome (15:22–29):

> [22]This is the reason that I have so often been hindered from coming to you. [23]But now, with no further place for me in these regions, I desire, as I have for many years, to come to you [24]when I go to Spain. For I do hope to see you on my journey and to be sent on by you, once I have enjoyed your company for a little while. [25]At present, however, I am going to Jerusalem in a ministry to the saints; [26]for Macedonia and Achaia have been pleased to share their resources with the poor among the saints at Jerusalem. [27]They were pleased to do this, and indeed they owe it to them; for if the Gentiles have come to share in their spiritual blessings, they ought also to be of service to them in material things. [28]So, when I have completed this, and have delivered to them what has been collected, I will set out by way of you to Spain; [29]and I know that when I come to you, I will come in the fullness of the blessing of Christ.

Clearly, Paul hopes the Roman church will support him in this new venture and speed him on his way, serving, perhaps, as a new base of operations for his projected mission to Spain. The letter prepares the way for this by introducing Paul and setting forth a detailed presentation of his theology, on the basis of which he would be asking them for support. In such a letter, it would be to his advantage to greet everyone in Rome he can think of—all who are known to him, directly or through hearsay, thereby establishing that he is by no means a stranger but rather bound to them through many common friends, distinguished ones at that, who can vouch for him.[2] In short, he is "networking,"[3] and thereby getting "a preliminary foot in the door."[4] (Upon meeting new people, don't we, too, often try to identify "common friends" as a way of building rapport?)

Where would Paul have met so many Roman Christians? No doubt in conjunction with his extensive missionary labors in the east. First-century Christians lived in a remarkably mobile world and traveled with relative ease due to Roman engineering prowess, which built and maintained a comprehensive network of roads that embraced the entire empire, facilitating efficient movement of armies, government officials, and civilians, as well as trade and commerce, between the east and the west. In addition, a maritime transportation network facilitated sea travel, except during winter months when sailing was suspended. All roads, whether land or sea routes, did, quite literally, lead to Rome, radiating out from the capital city, which drew a constant flow of immigrants. In fact, many of the persons greeted in Romans 16 bear eastern names and were likely immigrants from the east. Some of the people singled out for greetings, however, may have met Paul while in exile from Rome. According to the Roman historian Suetonius, the Roman emperor Claudius expelled Jews (including Jews who believed in Jesus) from Rome in the year 49 CE for "constantly making disturbances at the instigation of Chrestus." This likely refers to controversies that erupted between Jews and Jewish Christians over the Christ. Acts 18 reports that Prisca and Aquila, the first to be greeted in Romans 16, were among those banished. They moved to Corinth, where they met Paul, provided lodging for him, partnered with him in tentmaking and ministry, and then accompanied him to Ephesus. Others greeted in Romans 16 may have been among those banished from Rome along with Prisca and Aquila, returning after Claudius's death in the year 54, when the edict was lifted.

In short, given the remarkable mobility of the Roman imperial world, the constant flow of immigrants into the capital city, and the expulsion of Jewish Christians such as Prisca and Aquila from Rome, it is not at all unlikely that Paul would have known a number of believers in Rome and heard of others from them. He would also have learned from them a great deal about circumstances with which the Roman house churches were grappling. Some of those circumstances were of real concern to him, for the letter serves not only to introduce him to the church, but also to address genuine pastoral concerns, quite specifically in the immediately preceding chapters (Rom. 14–15). In fact, a number of scholars now argue (persuasively, in my view) that the return of exiled Jewish Christians (and founding members of that church) to Rome and to a church that had become largely Gentile Christian in the intervening years—thus with a very different composition and ethos—illumines Paul's extended discussion of multicultural conflict in Romans 14–15 between "the weak" and the "strong" (Paul's terms). As N. T. Wright observes, when Jewish Christians returned, "we may properly assume that the (Gentile) church leadership would not exactly be delirious with excitement."[5] The returnees may have had difficulty adapting to the new situation and finding genuine acceptance. Indeed, it is worth noting that "welcome one another" is the key admonition in Romans 14–15. The fact that such admonishment is needed suggests that this was not happening, that they were meeting separately, not worshiping together, and nursing antagonism and suspicions about one another. These circumstances are pertinent to a reading of Romans 16 as well, where at least five different house churches are referenced (vv. 5, 10, 11, 14, 15). Given the likelihood of conflict between predominantly Jewish house churches on the one hand and predominantly Gentile house churches on the other, it is significant that Paul does not greet his acquaintances directly but rather entreats *the community* at Rome to greet, and in so doing to honor and welcome, others on his behalf. (In other words, he does not say, "I greet," but rather, "*ya'll* greet," using second-person plural imperatives!) As N. T. Wright puts it, this historical scenario is one "into which Romans fits like a glove"[6] and illumines a reading of the letter as a whole, for in it Paul sets out to explain the "both Jew and Gentile" character of the gospel and of the promises to Israel, encouraging the Roman Christians to work out the implications of this gospel and these promises in their life together.

Paul's long list of greetings to specific Roman Christians in Romans 16 may not initially strike you as stimulating reading, but it has played a crucial role in discerning the historical background of the letter and Paul's purposes in writing. One commentator, in fact, has suggested that to understand Romans, one should turn first to its closing chapters and begin reading at the end![7] And for those interested in women in the biblical world (as we have been throughout this volume), Romans 16 turns out to be a gold mine of information about the contribution of women to the growth and expansion of the early church and one of the most fascinating chapters in the New Testament! So with this historical background in mind, let us turn to this matter of special interest to us.

LISTENING TO THE TEXT

Women in Ministry in Romans 16

The most intriguing feature of Romans 16 is the large number of women Paul greets and commends as partners in ministry. Twenty-eight individuals are singled out, among them ten women: Phoebe, Prisca, Mary, Junia, Tryphaena, Tryphosa, Persis, Julia, the mother of Rufus, and the sister of Nereus. This number is striking in and of itself, but Paul's generous praise of them is even more so, for as Brendan Byrne has observed, "women bear more than half the epithets denoting service and 'labor' on behalf of the community and the gospel."[8] Three women in particular stand out in this regard: Phoebe, Prisca, and Junia.

Phoebe

The chapter opens with Paul's commendation of Phoebe (vv. 1–2), who was almost certainly the bearer of Paul's letter to the church at Rome: "*I commend to you our sister Phoebe, a deacon of the church at Cenchreae, so that you may welcome her in the Lord as is fitting for the saints, and help her in whatever she may require from you, for she has been a benefactor of many and of myself as well.*" The Roman postal service was available only for governmental correspondence, and so delivery of all other mail required a courier. Paul entrusted Phoebe with this crucial task and urges the believers at Rome to "welcome her in the Lord as is fitting for the saints, and help her in whatever she may require from you" (16:2). Authors of letters often commended their couriers in order to secure hospitality and assistance for them in a community where they might not be known. Paul emphasizes that Phoebe is more than deserving of Roman hospitality and aid, highlighting her credentials as "our sister," as "a deacon of the church at Cenchreae," and as "a benefactor of many and of myself as well." Each of these credentials merits attention.

Bearing a name with origins in Greek mythology, Phoebe was likely a Gentile Christian, but Paul identifies her nonetheless as "our sister," invoking the familial language of Christian fellowship and solidarity, the language of "fictive kinship." Whatever their ethnic background and wherever their home, believers, through their baptism, are bound together in a new family as brothers and sisters in Jesus Christ. This language identifies Phoebe as one who is fully integrated into the new Christian family and who is to be received by Roman Christians as such.

She is further identified as "a deacon of the church at Cenchreae." In fact, Phoebe is the first named deacon in Christian history! Sadly, translators have tampered with Phoebe's official status as a deacon in her home church, demoting her to "servant" (KJV, NIV, NEB, CEV, ASV, NASB) or even "deaconess" (RSV, NJB, Phillips). However, when the same word (*diakonos* in Greek) is used in reference to (presumably male) others, it is usually translated as "deacon" (e.g., Phil. 1:1; 1 Tim. 3:8, 10, 12) or associated with explicit language of ministry. Paul, for example, uses the term in reference to his own labor on behalf of the church (e.g., 1 Cor. 3:5; 2 Cor. 3:6; 6:4; 11:23) and that of associates in ministry (e.g., Apollos in 1 Cor. 3:5). Interestingly, the gender-specific office of "deaconess" (*diakonissa*) does not appear in the New Testament and is not attested in Christian literature before the third and fourth centuries. Any reference to Phoebe as a "deaconess" in Romans 16, a first-century text, is thus anachronistic, and so we should not presume that her ministry, like that of later deaconesses, was subordinate to male deacons or primarily entailed ministry to other women.[9] The office of deacon was in its nascent stages at this point in early church history, so it is hard to specify duties such an office entailed,[10] but the language of the text clearly conveys that Phoebe exercised some sort of diaconal ministry in a continuing and officially recognized capacity in her home church at Cenchreae.[11] Paul emphasizes this in order to impress upon Roman Christians Phoebe's stature in an eastern church. Cenchreae was the eastern seaport of Corinth. Paul composed his letter to Rome while in Corinth, where he sojourned for extended periods of time and would have had occasion to become well acquainted with Phoebe.

Having established her official stature in the church at Cenchreae, Paul identifies Phoebe, additionally, as "a benefactor [*prostatis*] of many and of myself as well." Because the Greek word *prostatis* (a feminine grammatical form) does not appear elsewhere in the New Testament (in either masculine or feminine form), translators are not of one mind as to how to convey its meaning. Many settle for "helper" as the descriptor of Phoebe's relationship to Paul and the "many" others he references (e.g., RSV, NIV, ASV, NASB, NJB), but there is reason to suspect that this fails to do full justice to the implications of this language. The cognate verb form of the noun *prostatis* is *proistēmi*, a compound verb formed by the preposition *pro* ("before") and the verb *histēmi* ("to stand"), thus "to stand before." The verb appears eight times in the New Testament and bears a range of meanings, including connotations of leadership ("to direct, be at the head of, preside over, or manage") as well as benefactor ("to care for, be concerned about, or give aid"). Paul's use of the verb in Romans 12:8 and 1 Thessalonians 5:12 inclines toward the leadership sense rather than the benefactor sense, as does its appearance in the Pastoral Epistles (1 Tim. 3:4, 5; 5:17), though these are not mutually exclusive connotations since one can shade into the other. Many find it hard to imagine that Paul would speak of Phoebe as *his* leader, director, or manager and thus favor the common use of the word in secular Greek in reference to "patrons" and "benefactors." (The CEV translation bucks this trend, emphasizing Phoebe's leadership credentials: "I have good things to say about Phoebe, who is a leader in the church at Cenchreae. Welcome her in a way that is proper for someone who has faith in the Lord and is one of God's own people. Help her in any way you can. After all, she has proved to be a respected leader for many others, including me.") Whatever the case may be, "helper" says far too little about Phoebe, implying "assistant" status of some sort. Her role was likely much more influential. Clearly, Phoebe had the means to travel and was presumably a financially independent woman of some standing who placed her resources, time, and social clout in service of the early Christian mission. Paul acknowledges that he and "many" others as well were beneficiaries of her largesse and reliant on her sphere of influence.

Given these worthy credentials, Paul urges the Roman Christians to "help her in whatever she may require from you" (16:2). The unspecified matter (*pragmati*) in which Phoebe might have required assistance is itself a matter of debate. Most presume that she was a businesswoman who traveled to Rome primarily in connection with commercial (or perhaps personal) matters, agreeing to deliver Paul's letter en route. Robert Jewett, however, proposes an intriguing scenario, speculating that Phoebe may have taken on the role of patroness of Paul's upcoming Spanish mission announced in the immediately preceding chapter (15:22–29) and therefore traveled to Rome for strategic purposes, to secure necessary resources and create for him a logistical base of support.[12] As Jewett notes, a mission to Spain would require substantial advance planning, for sparse Jewish settlement in Spain meant that Paul would be without his customary synagogal springboard for missionary operations. Neither could Paul assume fluency in Greek in this region, as he had in the east, since the population spoke a bewildering variety of languages and dialects; the Romans had imposed Latin as a means of administration. Consequently, mission in Spain would also entail linguistic challenges that Paul heretofore had not faced, requiring the assistance of translators. Christians in Rome were in a position to be of considerable help in such matters as Paul ventured westward, and his long list of greetings would have provided Phoebe with a ready-made list of potential supporters and advisers.

Whatever the primary purpose of her trip to Rome, Phoebe's responsibilities as the bearer of Paul's letter would have entailed much more than a drop-off. It goes without saying that her responsibilities required, first of all, an arduous, extended (and nonmotorized!) journey of well over 600 miles, probably by both land and sea. Given the hazards, wear and tear of extended travel, and unpredictable weather, many ancient letters never reached their destinations. But Phoebe and the letter with which she had been entrusted arrived safely in Rome. Ancient epistolary conventions suggest that her responsibilities then would have included reading or "performing" the letter—not once, but several times, as she circulated among the various house churches of Rome, ensuring that it was properly heard and understood.[13] As one familiar with Paul's purposes in writing and the letter's content, she also would have been in a position to answer questions or concerns about it and to elaborate upon it as needed (in the same manner as Tychicus, the bearer of Colossians and Ephesians, is identified as one who can provide additional news in Col. 4:7–9 and Eph. 6:21–22). As Allan Chapple states, "Reading the letter was a rhetorical act":

That is, the bearer of the letter was also its interpreter—when it was being read out for the first time, the letter was also receiving its first public interpretation. Such things as the reader's intonation, facial expressions, and use of pauses and gestures were all vital ways of communicating the intended meaning of the words. So much so, that the hearers could safely assume that the reader, as bearer of the letter, had been coached by the sender in how to read it. With so much riding on the positive reception of *Romans*, there is thus little doubt that Paul would have gone through it carefully with Phoebe so that she was able to communicate its contents as he wanted. Her reading of the letter can thus be seen as an authorised interpretation of its contents.[14]

Phoebe, then, is rightly identified as the first interpreter of Romans, the first public commentator upon it,[15] as well as the one who ensured that it reached its destination. And given the importance of this letter to Paul, the hopes attached to it for his Spanish mission as well as for the well-being of the church at Rome, he surely would have taken great care in selecting his courier, securing the best possible person for this crucial task—someone with stature who would be well received and whom he could trust to function, in a sense, as his surrogate voice. We would not know of Phoebe if Paul had not commended her in Romans 16, for her name appears nowhere else in the New Testament. But thanks to her commitment to the early Christian mission and her service on behalf of the church, the most influential letter in Christian history was delivered, and preserved, for the ages.

Prisca

After commending his letter bearer to the Roman Christians, Paul turns to his closing greetings. As we have noticed, he does not address his acquaintances in Rome directly; rather, using second-person plural imperatives, he urges the Roman Christians to greet twenty-seven persons on his behalf—in other words, "*Ya'll* greet . . ."! In so doing, he facilitates public recognition of an extraordinary number of persons and of his connection with them, establishing that he is by no means a stranger in Rome. But equally as important, if the various house churches in Rome were experiencing multicultural strain between Jewish Christians and Gentile Christians (as Rom. 14–15 suggests), he endeavors to build up the unity of the church, entreating the community at Rome to greet, and in so doing to publicly honor and welcome, others with whom they may not be in close fellowship.

Pride of place on Paul's long list of greetings belongs to Prisca and Aquila, distinguished colleagues in ministry of long standing, to whom his most extensive and effusive greetings are to be conveyed: "*Greet Prisca and Aquila, who work with me in Christ Jesus, and who risked their necks for my life, to whom not only I give thanks, but also all the churches of the Gentiles. Greet also the church in their house*" (16:3–5). Prisca, known by the diminutive "Priscilla" in Acts, is one of the handful of women mentioned more than once in the New Testament (Acts 18:2–3, 18–19, 24–26; Rom. 16:3–5; 1 Cor. 16:19; 2 Tim. 4:19). It is hard to know what to make of the variation in name. Is the Acts reference to her as "Priscilla" ("little Prisca") a reflection of the affection in which she was held or of Luke's diminution of women? Is Paul's reference to her as "Prisca" an indication that he treats women as "grown-ups"?[16] Perhaps this is straining at gnats and the variation should not be pressed for significance!

Of greater interest is the fact that Prisca is always mentioned in conjunction with her husband, Aquila, and in four of the six references to them in the New Testament, her name appears first, in strikingly unconventional fashion. Some speculate that the atypical ordering of their names reflects that she was of higher social status than her husband; but such distinctions are of far less interest to Paul than ecclesial commitment and endeavor, demonstrated by the fact that greetings from high-status Corinthians—Gaius, host to the "whole church" in Corinth and Erastus, the city treasurer—do not appear until the tail end of the chapter, in Romans 16:23. Moreover, Luke tells us that Prisca and Aquila engaged in manual labor (Acts 18:3); if she had been a woman of elevated status, Luke likely would have mentioned such a distinction, as he does for others (Luke 8:3; Acts 16:14; 17:4, 12, 34). The unusual ordering more likely reflects Prisca's prominence in ministry, or perhaps, as Scott Spencer suggests, the genuine mutuality that characterized their joint labor, for the two clearly functioned as a missionary team, as "interchangeable, collegial partners" in "marriage, occupation, and association with Paul and his mission."[17]

To our knowledge, Prisca and Aquila were the most prominent couple engaged in the Pauline mission field, for their memory is honored in multiple New Testament documents (Acts, Romans, 1 Corinthians, 2 Timothy) and in association with three of the most important centers of early Christianity—Corinth, Ephesus, and Rome. Indeed, the most striking feature of Prisca and Aquila's ministry was its itinerancy, which took them from Italy to Greece, then on to Asia Minor (modern Turkey), and eventually back to Rome. They have "one of the most complete surviving migration histories of any individuals of similar status"—one that illustrates "the distances it was possible for migrants to travel and the range of contacts they could make."[18] As noted, they were Jews and among the first followers of Jesus in Rome, banished from the city for disturbances in the synagogue (Acts 18), probably related to proclamation of Jesus Christ. Evidently they did not shrink from public witness to their faith despite any conflict it evoked, and they paid a price for it.

But exile set in motion expansive opportunities for ministry. Upon expulsion, they migrated east to Corinth, where they first encountered Paul, offered him hospitality, and partnered with him in tentmaking and ministry. Only Acts tells us that they (and Paul) were independent artisans, tentmakers by trade. As such, they worked with linen, canvas, or leather. Scholars debate the implications of this work for their economic status.[19] Some presume that the couple was relatively prosperous, but there is little evidence that tentmaking was associated with great wealth, reputation, or prestige.[20] Paul speaks of it as wearying labor (1 Cor. 4:12; 1 Thess. 2:9). Moreover, Prisca and Aquila's hosting of house churches (in both Rome and Ephesus, and perhaps Corinth as well) did not necessarily entail home ownership but rather the ability to share access to whatever space (owned or rented) they inhabited.

In fact, their travel does not appear to have been constrained by real estate ventures, for when Paul departed from Corinth after an extended sojourn there of eighteen months, Prisca and Aquila accompanied him to Ephesus. Perhaps it was in Ephesus where they "risked their necks" for Paul's life (16:4), when he found himself in danger of mob violence incited by silversmiths whose business at the great shrine of Artemis was threatened by his preaching (Acts 19:21–41); yet while undergoing the many hardships and dangers to which Paul bears witness, in Ephesus and elsewhere (e.g., 1 Cor. 15:32; 2 Cor. 1:8–9; 11:22–33), there were various occasions when he would have found himself in need of protection. Whatever the dangerous circumstances may have been, Paul's striking testimony to Prisca and Aquila's heroic risking of life and limb on his behalf (like their earlier expulsion from Rome) reflects the perils associated with early Christian mission and their willingness to bear suffering, if need be, for the sake of the gospel.

They established a house church in Ephesus, referenced in 1 Corinthians 16:19, and when Paul departed from Ephesus, Prisca and Aquila remained. Acts tells us that in Ephesus they also tutored the eloquent and erudite Apollos, a "well-versed" teacher in his own right, taking him "aside" (privately, in discreet, respectful, and pastoral fashion) and explaining "the Way of God to him more accurately" (18:24–28), thereby providing advanced training for his powerfully effective missional endeavor.[21] The historicity of this incident is in question, but as Jouette Bassler insists, it surely reflects "an enduring memory that Prisca was an authoritative teacher who not only performed missionary work herself, but also helped train others."[22] At some point (presumably after the emperor Claudius's death in 54 CE, when his edict was lifted and the coast was clear), they returned to Rome, where they once again hosted a "church in their house," to which Paul extends greetings in Romans 16:5. Given their close collaboration with Paul, some have speculated that the couple's return to Rome was strategic—that they returned as his "advance team"[23] to help him establish a foothold for his gospel before he ventured on to Spain.

Whatever the case may have been, Prisca evidently was in no way subordinate to her husband, Aquila; theirs was a genuine team ministry. And neither of them were subordinate to Paul as "assistants" or "helpers." Paul identifies them upfront in 16:3 (RSV) as "my fellow workers in Christ Jesus" (*tous synergous mou en Christō Iēsou*), "a distinctive and unique Pauline expression" for persons who work "together with Paul as agent[s] of God in the common 'work' of missionary proclamation"[24] (cf. 1 Cor. 3:9; 2 Cor. 1:24, 8:23; Phil. 2:25, 4:3; 1 Thess. 3:2; Phlm. 1, 24). In short, as Carolyn Osiek and Margaret MacDonald note, Prisca and Aquila were clearly "movers and shakers in Pauline circles" in their own right: "As missionaries, teachers, collaborators of Paul and others, and patrons of house churches in three different cities, they helped people get where they wanted to go and obtain needed information, and they created spaces that offered vital infrastructure for the expansion and support of the movement—taking risks in the process."[25] And as Marie Noël Keller observes, as exiles from Rome they undoubtedly knew the importance of being welcomed, and clearly honed the art of hospitality everywhere they went, creating space that "formed, nurtured, and sustained numerous believers in the various places they lived and ministered."[26] This Jewish Christian couple was so widely known that Paul notes (in striking and somewhat hyperbolic fashion) that they are universally recognized—that not only he, but also "all the churches of the Gentiles" give thanks for their ministry.[27] By entreating the recipients of his letter to convey to Prisca and Aquila his effusive words of praise, Paul there facilitates public recognition of their distinguished service on behalf of the whole church.

Junia

A third prominent woman, Junia, stands out in Paul's greeting to another missionary team in 16:7: *"Greet Andronicus and Junia, my relatives who were in prison with me; they are prominent among the apostles, and they were in Christ before I was."* Striking similarities between the two missionary couples can be observed. In all probability, Junia, like Prisca, was married to her partner in mission, Andronicus. Yet Paul himself does not explicitly identify either Prisca or Junia as "wives." Only Acts describes Prisca as a "wife." Throughout the entire list of greetings, Paul focuses not on their marital status but on their significant contributions to the life of the church. "In light of that culture's obsession with classifying women by sexual status, it is striking that so many women are named . . . without any such designation."[28] Moreover, like Prisca and Aquila, Andronicus and Junia were Jewish Christians. In the case of Prisca and Aquila, we learn this from Acts (18:2). But Andronicus and Junia are explicitly identified as Jewish Christians by Paul's pointed reference to them as "my relatives" or "compatriots" (*syngeneis* in Greek). Paul uses the same word in Romans 9:3 when he refers to the Jewish people as a whole as "my own people, my kindred [*syngenōn*] according to the flesh," whose rejection of the gospel evokes in him sorrow, anguish, and extended theological reflection (Rom. 9–11). (Another Roman Christian, Herodion, is also greeted as a "relative" or "compatriot" in 16:11, and Paul's singling out of five Jewish Christians for public affirmation is not insignificant if multicultural tension between Jewish Christians and Gentile Christians—in particular, discrimination against Jewish believers by a Gentile Christian majority—was disrupting the peace and unity of the community, as seems likely in Rom. 14–15.)[29] Finally, Andronicus and Junia, like Prisca and Aquila, endured the perils of Christian mission, suffering on behalf of the gospel, for Paul remembers that they "were in prison with me" (16:7). We do not know whether they shared a period of imprisonment with Paul, incarceration at the same time and in the same place, or whether he is acknowledging that they have endured imprisonment, as he has, for the sake of the gospel. In either case, Junia was clearly a woman whose witness to Jesus Christ (along with that of Andronicus) evoked public attention and judicial backlash.

Yet Junia (along with Andronicus) is also singled out in unparalleled fashion as "outstanding" or "prominent among the apostles" (16:7). This is the most astonishing feature of Romans 16 since it is the New Testament's only reference to a woman as an apostle, and a distinguished one at that! However, Junia's apostleship has struck many as so unlikely that her gender identity has been called into question. Interpreters who could not imagine that Paul would have described a woman as an apostle presumed that Junia must have been a man, and arbitrarily replaced the female name with a masculine one ("Junias").[30] Thus, in the course of the text's transmission, Junia was subject to what Elizabeth Castelli aptly refers to as "sex-change-by-translation."[31] And as Bernadette Brooten has noted, the logic behind this change was decidedly circular: "a woman could not have been an apostle. Because a woman could not have been an apostle, the woman who is here called apostle could not have been a woman."[32]

Interestingly, there seems to have been no question about Junia's gender identity during the first thirteen centuries of the church's existence. Early church fathers clearly acknowledged Andronicus's partner in ministry as a woman. Origen of Alexandria (ca. 185–254 CE), the earliest commentator on Romans 16:7, took the name to be feminine, as did Ambrosiaster (ca. 375), Jerome (ca. 340–419), John Chrysostom (ca. 345/54–407), Theodoret of Cyrrhus (ca. 393–ca. 458), John of Damascus (ca. 675–ca. 749), Hraban of Fulda (780–856), Atto of Vercelli (924–961), Theophylact (fl. 1070–1081), Peter Abelard (1079–1142), and Peter Lombard (ca. 1095–1169), among others.[33] John Chrysostom (ca. 344/54–407) underlined this fact in unambiguous fashion, exclaiming, "Think how great the devotion of this woman Junia must have been, that she should be worthy to be called an apostle!"[34] To our knowledge, the first to question Junia's gender identity was Aegidius of Rome (1245–1316), a thirteenth-century archbishop, who took the name to be masculine.[35] In the sixteenth century, Martin Luther identified Andronicus and Junias as "men of note among the apostles"; and when his influential and long-standing translation of the Bible rolled off the printing press in 1522, it conveyed the same. Translations thereafter followed suit. In sum, as Luise Schottroff reports, "Only since the Middle Ages, and primarily because of Luther's translation, has the view prevailed that Junia was not a woman but a man by the name of Junias."[36]

Thankfully, Bernadette Brooten has now restored Junia to her rightful gender by demonstrating conclusively that the male name "Junias" is not attested in Greco-Roman antiquity. Indeed, there is not a shred of evidence that such a name ever existed, whereas the female name "Junia" occurs over 250 times among inscriptions from ancient Rome alone. In short, to put it bluntly, "Junias" is "a figment of chauvinistic imagination"[37]—and as James D. G. Dunn observes, "a striking indictment of male presumption regarding the character and structure of earliest Christianity."[38] Brooten made this convincing case in the 1970s;[39] and in 2005 Eldon Epp backed it up with a meticulously detailed study representing a definitive "last word" on the matter.[40] New Testament scholars no longer need to be convinced that Junia was a woman; thus it is puzzling that a number of contemporary translations, including the Contemporary English Version (CEV) and *The Message*, continue to propagate the notion that Andronicus's partner in ministry was a man named Junias.[41]

The question of Junia's gender is thus largely settled (among New Testament scholars, at least). But once Junia regained her identity as a woman, her apostleship faced challenges: What does it mean, exactly, to say that she and Andronicus were "prominent among the apostles"? The Greek adjective *episēmos* means "marked out, distinguished, outstanding, prominent,"[42] and most understand this, in straightforward fashion, to convey that Paul is recognizing Andronicus and Junia as apostles whose service on behalf of the gospel and the church has been exceptional. Some, however, insist that Junia and Andronicus were not themselves apostles, but rather were held in high regard *by* the apostles—in short, they were respected by a circle to which they did not belong! Thus some translations concede that Junia is a woman but deprive her of apostolic status, with the result that Paul conveys greetings to Andronicus and Junia who are "well known to the apostles" or "noteworthy in the eyes of the apostles" (e.g., New English Translation [NET], English Standard Version [ESV], Holman Christian Standard Bible, Lexham English Bible).

While this alternate reading of the text is not outside the realm of grammatical possibility,[43] it is worth noting that early church fathers who comment on the matter—and who surely had more clarity about the nuances of New Testament Greek syntax than do we—regarded Andronicus and Junia as apostles in their own right rather than as individuals who were held in high regard *by* them. Moreover, "Paul nowhere else appeals to the opinion of 'the apostles' as a group";[44] nor would he have been likely to refer to "the apostles" as a third party to which he himself did not belong (as the alternate translations seem to convey).[45] Paul vigorously defended his own apostleship on occasions when it was called into question (especially in Galatians and 2 Corinthians) and did not use the language of apostleship lightly or loosely. In his view, apostleship was not limited to the original twelve disciples who accompanied Jesus during his ministry (1 Cor. 15:3–11). To be an apostle meant that one had encountered the risen Lord (1 Cor. 9:1; Gal. 1:1, 15–17) and received from him a commission to proclaim the gospel (Rom. 1:1–5; 1 Cor. 1:1; Gal. 1:1, 15–17). It also entailed "the conscious acceptance and endurance of the labors and sufferings connected with missionary work"[46] and evident fruit of such toil (1 Cor. 15:9–10; 2 Cor. 12:11–12). As Epp insists, "Unless Paul recognized these traits in others, he would not deign to call them 'apostles,' but Andronicus and Junia obviously met and exceeded his criteria."[47] Moreover, Paul acknowledges their seniority to him and admits, "They were in Christ before I was" (Rom. 16:7). As Jews who believed in Jesus before Paul's conversion and who had encountered and been commissioned by the risen Lord, Andronicus and Junia may well have been among the earliest group of believers in Jerusalem and perhaps among those whose missionary labors brought the gospel to Rome. Given their venerable status, it is no wonder that they, along with Phoebe, Prisca, and Aquila, are singled out for special acknowledgment and public recognition in Paul's closing greetings to the church at Rome.

Other Women in Romans 16:1–16

Other women (and men) are included in the list of friends and acquaintances in Rome who are to be greeted on Paul's behalf. While the praise that accompanies mention of them is relatively brief (in comparison with the accolades showered on Phoebe, Prisca and Aquila, Andronicus and Junia), the language Paul uses in commending them is nonetheless revealing and bears witness to the significant contributions they were making to the life and ministry of an early church. Four women—Mary, Tryphaena and Tryphosa, and Persis— are commended for their "hard work" on behalf of the Lord and the church:

Greet Mary, who has *worked very hard* among you. (v. 6)

Greet those *workers* in the Lord, Tryphaena and Tryphosa. Greet the beloved Persis, who has *worked hard* in the Lord. (v. 12)

The repeated language of labor that Paul uses in describing each of these women (*kopiaō* in Greek) speaks of ministry and mission and conveys hard labor, wearying toil. It is Paul's preferred language when describing his own missionary activity, his apostolic labor on behalf of the gospel (1 Cor. 15:10; Gal. 4:11; Phil. 2:16), which included preaching, teaching, and evangelizing. He also employs it to describe the labor of leaders within local congregations (1 Thess. 5:12), labor that entailed expenditure of time and energy to meet needs within the congregation.[48] It is a word that reflects Paul's understanding of ministry as burden-bearing, suffering service for the gospel that one willingly shoulders.[49] Strikingly, this language is used exclusively of women in Romans 16. By means of it, Paul characterizes Mary, Tryphaena and Tryphosa, and Persis as "leaders of the community who . . . deserve respect and recognition for their tireless evangelizing and community-building ministry."[50]

We wish we knew more about these women and their ministries, but only a few clues present themselves. We cannot say for certain whether Mary was a Jewish Christian or Gentile Christian, for the name has both a Hebrew (Miriam) and Latin (Maria) background and was common among both. The ancient Greek manuscripts vary as to whether Paul describes Mary as having worked very hard "among *us*" or "among *you*," though the strongest manuscript evidence supports the latter reading, and thus recognition of Mary's leadership and labor within the Christian community at Rome.

Tryphaena and Tryphosa are also commended as hard workers. They are greeted as a pair (one verb conveys greeting to both, and one participle describes their labor) and so quite likely are missionary partners—the third missionary team recognized in Romans 16 (along with Prisca and Aquila, Andronicus and Junia).[51] They may have been sisters (perhaps even twins!), since it was not uncommon for parents to bestow upon their children names that shared the same Greek root; though Mary Rose D'Angelo notes that the meaning of the verb from which their names derive suggests that they were slaves or freedwomen of the same patron.[52] The verb *tryphaō* means "to live delicately, luxuriously," and it can have sexual overtones when applied to women.

The name "Tryphaena" means "dainty" and "Tryphosa" means "luscious";[53] thus D'Angelo wonders if they once may have been sex workers.[54] Peter Lampe's extensive research on the use of these names in Roman inscriptions and papyri (Tryphaena appears sixty times, and Tryphosa thirty-two times) also supports the probability that they came from slave backgrounds (though he makes no mention of sexual implications associated with these names).[55] Whatever the case may be, the etymology of their names, which connotes delicate or luxurious living, stands in stark contrast with Tryphaena and Tryphosa's hard work, their tireless missional labor on behalf of the gospel.

Persis, the fourth woman commended for her hard work in the Lord, almost certainly bears a name with affinity to slave origins. The name denotes a woman from Persia, and ethnic names were typical first names of slaves. As Lampe explains, "The origin of this type of name lies in the custom of calling slaves, who were merchandise, according to their country of export."[56] And as Jouette Bassler astutely observes, the fact that Paul refers to her as "*the* beloved Persis" (rather than as "*my* beloved Persis"; compare 16:5, 8–9) probably indicates the esteem in which she was held by Roman Christians.[57] She was widely loved and respected, and though a slave or freedwoman, "she was clearly a pillar, if not one of the founders, of the Roman church."[58]

In addition to the four women singled out for their "hard work" in the Lord, three remaining women appear in Paul's closing greetings. In 16:13, he asks that his readers "*Greet Rufus, chosen in the Lord; and greet his mother—a mother to me also.*" Though Rufus's mother is not named, she was evidently quite dear to Paul, and his affectionate maternal reference to her suggests that at some point in his career he became "virtually a member of the family."[59] We do not know how she "mothered" him. Perhaps, as Fred Craddock imagines, he is recalling her generous hospitality to him: "I don't care if you are an apostle— you still have to eat!"[60] However, Paul elsewhere uses maternal imagery to convey his own ministry of evangelism and Christian nurture rather than domestic care (1 Cor. 3:2; Gal. 4:19; 1 Thess. 2:7).[61]

One other tantalizing possibility presents itself in connection with Rufus's mother: could she have been the wife of Simon of Cyrene, whom the Gospels identify as the man conscripted by Roman soldiers to carry Jesus' cross en route to Golgotha? Mark 15:21 narrates, "They compelled a passer-by, who was coming in from the country, to carry his cross; it was Simon of Cyrene, the father of Alexander and Rufus." This may seem like a long shot, since the Latin name "Rufus" (denoting a "redhead") was not uncommon in the Roman Empire. Still, the designation of Rufus as "chosen in the Lord" (Rom. 16:13) is unusual, as Paul does not typically refer to individual believers in this manner; in Romans 1:6–7; 8:33; and 9:24, for example, "chosen," "elect," or "called" status applies to all believers. This unusual designation lends at least a measure of plausibility (however slim!) to a connection between this family and Simon of Cyrene, for as Jewett notes, it "sustains the impression that a specific calling or biographical distinction was attached to Rufus" (and by association, his mother) and "could well refer to a class of believers who had a direct link with the historical Jesus."[62] But admittedly, we are in the realm of speculation!

The final two women appear in 16:15: "*Greet Philologus, Julia, Nereus and his sister, . . . and all the saints who are with them.*" There is little we can say about them since their names are not accompanied by further words of commendation. Philologus and Julia are likely the third married couple referred to in Romans 16 for a *kai* ("and" in Greek) explicitly connects their names ("Greet Philogus *and* Julia"—though this is obscured in many translations (as in the NRSV). Neureus and his sister could be their children, though sister language was also used of fellow believers and coworkers (e.g., Rom. 16:1) and of Christian wives or missionary partners (1 Cor. 9:5 KJV, Greek). What we can discern is that both Julia and the sister of Neureus, along with others specifically mentioned in this verse (Philologus, Neureus, and Olympas), constituted the nucleus of one of several house churches meeting in Rome,[63] since Paul greets "all the saints who are with them." This small house church, along with others referenced in Paul's long list of greetings (16:5, 10, 11, 14), no doubt included many other unnamed women, for we should never assume that women were present only when they are explicitly mentioned. The generic use of male language (e.g., "mankind," "men," "brothers," "bishops," "deacons," etc.) in reference to mixed-gender groups often masks the presence of women.

Final Words of Exhortation
and Salutation

Paul brings his long list of greetings to a close with final words of exhortation and salutation: "*Greet one another with a holy kiss. All the churches of Christ greet you*" (16:16). As we have noted, Paul has not addressed any of his acquaintances in Rome directly; rather, he has urged the Roman Christians to greet twenty-seven persons on his behalf ("*Ya'll* greet . . .")! In so doing, he has established that he is by no means a stranger in Rome. Yet equally as important, if the various house churches in Rome are experiencing multicultural strain between Jewish Christians and Gentile Christians (as Rom. 14–15 suggests), he has endeavored to build up the unity of the church, entreating the community at Rome to greet, and in so doing to publicly honor and welcome, others with whom they may not be in close fellowship. That latter end is also served by his concluding exhortation that they greet each other with a holy kiss. In antiquity, kissing was a sign of affection and welcome normally reserved for greeting family members. Thus, in much the same way that we might urge disputing parties to "kiss and make up," Paul urges the Roman Christians to kiss and thereby acknowledge each other as family—as people related to each other by baptism into Jesus Christ—and to be reconciled to one another. If the house churches in Rome were experiencing discord (and there is reason to believe that they were), a holy kiss would represent a significant visible expression of unity. This exhortation is accompanied by a final word of salutation, remarkably global in scope: "All the churches of Christ greet you." Paul probably has in mind all the congregations in the east with which he has been associated. This final greeting would stretch the horizons of their vision, no doubt reminding Roman Christians of the larger body of Christ, of which they are a part. It may also serve as a reminder that the eyes of other churches are upon them as they negotiate the tensions with which they are living and struggle to embody the implications of the gospel for their life together in Christ.

DIALOGUE WITH THE TEXT

After engagement with five tyrannical texts in chapters 1–5, it may come as a relief to be in the presence of a text with which we may not feel a need to argue (Recommendation 2)! So let us proceed to the discernment of insights and dangers (Recommendations 3 and 4) that might facilitate reflection on the significance of the text for our own lives and ministries.

Discerning Insights and Dangers

An understatement: Romans 16 has enjoyed far less public attention and influence than other texts with which we have grappled in this volume. It has not figured prominently in ongoing ecclesial controversies over appropriate roles for women in church and society, though it should have. In fact, the greatest danger that attends it may be the likelihood that it will be ignored! Not because it is considered tyrannical, but because it is considered irrelevant and *boring*. Long lists of names in the Bible do not typically set one's heart aflutter.[64] And in the history of scholarship, the last chapter of Romans has (until recently) long been ignored, regarded as a mere appendix to the far more important theological matters Paul engages in Romans 1–15. But whatever one may think about the apostle Paul, there is no denying that he was a pastor-theologian par excellence. *Every* word he wrote had a pastoral and theological purpose: the formation of better Christian people and communities.[65] Even mundane matters were, for him, occasions for deep theological reflection; indeed, "some of Paul's most striking insights come when he is speaking most practically."[66] Thus, part of his legacy to us is that he prods us, too, to reflect pastorally and theologically on every single aspect of the church's life and ministry. Romans 16 is no exception. So this baby, like those we have engaged in preceding chapters, ought not to be thrown out with the bathwater!

So what insights emerge from this long list of greetings that might be significant for our own lives and ministries? Most obviously, Romans 16:1–16 represents a striking counterpoint to all the prescriptive texts we have considered in this volume and needs to be placed in conversation with them. It bears indisputable witness to the fact that women, as well as men, exercised leadership in the earliest Christian communities. Indeed, one of the most intriguing things about it is the matter-of-fact fashion in which Paul identifies ten women as valued colleagues in mission and ministry. The text clearly reflects an assumption on his part—one that did not need to be argued or defended—that they played crucial roles both in local congregations and in Pauline mission fields. As Beverly Roberts Gaventa puts it, "Whatever Paul writes or does not write elsewhere, here he simply assumes that women too are God's agents on behalf of the gospel of Jesus Christ."[67] And Romans 16 reflects female agency in service of that gospel in an astonishing variety of capacities: it provides glimpses of women at work individually, with partners, and as members of extended families. We learn from it that they proclaimed the gospel and in some cases suffered for it, enduring exile or imprisonment and risking life and limb on its behalf. They served as letter couriers and interpreters, emissaries, and patrons and traveled widely in conjunction with missionary endeavors. They also played indispensable roles in local congregations, hosting house churches and laboring tirelessly and tenaciously in community-building ministries. They were influential leaders who exercised emerging offices in the church, serving as deacons and even as apostles under the direct commission of the risen Lord. In short, their contributions were essential to the formation and expansion of the early church.[68]

With the exception of Prisca, we would not know of these women and their significant labor on behalf of the gospel and the church if Paul had not mentioned them in his closing greetings to the church at Rome. Thank heavens he did, thereby providing for us a glimpse of "the tip of an iceberg,"[69] "a small window onto what we must imagine was a much larger reality."[70] For many Christians to this day, concerns about women in leadership roles is tied to the question of whether women actually served as leaders during the church's formative years.[71] For those harboring such reservations, Romans 16 provides indisputable, eye-opening food for thought. Of course, as we have seen throughout this volume, the New Testament and its interpretation also reflect a history of resistance to women's ecclesial leadership and of increasing restriction on their exercise of ministry. Nowhere is this more apparent than in the Pastoral Epistles, which feature texts like 1 Timothy 2:8–15 and 5:3–16 (see chaps. 1 and 5 above). As we have recognized, such texts preserve the sites of ancient arguments that invite our continued participation and collective discernment of God's will for our own time and place—and Romans 16 reminds us that they by no means represent all that the New Testament has to say on the matter of women's religious leadership.

While our engagement with Romans 16 has focused primarily on foremothers in the faith and what we can learn of their contributions to early Christian life and mission, we would be remiss if we did not note the broader diversity of the early church to which this text also bears witness. Judging from the names that appear in Paul's extensive list of greetings to them, the Roman Christians were an astonishingly heterogeneous mix of people. Peter Lampe's magisterial study of Christianity at Rome in the first two centuries includes meticulous examination of the names in Romans 16, taking all available evidence (literary, archaeological, and epigraphical) for them into account.[72] What he demonstrates in compelling fashion is that a disproportionate number of the names (two-thirds of them) are of Greek rather than Latin origin. In conjunction with other available data, this suggests that a majority of Roman Christians were not indigenous to Rome but rather were Greek-speaking immigrants from the east and of low socio-economic status. Moreover, over two-thirds of the names bear affinities with slave origins. In conjunction with other data, this too suggests that a majority of Roman Christians were likely slaves or freedmen and women with slave ancestry. This evidence coheres with the diverse demographics of ancient Rome in general: as the capital city, it drew immigrants of different nationalities from across the entire empire, and slaves constituted a huge percentage of the total population.[73] Because Paul explicitly identifies several Roman Christians as "relatives" (and thus as fellow Jews), it is also clear that both Jewish and Gentile Christians were among their number, the latter increasingly in the majority.

We should not suppose, then, that the challenges of living with "multiculturalism" and socioeconomic diversity are peculiar to the contemporary church and our own historical context. The snapshot of ancient Roman Christianity that we glimpse in Romans 16 reflects a community living into the baptismal reality of life in Christ, in whom "there is no longer Jew or Greek, there is no longer slave or free, there is no longer male and female; for all of you are one in Christ Jesus" (Gal. 3:28). That life was not without its strains, and thus we see Paul striving to build up the unity of the Roman Christian community. In Romans 16, "his theology of inclusion is mirrored closely in his practice" as he enumerates greetings that transcend all ethnic, social, and gender barriers.[74] By means of these greetings, he facilitates public recognition and welcome of diverse others and strives to nurture their sense of new familial identity as brothers and sisters in Christ.

Paul also nurtures their awareness that they are part of a larger Christian fellowship beyond Rome, a community within which God's Spirit is at work to accomplish God's purposes. Indeed, the astonishing diversity of the Christian community, both locally in Rome and throughout the empire, is, for Paul, a crucial matter at the heart of the church's witness in the world. As risen lord, Christ reigns within the church, where he is confessed and where his resurrection power is at work, creating a "strange new community in which Jew and Gentile, slave and free, male and female stand together in harmonious praise of the one God of Israel."[75] That community exists in this world as an embodiment of Christ's lordship, an outpost of the coming future, and a witness to the reconciliation that God intends for all. It should not escape our attention that the community to whom Romans was first addressed was living in the capital city of the Roman Empire; as N. T. Wright observes, Paul was interested in maintaining communities united in loyalty to Jesus as Lord, right under Caesar's nose: "A church that all too obviously embodies the social, ethnic, cultural, and political divisions of its surrounding world is no real challenge to the Caesars of this world. It is only when representatives of many nations worship the world's true Lord in unity that Caesar might get the hint that there is after all 'another king.'"[76] The astonishing diversity of the early church at Rome to which this text bears witness thus prompts reflection on the heterogeneity (or lack thereof) of our own Christian communities and its implications for the credibility of our own communal witness to the world's true Lord—our own participation, by divine grace at work within us, to the cosmic, reconciling purposes of God.

What other implications of Romans 16 for our own lives and ministries can be discerned? Two final aspects of Paul's ministry reflected in Romans 16 are worth noting. As Douglas Moo observes, one of the important lessons we learn from this text is that Paul was not a "lone ranger"! His ministry looms so large in the New Testament witness and in the church's history and imagination that we may be inclined to think of him that way, as single-handedly engineering the growth and expansion of the early church. But as Romans 16 demonstrates, this was not the case: "At every point in his ministry, Paul depended on a significant number of others who were working along with him. And if Paul needed such help, how much more do we! There is no room in modern ministry for the lone ranger approach either."[77] Amen! Ministry is always shared labor, and it is important that we recognize and acknowledge the partners with whom we work in the Lord's vineyard, without whom our own service to the gospel would not bear fruit.

It is surely also worth noticing the generosity with which Paul characterizes the labor of colleagues in ministry in Romans 16, honoring their service on behalf of the church. Is it just my imagination, or would it be fair to say that those who labor in professional ministry often seem to find it hard to acknowledge or express appreciation for the contributions of colleagues? Maybe a sense of professional jealousy or superiority ("I would have preached a *much* better sermon!") makes us stingy with our praise; or perhaps a sense that there is only so much praise to go around, and if the labor of others is celebrated, our own efforts are somehow diminished. But as Romans 16 reminds us, and as all who devote themselves to ministry (lay or professional) well know, it is hard work, burden-bearing toil, and all who labor in the Lord's vineyard need to be encouraged in their endeavors—need to hear, upon occasion, "Well done, good and faithful servant!" Perhaps as we reflect on Romans 16, Paul's striking generosity in commending the ministries of others, facilitating public recognition and honoring of their contributions to the life of the church, can expand our own parsimonious spirits. In fact, would it not behoove every one of us to make a list of our own—to "reflect with gratitude on those fellow believers who have significantly impacted our lives" and "to consider how we would describe them"? As William Greathouse reminds us, "Perhaps, like Paul, we would do well to commend them while they are still alive, before we eulogize them at their funerals."[78]

Holy Wrestling

This hardly exhausts the implications of Romans 16 for our own lives and ministries. Others will no doubt emerge from your own reflection on the text. But I hope the point has been made: blessings can emerge from tyrannical texts and also from ones that strike us initially as boring or irrelevant—*if* we but take the time to listen patiently, carefully to them, to dialogue with them (arguing, if need be), being instructed by both the dangers and insights they present. God is present in all our engagements with Scripture, which is, after all, why we call it "Holy." God is present whenever we wrestle with Scripture, both with and against its claims. So don't let go of it. It is holy wrestling. Hang on to that text and do not let it go until it has a chance to bless you![79]

QUESTIONS FOR DISCUSSION AND REFLECTION

What has been your prior experience with Romans 16? In what contexts have you encountered it?

What strikes you most about Paul's long list of greetings in Romans 16? What questions does it raise for you?

What new insights have emerged from your engagement with Romans 16? Why are they important to you? What questions linger?

Of all the women commended in Romans 16, which one most captures your attention, and why? What questions would you like to ask her?

What does Romans 16 contribute to your understanding of the apostle Paul?

Would you be inclined to preach or teach on Romans 16? Why, or why not? If you are so inclined, what connections are you likely to articulate between the claims of the text and the life of your congregation? Why might it be important for them to engage Romans 16?

Share your response to N. T. Wright's observation: "A church that all too obviously embodies the social, ethnic, cultural, and political divisions of its surrounding world is no real challenge to the Caesars of this world." What implications does this bear for the life of your own congregation or denomination?

If you were to make a list of fellow believers who have significantly impacted your life and faith experience, who would be on it? How would you describe them? Have you shared your gratitude with them? Why, or why not?

Who would you identify as significant colleagues in ministry (lay or professional), without whom your own labor in the Lord's vineyard would not bear fruit? Have you shared words of appreciation with them? Why, or why not?

Of the six texts engaged in this volume, which one has made the deepest impression on you—and why?

Epilogue

To readers I offer a few final words in closing. First, to those who have been inclined to avoid texts featured in this volume because of their obscure and problematic aspects, I hope you have found encouragement to address them directly and publicly—to engage them with others in your practice of ministry (lay or ordained) in the community of faith, with the expectation of encountering God and with the confidence that wrestling with them is part of God's own work in us, forming the mind of Jesus Christ in us.

Second, to those who have been in close conversation with these texts and who may interpret them quite differently—especially with regard to what we understand them to convey about God's will for relationships between male and female (in the home and in the community of faith)—I hope this volume has provided food for thought and helped you understand the logic and integrity of other points of view, even if you consider them misguided. I also hope you have been able to recognize that I am trying to honor Scripture and striving as best I can to be faithful to it—in short, that those with whose interpretations you disagree may indeed take the authority of Scripture no less seriously than you do.

Finally, I wish for all of us a measure of interpretive humility, for none of our interpretations are definitive and have the last word. None of them fully exhaust the depths and richly generative capacity of the living word that is Scripture. I also wish for all of us a measure of charity, not only toward the text, but also toward those with whose interpretations we disagree.[1] There is, after all, perhaps no more evident sign that God's work in us through Scripture is bearing fruit—that we are maturing, growing into "the measure of the full stature of Christ" (Eph. 4:13). Blessings on your wrestling with Scripture!

Notes

Introduction

1. Robert P. Carroll, *The Bible as a Problem for Christianity* (Philadelphia: Trinity Press International, 1991), 2.

2. A phrase coined by Phyllis Trible, one of the pioneering figures of modern feminist biblical criticism, in her groundbreaking work titled *Texts of Terror: Literary-Feminist Readings of Biblical Narratives* (Philadelphia: Fortress Press, 1984).

3. The undisputed letters can be attributed with confidence to the apostle Paul. His seven undisputed letters include Romans, 1 and 2 Corinthians, Galatians, Philippians, 1 Thessalonians, and Philemon.

4. The following six letters are identified by a majority of scholars as pseudonymous—letters written in Paul's name after his death in order to bring his legacy to bear on new circumstances: Colossians, Ephesians, 1 and 2 Timothy, Titus, and 2 Thessalonians. They are referred to as "disputed" because their authorship is still a matter of debate—in some cases more than others. An estimated 60 percent of scholars, e.g., regard Colossians as pseudonymous. But the percentage is much greater in the case of Ephesians and 1 Timothy, the two letters we will especially consider in this volume: an estimated 80 percent regard Ephesians as pseudonymous, and 90 percent regard 1 Timothy as pseudonymous.

5. "Deutero" means "secondary." The deuteropauline letters are thus "secondary letters of Paul." As Mark Allan Powell notes, this label can be confusing since it seems to be used in different ways: "For many, the deutero-Pauline letters are simply 'secondary' in the chronological sense: they were written later than the others. For other interpreters, however, the label seems to imply a value judgment: the 'secondary letters' are less important or authoritative than Paul's 'undisputed letters.' Still others adopt a mediating position: the deutero-Pauline letters are less important for the specific task of 'understanding how Paul thought,' but they are not less important in any other sense (e.g., for receiving God's word of scripture to the church)" (*Introducing the New Testament: A Historical, Literary, and Theological Survey* [Grand Rapids: Baker Academic, 2009], 223). I am using the term in both the first and third senses, but not in the second sense. In my view, the disputed or deuteropauline letters are no less important or authoritative than Paul's undisputed letters for the life of the church.

6. For an accessible discussion of the extended and complex process of canon

formation, see Lee Martin McDonald, *Formation of the Bible: The Story of the Church's Canon* (Peabody, MA: Hendrickson Publishers, 2012). McDonald's narrative helps readers grasp the range of factors (historical and technological) and "criteria" that bore on the complex process of canon formation over the course of several centuries, and it engenders renewed appreciation for the collective wisdom of the church from which the canon eventually emerged.

7. Holly Hearon aptly describes 1 Cor. 14:33b–36 as such, and this observation could also be said to describe other texts featured in this volume! See Hearon, "1 and 2 Corinthians," in *The Queer Bible Commentary*, ed. Deryn Guest, Robert E. Goss, Mona West, and Thomas Bohache (London: SCM Press, 2006), 617.

Chapter 1: Beyond Textual Harassment: Engaging Tyrannical Texts

1. Ellen F. Davis, "Critical Traditioning: Seeking an Inner Biblical Hermeneutic," in *The Art of Reading Scripture*, ed. Ellen F. Davis and Richard B. Hays (Grand Rapids: Wm. B. Eerdmans Publishing Co., 2003), 163–64.

2. A phrase coined by Mary Jacobus, "Is There a Woman in This Text?," *New Literary History* 14 (1982): 119.

3. A phrase coined by Phyllis Trible, one of the pioneering figures of modern feminist biblical criticism, in her groundbreaking work titled *Texts of Terror: Literary-Feminist Readings of Biblical Narratives* (Philadelphia: Fortress Press, 1984).

4. Davis, "Critical Traditioning," 164.

5. Since 2011, the PC(USA) now refers to ministers of Word and Sacrament as "teaching elders" and to elders as "ruling elders."

6. Joel B. Green, *Seized by Truth: Reading the Bible as Scripture* (Nashville: Abingdon Press, 2007), 51.

7. Ibid., 50–62; see also Michael J. Gorman, *Reading Paul* (Eugene, OR: Cascade Books, 2008), 2–7.

8. Deborah Krause, *1 Timothy*, Readings: A New Biblical Commentary (London: T&T Clark, 2004), xiv.

9. Ibid., 9.

10. Ibid., 10.

11. Ibid., 11.

12. On these points, see ibid., 11–18; also Deborah Krause, "Paul and Women: Telling Women to Shut Up Is More Complicated Than You Might Think," in *Paul Unbound: Other Perspectives on the Apostle*, ed. Mark D. Given (Peabody, MA: Hendrickson Publishers, 2010), 172–73. If, as the PC(USA)'s "A Brief Statement of Faith" affirms, "the Spirit gives us courage to hear the voices of peoples long silenced" (line 70), this is one of those places we can go to hear them. (See "A Brief Statement of Faith," in the PC[USA]'s Book of Confessions, http://www.presbyterianmission.org/ministries/101/brief-statement-faith/.)

13. Carolyn Osiek and David Balch, *Families in the New Testament World: Households and House Churches* (Louisville, KY: Westminster John Knox Press, 1997), 122.

14. David C. Verner, *The Household of God: The Social World of the Pastoral Epistles* (Chico, CA: Scholars Press, 1983), 169.

15. N. T. Wright proposes this translation in *Paul for Everyone: The Pastoral Letters; 1 and 2 Timothy and Titus*, 2nd ed. (Louisville, KY: Westminster John Knox Press, 2004), 21. See also N. T. Wright, "Women's Service in the Church: The Biblical Basis," a conference paper for the symposium "Men, Women and the Church," at St John's College, Durham, September 4, 2004, http://ntwright page.com/Wright_Women_Service_Church.htm. Wright translates vv. 11–12 as a whole as follows: "They must be allowed to study undisturbed, in full submission to God. I'm not saying that women should teach men, or try to dictate to them; they should be left undisturbed."

16. E.g., James B. Hurley, *Man and Woman in Biblical Perspective* (Grand Rapids: Zondervan, 1981), 203.

17. For astute critiques of anti-Judaism in Christian biblical interpretation, see Judith Plaskow, "Anti-Judaism in Feminist Christian Interpretation," in *Searching the Scriptures*, vol. 1, *A Feminist Introduction*, ed. Elisabeth Schüssler Fiorenza (New York: Crossroad, 1993), 117–29; and Amy-Jill Levine, *The Misunderstood Jew: The Church and the Scandal of the Jewish Jesus* (San Francisco: HarperSan-Francisco, 2006), 119–66.

18. Adolf von Schlatter, *Erläuterungen zum Neuen Testament*, vol. 2, *Die Briefe des Paulus* (Stuttgart: Calwer, 1928), 42; referenced by Jouette M. Bassler, "Adam, Eve, and the Pastor: The Use of Genesis 2–3 in the Pastoral Epistles," in *Genesis 1–3 in the History of Exegesis: Intrigue in the Garden*, ed. Gregory Allen Robbins (Lewiston, NY: Edwin Mellen Press, 1988), 44.

19. Davis, "Critical Traditioning," 178.

20. Ibid.

21. Elsa Tamez, *Struggles for Power in Early Christianity: A Study of the First Letter to Timothy* (Maryknoll, NY: Orbis Books, 2007), 8.

22. Ibid., 16.

23. Ibid., 36.

24. Frances Young, *The Theology of the Pastoral Letters*, New Testament Theology (Cambridge: Cambridge University Press, 1994), 99. Philip H. Towner's work on the Pastoral Epistles also places helpful emphasis on this point, as in *The Letters to Timothy and Titus*, New International Commentary on the New Testament (Grand Rapids: Wm. B. Eerdmans Publishing Co., 2006).

25. Towner, *The Letters to Timothy and Titus*, 193.

26. Levine, *The Misunderstood Jew*, 205.

27. Walter Brueggemann, "Biblical Authority: A Personal Reflection," in Walter Brueggemann, William Placher, and Brian K. Blount, *Struggling with Scripture* (Louisville, KY: Westminster John Knox Press, 2002), 16.

28. William Placher, "Struggling with Scripture," in Brueggemann, Placher, and Blount, *Struggling with Scripture*, 49.

29. J. R. Daniel Kirk, *Jesus Have I Loved, But Paul? A Narrative Approach to the Problem of Pauline Christianity* (Grand Rapids: Baker Academic, 2011), 137.

30. Ellen F. Davis, "The Soil That Is Scripture," in *Engaging Biblical Authority: Perspectives on the Bible as Scripture*, ed. William P. Brown (Louisville, KY: Westminster John Knox Press, 2007), 38, 40.

31. Thomas C. Oden, *First and Second Timothy and Titus*, Interpretation (Louisville, KY: John Knox Press, 1989), 94.

32. Luke Timothy Johnson, *The First and Second Letters to Timothy: A New Translation with Introduction and Commentary*, Anchor Bible 35A (New York: Doubleday, 2001), 204.

33. Raymond E. Brown, *The Community of the Beloved Disciple: The Life, Loves, and Hates of an Individual Church in New Testament Times* (New York: Paulist Press, 1979), 135.

34. Davis, "The Soil That Is Scripture," 39.

35. Rowan Williams, *A Ray of Darkness: Sermons and Reflections* (Cambridge, MA: Cowley Publications, 1995), 135.

36. Ibid., 136.

37. On this point, see Sarah Heaner Lancaster, *Women and the Authority of Scripture: A Narrative Approach* (Harrisburg, PA: Trinity Press International, 2002), 169.

38. With thanks to Phyllis Trible for this imagery. In the introduction to her classic *Texts of Terror* (4–5), Trible invokes the story of Jacob's nocturnal wrestling at the Jabbok (Gen. 32:22–32) as a metaphor for feminist biblical criticism as it seeks to wrestle something redemptive out of horrific texts. And in an essay titled "Wrestling with Scripture," Trible sagely advises: "Do not abandon the Bible to the bashers and thumpers. Take back the text. Do not let go until it blesses you. Indeed, make it work for blessing, not for curse, so that you and your descendants, indeed so that all the families of the earth, may live" (*Biblical Archaeology Review* [March/April 2006]: 52).

Chapter 2: Wives, Be Subject? Articulating Biblical Authority

1. Used by permission of this former student, who wishes to remain anonymous! She has since been ordained and is one of the most extraordinary young clergywomen I know.

2. John P. Burgess, *Why Scripture Matters: Reading the Bible in a Time of Church Conflict* (Louisville, KY: Westminster John Knox Press, 1998), 24.

3. For further discussion of the propositional notion of revelation, see Sarah Heaner Lancaster, *Women and the Authority of Scripture: A Narrative Approach* (Harrisburg, PA: Trinity International Press, 2002), 67–74; and Sandra

Schneiders, *The Revelatory Text: Interpreting the New Testament as Sacred Scripture* (San Francisco: HarperSanFrancisco, 1991), 53–55.

4. On this point, see Paul J. Achtemeier, *Inspiration and Authority: Nature and Function of Christian Scripture* (Peabody, MA: Hendrickson Publishers, 1999), 82; and G. C. Berkouwer, *Holy Scripture: Studies in Dogmatics* (Grand Rapids: Wm. B. Eerdmans Publishing Co., 1975), 16–17, 28, 73–74. In the same vein, Sandra Schneiders critiques what she views as a kind of "biblical Docetism," parallel to christological Docetism: "Just as an omniscient or immortal Jesus only appears to be a genuine human being (since human beings are, by nature, limited in knowledge and mortal), an inerrant Bible would only appear to be a genuine human text" (*The Revelatory Text*, 54).

5. This quotation from the Confession of 1967 comes from Part I, section 9.29 in *The Book of Confessions of the Presbyterian Church (U.S.A.)* (Louisville, KY: Office of the General Assembly of the Presbyterian Church (U.S.A.), 2002).

6. See Sandra M. Schneiders on this point; she maintains that "the New Testament is not a catechism or an answer book supplying prescriptions for the solution of problems not even envisioned by its authors. Rather, our engagement with the biblical text is meant to form in us the mind of Christ, so that we can confront the issues of our own time in the spirit of Jesus, who is for all Christians throughout the ages the way, the truth, and the life" (*Written That You May Believe: Encountering Jesus in the Fourth Gospel*, rev. and expanded ed. [New York: Crossroad, 2003], 95).

7. For further discussion of the dialogical notion of revelation and the Bible as the medium of encounter with God, see Lancaster, *Women and the Authority of Scripture*, 74–90; and Schneiders, *The Revelatory Text*, 55–61, 174–78.

8. John Calvin, *Institutes of the Christian Religion*, ed. John T. McNeill, trans. Ford Lewis Battles, Library of Christian Classics (Philadelphia: Westminster, 1960), 1.6.1.

9. Serene Jones, "Inhabiting Scripture, Dreaming Bible," *Engaging Biblical Authority: Perspectives on the Bible as Scripture*, ed. William P. Brown (Louisville, KY: Westminster John Knox Press, 2007), 77.

10. Burgess, *Why Scripture Matters*, 48.

11. Jones, "Inhabiting Scripture," 77.

12. Rowan Williams, *A Ray of Darkness: Sermons and Reflections* (Cambridge, MA: Cowley Publications, 1995), 135.

13. On this point, see Lancaster, *Women and the Authority of Scripture*, 25.

14. Karl Allen Kuhn, *Having Words with God: The Bible as Conversation* (Minneapolis: Fortress Press, 2008), 5.

15. Walter Brueggemann, "Biblical Authority: A Personal Reflection," in Walter Brueggemann, William Placher, and Brian K. Blount, in *Struggling with Scripture* (Louisville, KY: Westminster John Knox Press, 2002), 16.

16. On these important points, see ibid., 13–19; and Brian K. Blount, "The Last Word on Biblical Authority," in Brueggemann, Placher, and Blount, *Struggling with Scripture*, 51–69.

17. Schneiders, *The Revelatory Text*, 175–76. See also Sandra Schneiders, "Feminist Ideology Criticism and Biblical Hermeneutics," *Biblical Theology Bulletin* 19 (January 1989): 7.

18. Schneiders, *The Revelatory Text*, 176.

19. Ibid., 177, emphasis added.

20. This is how the *Book of Order* of the Presbyterian Church (U.S.A.) puts it in its new Form of Government. See *Book of Order: The Constitution of the Presbyterian Church* (U.S.A.), Pt. II, 2013–15 (Louisville, KY: Office of the General Assembly of the Presbyterian Church (U.S.A.), 2013), F-2.02. See Anna Case-Winters's emphasis on God's agency and initiative, through Scripture and the calling of the Spirit, in "What Do Presbyterians Believe about 'Ecclesia Reformata, Semper Reformanda?': Our Misused Motto, *Presbyterians Today* (May 2004), http://www.presbyterianmission.org/ministries/today/reformed/.

21. Letty R. Russell, "Authority and the Challenge of Feminist Interpretation," in *Feminist Interpretation of the Bible*, ed. Letty R. Russell (Philadelphia: Westminster Press, 1985), 138.

22. Sandra Schneiders, "Author's Response" to a Review Symposium of *The Revelatory Text*, in *Horizons* 19 (1992): 306–7.

23. Phyllis Trible, "Wrestling with Scripture," *Biblical Archaeology Review* (March/April 2006): 52. The truth of Trible's observation was impressed upon me years after my excision of Eph. 5 from my Bible, when I encountered Rowan Williams's use of it in a brilliant essay to argue for the church's consecration of gay unions (see Rowan Williams, "The Body's Grace," in *Theology and Sexuality: Classic and Contemporary Readings*, ed. Eugene F. Rogers [Malden, MA: Blackwell Publishers, 2002], 309–21). I would never have imagined its relevance for reflection on this matter!

24. Jouette M. Bassler, "Limits and Differentiation: The Calculus of Widows in 1 Timothy 5:3–16, in *A Feminist Companion to the Deutero-Pauline Epistles*, ed. Amy-Jill Levine with Marianne Blickenstaff (Cleveland: Pilgrim Press, 2003), 131.

25. E.g., Margaret Y. MacDonald, "Rereading Paul: Early Interpreters of Paul on Women and Gender," in *Women and Christian Origins*, ed. Ross Shepard Kraemer and Mary Rose D'Angelo (New York: Oxford University Press, 1999), 251.

26. Andrew Lincoln, *Ephesians*, Word Biblical Commentary (Nashville: Thomas Nelson, 1990), 365. As Carolyn Osiek notes, "The text very quickly moves away from marriage to ecclesiology" ("The Bride of Christ [Ephesians 5:22–33]: A Problematic Wedding," *Biblical Theology Bulletin* 32 [2002]: 32).

27. Ian McFarland, "A Canonical Reading of Ephesians 5:21–33: Theological Gleanings," *Theology Today* 57 (October 2000): 357.

28. Sarah J. Tanzer, "Ephesians," in *Searching the Scriptures*, vol. 2, *A Feminist Commentary*, ed. Elisabeth Schüssler Fiorenza (New York: Crossroad, 1994), 331.

29. Ibid., 330. See also Peter Lampe, "'Family' in Church and Society of New Testament Times," *Affirmation* 5 (Spring 1992): 20 n. 57.

30. Lincoln, *Ephesians*, 363.

31. Susan Brooks Thistlethwaite, "Every Two Minutes: Battered Women and Feminist Interpretation," in Russell, *Feminist Interpretation of the Bible*, 104.

32. Ibid., 100, emphasis added in the first quotation.

33. Virginia Ramey Mollenkott, "Emancipative Elements in Ephesians 5.21–33: Why Feminist Scholarship Has (Often) Left Them Unmentioned, and Why They Should Be Emphasized," in Levine with Blickenstaff, *A Feminist Companion to the Deutero-Pauline Epistles*, 42.

34. Ibid., with original emphasis. As a prescriptive text that presents an "ideal," Eph. 5 neglects the real, failing to take into account sinful human realities that impact the institution of marriage.

35. See McFarland, "A Canonical Reading," 349.

36. As Carolyn Osiek notices, in Eph. 5 sacrifice seems to be a "guy-thing" and submission a "woman-thing" ("The Bride of Christ," 31).

37. Tanzer, "Ephesians," 341.

38. McFarland, "A Canonical Reading," 354.

39. Gail O'Day, "John," in *The Women's Bible Commentary*, ed. Carol A. Newsome, Sharon H. Ringe, and Jacqueline E. Lapsley, 3rd ed. (Louisville, KY: Westminster John Knox Press, 2012), 525.

40. William R. Herzog II, "The 'Household Duties' Passages: Apostolic Traditions and Contemporary Concerns," *Foundations* 24 (1981): 215.

41. Clarice J. Martin, "The *Haustafeln* (Household Codes) in African American Biblical Interpretation: 'Free Slaves' and 'Subordinate Women,'" in *Stony the Road We Trod: African American Biblical Interpretation*, ed. Cain Hope Felder (Minneapolis: Fortress Press, 1991), 226.

Chapter 3: Women and Worship Wars (I)

1. Jouette M. Bassler, "1 Corinthians," in *The Women's Bible Commentary*, ed. Carol A. Newsom, Sharon H. Ringe, and Jacqueline E. Lapsley, 3rd ed. (Louisville, KY: Westminster John Knox Press, 2012), 562. A handful of scholars have tried to make the case that Paul did not write 1 Cor. 11:2–16—that it is an "interpolation" (material inserted into the text in the process of scribal transmission), but few have found this argument convincing. But even if 1 Cor. 11:2–16 were a later addition to the text, this would not eliminate the difficulties it represents, for it is still in the canon. Its authority derives not from its authorship, but from its canonical status, so it would still demand engagement.

One other proposal circumvents Pauline authorship of the most problematic verses: David W. O'Dell-Scott contends that vv. 2–10 and vv. 12b–15 represent the views of Corinthian Christians, which Paul quotes from their letter to him and then refutes in vv. 11–12a and 16 (see O'Dell-Scott, *A Post-Patriarchal*

Christology [Atlanta: Scholars Press, 1991], 179–81). Few have found this argument convincing, for there is no clear signal that Paul is quoting a Corinthian point of view, as in 7:1, e.g., where he begins with "Now concerning the matters about which you wrote . . ." (see also 7:25; 8:1). Moreover, earlier citations of Corinthian points of view in 1 Cor. 7–10 are brief and to the point—on the order of "slogans," in contradistinction to the elaborate discourse in 11:2–10.

2. The adaptations of the NRSV include the following: NRSV adds "veil" in 11:6 although the Greek word for "veil" (*kalymma*, which Paul uses elsewhere, in 2 Cor. 3:12–18) does not appear in the text. (Though *kalymma* is inserted in some ancient manuscripts in v. 10, textual critics are confident in their judgment that it was not part of the original text.) Thus, instead of the language of veiling, I am using the more usual language of covering/uncovering. In v. 3, the NRSV reads "the husband is head of his wife," but the Greek word *anēr* means "man" or "husband," and the Greek word *gynē* means "woman" or "wife." Most translations and commentators believe that generic references are more appropriate and that all the men and women of the Corinthian church are in view (not just married members). Finally, in vv. 7–8, the NRSV's "reflection" has been replaced with "glory," the usual translation of the Greek *doxa* and one that more clearly captures the cultural language of honor and shame that pervades the text.

3. See David E. Garland, *1 Corinthians*, Baker Exegetical Commentary on the New Testament (Grand Rapids: Baker Academic, 2003), 582, 632; Raymond Collins, *1 Corinthians*, Sacra pagina (Collegeville, MN: Liturgical Press, 1999), 491. Some scholars limit prophecy to spontaneous utterance, but Garland notes that "the moment of revelation should not be restricted to flashes that come only during worship. Revelation can come at other times, allowing the individual to ponder it and share it later, in the next worship" (633).

4. In some ancient manuscripts (translations and patristic witnesses), the word "veil" (*kalymma* in Greek) is inserted in v. 10.

5. See, e.g., Richard Horsley, *1 Corinthians*, Abingdon New Testament Commentaries (Nashville: Abingdon, 1998), 152–57; and Richard B. Hays, *First Corinthians*, Interpretation (Louisville, KY: John Knox Press, 1997), 182–90. The "hairstyle" option simplifies the interpretive challenge in some respects, for all the evidence from the first-century world suggests that short hair was the cultural norm for men and long hair the norm for women; the evidence for cultural norms regarding female headwear is far more ambiguous. However, the hairstyle option is not entirely convincing. If the references to "covered" and "uncovered" heads are better understood as references to "bound" or "unbound" hair, what are we to make of the contrast in v. 7? As Dennis MacDonald notes, it is hard to imagine that v. 7 should read: "for a man ought not have his hair piled up in a bun" (*There Is No Male and Female: The Fate of a Dominical Saying in Paul and Gnosticism*, Harvard Dissertations in Religion [Philadelphia: Fortress Press, 1987], 87). Moreover, "when Paul refers to hair lengths in vss 14–15 he does so not because hair itself was at issue but in order to argue by analogy. Nature has

supplied woman with a natural 'garment,' her long hair. What nature began let women complete by retaining fabric garments on their heads" (ibid.). Verse 4, which describes a man as praying and prophesying "with [something] down the head" (*kata kephalēs echōn* in Greek), is notoriously obscure. While it could refer to long hair, it could also refer to something resting on the head.

6. Jerome Murphy-O'Connor, "Sex and Logic in 1 Corinthians 11:2–16," *Catholic Biblical Quarterly* 42 (1980): 488; and Gillian Beattie, *Women and Marriage in Paul and His Early Interpreters*, Journal for the Study of the New Testament: Supplement Series 296 (London: T&T Clark, 2005), 43 n. 23.

7. Hays, *First Corinthians*, 182–83.

8. The only "imperatives" Paul articulates, in vv. 6 and 13, concern the management of female heads. Structural analysis also confirms that the state of female heads (rather than male ones) is the focus of Paul's concern. As Patrick Gray notes, the use of chiasm (reverse parallelism) can be observed in vv. 8–12, with v. 10 at the center as the focal point:

A Indeed, man was not made from woman, but woman from man. (v. 8)

  B Neither was man created for the sake of woman, but woman for the sake of man. (v. 9)

    C For this reason a woman ought to have authority over her head, because of the angels. (v. 10)

  B' Nevertheless, in the Lord woman is not independent of man or man independent of woman. (v. 11)

A' For just as woman came from man, so man comes through woman; but all things come from God. (v. 12)

See Patrick Gray, *Opening Paul's Letters: A Reader's Guide to Genre and Interpretation* (Grand Rapids: Baker Academic, 2012), 51–52.

9. Ellen F. Davis, "Critical Traditioning: Seeking an Inner Biblical Hermeneutic," in *The Art of Reading Scripture*, ed. Ellen F. Davis and Richard B. Hays (Grand Rapids: Wm. B. Eerdmans Publishing Co., 2003), 178.

10. Margaret M. Mitchell, *Paul and the Rhetoric of Reconciliation: An Exegetical Investigation of the Language and Composition of 1 Corinthians* (Tübingen: J. C. B. Mohr [Paul Siebeck], 1991), 259.

11. This opening word of commendation stands in sharp contrast to Paul's broaching of the second item on his liturgical agenda—the subject of abuses at the Lord's Supper in the section that follows ("Now in the following instructions I do not commend you, because when you come together it is not for the better but for the worse" [11:17; see also 11:22]). Thus, Gordon D. Fee describes Paul's attitude toward the headwear dispute as relatively "relaxed" in comparison to his attitude toward abuses of the poor by the rich at the Lord's Supper, which he addresses vociferously in the next section as threats to the heart of the gospel (Fee, "Praying and Prophesying in the Assemblies: 1 Corinthians 11:2–16," in *Discovering Biblical Equality: Complementarity without Hierarchy*, ed. Ronald W. Pierce and Rebecca Merrill Groothuis, 2nd ed. [Downers Grove, IL: InterVarsity

Press, 2005], 142). That may be the case, though "relaxed" is not a word that leaps to mind as an apt descriptive for this driven apostle, and the vigorous, labored argument that follows suggests that the matter under discussion is of real concern to him.

12. J. Paul Sampley, "The First Letter to the Corinthians," in *The New Interpreter's Bible*, ed. Leander E. Keck (Nashville: Abingdon Press, 2002), 10:928.

13. Mary Rose D'Angelo, "Veils, Virgins, and the Tongues of Men and Angels: Women's Heads in Early Christianity," in *Off with Her Head! The Denial of Women's Identity in Myth, Religion, and Culture*, ed. Howard Eilberg-Schwartz and Wendy Doniger (Berkeley: University of California Press, 1995), 133. Occasionally a third possible meaning of headship language is suggested: that it can convey that which is preeminent, prominent, or foremost, without necessarily entailing obedience or submission. David Garland, e.g., argues for this possibility, which would designate the man as the prominent partner in the relationship between male and female—the public face and representative of the whole (an argument presuming that "man" and "woman" are not used generically, but much more specifically in reference to the relationship between "husband" and "wife"; see Garland, *1 Corinthians*, 514–16).

14. Garland, *1 Corinthians*, 514.

15. E. Elizabeth Johnson, "Ephesians," in Newsome, Ringe, and Lapsley, *Women's Bible Commentary*, 579.

16. Horsley, *1 Corinthians*, 156.

17. Cynthia L. Thompson, "Hairstyles, Head-Coverings, and St. Paul: Portraits from Roman Corinth," *Biblical Archaeologist* 51 (June 1988): 104.

18. This is Elisabeth Schüssler Fiorenza's view of the matter; see *In Memory of Her: A Feminist Theological Reconstruction of Christian Origins* (New York: Crossroad, 1983), 226–30.

19. Cf. Kenneth E. Bailey, *Paul through Mediterranean Eyes: Cultural Studies in 1 Corinthians* (Downers Grove, IL: IVP Academic, 2011), 301; Garland, *1 Corinthians*, 521; and Walter F. Taylor, *Paul: Apostle to the Nations: An Introduction* (Minneapolis: Fortress Press, 2012), 178. Along similar lines, Sarah Ruden has argued, "The veil was the flag of female virtue, status, and security. In the port city of Corinth, with its batteries of prostitutes—including the sacred prostitutes of the temple of Aphrodite—the distinction between veiled and unveiled women would have been even more crucial." She further suggests, "Paul's rule" regarding veiling "aimed toward an outrageous equality. All Christian women were to cover their heads in church, without distinction of beauty, wealth, respectability—or of privilege. . . . Perhaps the new decree made independent women of uncertain status, or even slave women, honorary wives in this setting" (Ruden, *Paul among the People: The Apostle Reinterpreted and Reimagined in His Own Time* (New York: Pantheon, 2010), 87–88. If this were the case, Paul could have said this (and thereby made a much more convincing argument for head coverings); but he does not make his argument in these terms, and this strikes me as an attempt to put way too much lipstick on a pig.

20. N. T. Wright, "Women's Service in the Church: The Biblical Basis," a conference paper for the symposium "Men, Women and the Church," at St John's College, Durham, September 4, 2004, http://ntwrightpage.com/Wright_ Women_Service_Church.htm.

21. Thompson, "Hairstyles, Head-Coverings, and St. Paul," 112.

22. Ibid.

23. N. T. Wright, "Women's Service in the Church."

24. Francis Watson, *Agape, Eros, Gender: Towards a Pauline Sexual Ethic* (Cambridge: Cambridge University Press, 2004), 55.

25. Carolyn Osiek, *What Are They Saying about the Social Setting of the New Testament?* (Ramsey, NJ: Paulist Press, 1984), 26.

26. This could be said to argue against secondary and inferior existence: "Her being can make good a being that is 'not good' without her" (see, e.g., Watson, *Agape, Eros, Gender*, 57–58).

27. As Michael Gorman notes, many modern translations convey hierarchical implications more forcefully than does the Greek text, translating "*but* woman is the glory of man" (instead of "*and* woman is the glory of man"), and conveying that woman was created "*for the sake of*" man (rather than "*on account of*" man); see Gorman, *Apostle of the Crucified Lord: A Theological Introduction to Paul and His Letters* (Grand Rapids: Wm. B. Eerdmans Publishing Co., 2004), 266.

28. Hays, *First Corinthians*, 186.

29. Ibid.

30. L. Ann Jervis, "'But I Want You to Know . . .': Paul's Midrashic Intertextual Response to the Corinthian Worshipers (1 Cor 11:2–16)," *Journal of Biblical Literature* 112, no. 2 (1993): 246.

31. Ibid.

32. Fee, "Praying and Prophesying in the Assemblies," 147.

33. Antoinette Clark Wire, *The Corinthian Women Prophets: A Reconstruction through Paul's Rhetoric* (Minneapolis: Fortress Press, 1990), 133.

34. Mitchell, *Paul and the Rhetoric of Reconciliation*, 262 n. 421.

35. Cf. 1QSa 2.5–9: "Everyone who is defiled in his flesh, . . . with a blemish visible to the eyes, . . . these shall not enter to take their place among the congregation of famous men, for the angels of holiness are among their congregation."

36. Angels played a mysterious role in Paul's cosmology: at other points in the letter, they are mentioned as spectators of apostolic ministry (4:9) and as those whom believers will one day judge (6:3); in other Pauline letters they are among the things that can separate us from the love of God in Christ (Rom. 8:38) and can have satanic associations (2 Cor. 12:7, *angelos*), so their presence is not always benign.

37. Gordon Fee, *The First Epistle to the Corinthians*, New International Commentary on the New Testament (Grand Rapids: Wm. B. Eerdmans Publishing Co., 1987), 518.

38. Judith M. Gundry-Volf, "Gender and Creation in 1 Corinthians 11:2–16:

A Study in Paul's Theological Method," in *Evangelium Schriftauslegung, Kirche: Festschrift für Peter Stuhlmacher*, edited by J. Adna et al. (Göttingen: Vandenhoek & Ruprecht, 1997), 170.

39. Ibid., 168.

40. Ibid., 169.

41. Ibid., 168.

42. Ibid., 169.

43. Ibid., with original emphasis.

44. Sampley, "The First Letter to the Corinthians," 929.

45. Margaret M. Mitchell, "1 Cor 11:2–16: Women Praying and Prophesying," in *Women in Scripture: A Dictionary of Named and Unnamed Women in the Hebrew Bible, the Apocryphal/Deuterocanonical Books, and the New Testament*, ed. Carol Meyers (Boston: Houghton Mifflin: 2000), 476–77.

46. Bassler, "1 Corinthians," 563.

47. Victor Paul Furnish, *The Moral Teaching of Paul: Selected Issues*, 3rd ed. (Nashville: Abingdon Press, 2009), 114.

48. Cynthia Thompson notes that "Paul's zeal for this distinction" is independently paralleled by the Greek historian Plutarch, who shares "the underlying conviction that in hairstyle and head-covering women and men must be different" ("Hairstyles, Head-Coverings, and St Paul," 104–5). Some studies have also explored the possibility that Paul's concern with this distinction reflects anxiety about appearances of deviant sexuality. Jerome Murphy-O'Connor, e.g., contends that long hair on men and short hair on women was associated with homosexuality ("Sex and Logic in 1 Corinthians 11," 485–90). Kirk R. MacGregor calls attention to Paul's explicit denunciation of homosexuality in 1 Cor. 6:9–10 and notes that blurring of the distinction between sexes was "a feat that homosexuality accomplished par excellence" ("Is 1 Corinthians 11:2–16 a Prohibition of Homosexuality?," in *Bibliotheca sacra* 166 [April–June 2009]: 215).

49. Fee, "Praying and Prophesying in the Assemblies," 148.

50. Sandra Hack Polaski, *A Feminist Introduction to Paul* (St. Louis: Chalice Press, 2005), 56, with original emphasis.

51. Hays, *First Corinthians*, 17.

52. Beattie, *Women and Marriage in Paul and His Early Interpreters*, 53–54.

53. However, some Christian communions, both in North America and abroad, do continue to insist on head coverings for women, citing 1 Cor. 11:2–16 as grounds for this custom. Visit, e.g., www.headcoveringmovement.com.

54. Mitchell, *Paul and the Rhetoric of Reconciliation*, 150–51.

55. Ibid., 150.

56. Bernadette Brooten, "Early Christian Women and Their Cultural Context: Issues of Method in Historical Reconstruction," in *Feminist Perspectives on Biblical Scholarship*, ed. Adela Yarbro Collins (Chico, CA: Scholars Press, 1984), 65–91.

57. Ibid., 82.

58. Deborah Krause, "Paul and Women: Telling Women to Shut Up Is More Complicated Than You Might Think," in *Paul Unbound: Other Perspectives on the Apostle*, ed. Mark D. Given (Peabody, MA: Hendrickson Publishers, 2010), 161.

59. Richard B. Hays, *The Moral Vision of the New Testament: A Contemporary Introduction to New Testament Ethics* (San Francisco: HarperSanFrancisco, 1996), 56.

60. Cynthia Brooks Kittredge, "Corinthian Women Prophets and Paul's Argumentation in 1 Corinthians," in *Paul and Politics: Ekklesia, Israel, Imperium, Interpretation; Essays in Honor of Krister Stendahl*, ed. Richard A. Horsley (Harrisburg, PA: Trinity Press International, 2000), 103.

61. Antoinette Clark Wire, "Response: The Politics of the Assembly in Corinth," in Horsley, *Paul and Politics*, 128. For a full-scale reconstruction of the perspective of the Corinthian women prophets and their contest with Paul, see Wire, *The Corinthian Women Prophets*.

62. Elisabeth Schüssler Fiorenza, "Paul and the Politics of Interpretation," in Horsley, *Paul and Politics*, 57.

63. See Ellen F. Davis, "The Soil That Is Scripture," in *Engaging Biblical Authority: Perspectives on the Bible as Scripture*, ed. William P. Brown (Louisville, KY: Westminster John Knox Press, 2007), 39.

64. Horsley, *1 Corinthians*, 156.

65. Bassler, "1 Corinthians," 562.

66. If Paul's own teaching on freedom in Christ did occasion the problem at hand, it may not be coincidental that his use of the baptismal formula in 1 Cor. 12:13 refers only to the reunification of "Jews or Greeks" and "slaves or free" in Christ, omitting the reunification of male and female.

67. However, Dennis MacDonald notes another possibility: perhaps Gal. 3:27–28 is not Paul's own novel creation, but a quotation from early Christian baptismal liturgy. Thus, perhaps the inconsistency between 1 Cor. 11 and Gal. 3 is "evidence of incongruity between a liberating pre-Pauline movement and Paul himself" (*There Is No Male and Female*, 5).

68. J. R. Daniel Kirk, *Jesus Have I Loved, but Paul? A Narrative Approach to the Problem of Pauline Christianity* (Grand Rapids: Baker Academic, 2011), 139.

69. Dale B. Martin, *The Corinthian Body* (New Haven, CT: Yale University Press, 1995), 232.

70. One other striking point of tension (and contradiction) within 1 Corinthians can be noted: while 1 Cor. 11:2–16 presumes that women exercise ministries of liturgical leadership, praying and prophesying publicly within the worship life of the congregation, 1 Cor. 14:34–36 declares that women "are not permitted to speak. . . . If there is anything they desire to know, let them ask their husbands at home. For it is shameful for a woman to speak in church." This glaring contradiction requires extended comment and will be addressed in the following chapter, on 1 Cor. 14:33b–36.

71. Davis, "The Soil That Is Scripture," 39.

72. *Presbyterian Understanding and Use of Holy Scripture*, A Position Statement Adopted by the 123rd General Assembly (1983) of the Presbyterian Church in the United States, 11, http://www.pcusa.org/media/uploads/_resolutions/scripture-use.pdf.

73. Ibid.

74. Ian McFarland, "A Canonical Reading of Ephesians 5:21–33: Theological Gleanings," *Theology Today* 57 (October 2000): 354.

75. See Fee, "Praying and Prophesying in the Assemblies," 142–43; Lone Fatum, "Image of God and Glory of Man: Women in the Pauline Congregations," in *The Image of God: Gender Models in Judaeo-Christian Tradition*, ed. Kari Elisabeth Børresen (1991; Minneapolis: Fortress Press, 1995), 117 n. 89.

76. J. Todd Billings, *The Word of God for the People of God: An Entryway to the Theological Interpretation of Scripture* (Grand Rapids: Wm. B. Eerdmans Publishing Co., 2010), 28–29.

77. Richard N. Soulen and R. Kendall Soulen, *Handbook of Biblical Criticism*, 4th ed. (Louisville, KY: Westminster John Knox Press, 2011), 185.

78. Billings, *The Word of God for the People of God*, 29.

79. To learn more about this evangelical debate, see both *Recovering Biblical Manhood and Womanhood: A Response to Evangelical Feminism*, ed. John Piper and Wayne Grudem (Wheaton, IL: Crossway, 2006); and Pierce, Groothuis, and Fee, *Discovering Biblical Equality*.

80. For a critique of the presumption of continuity between Scripture and creeds on the part of "evangelical feminists," see Michael J. Lakey, *Image and Glory of God: 1 Corinthians 11:2–16 as Case Study in Bible, Gender, and Hermeneutics* (London: T&T Clark, 2010).

81. Hays, *First Corinthians*, 192.

82. "A Brief Statement of Faith," in *The Constitution of the Presbyterian Church (U.S.A.), Part I: Book of Confessions*, lines 29–32, http://www.pcusa.org/resource/book-confessions/.

83. Joel B. Green nuances the relationship between the rule of faith and Scripture: "From a historical perspective, we cannot argue that the church's Rule of Faith is built on top of the foundation provided by the Old and New Testaments. To put things more pointedly, we cannot argue that the church has simply received its doctrine from the Bible. . . . The canon of Christian Scripture was not in place at the very time that the Rule of Faith—or Rule of Truth, as it was sometimes called—was taking shape among early church theologians. The New Testament as a canonical collection took shape alongside and in relationship to these kerygmatic formulations, so that the least we can say is that, historically, the Rule of Faith and the canon of Scripture took shape in a context of mutual influence. Indeed, one of the primary criteria by which these books, and not those, would comprise the New Testament was their coherence with the kerygma as this was articulated in the Rule of Faith" (*Practicing Theological Interpretation: Engaging Biblical Texts for Faith and Formation* [Grand Rapids: Baker Academic,

2011], 72–73). See also Tomas Bokedal, "The Rule of Faith: Tracing Its Origin," in *Journal of Theological Interpretation* 7, no. 2 (2013): 233–55. Following Bengt Hägglund, Bokedal describes the relationship between the two as follows: "The Rule of Faith is not constituted first by Scripture, but rather relates to the event of salvation, to which the prophetic and apostolic Scriptures make up the only original testimony" (249).

84. L. Ann Jervis, "'But I Want You to Know," 246. In Jervis's view, "What Paul wants his readers to know is that the unity of man and woman in Christ does not obliterate the diversity of the sexes, but rather establishes it in all of its glory—and believers should not disguise this."

85. Wire, *The Corinthian Women Prophets*, 129.

86. For an intriguing discussion of the bearing of this distinction on a reading of 1 Cor. 11–14, see Jorunn Økland, *Women in Their Place: Paul and the Corinthian Discourse of Gender and Sanctuary Space*, Journal for the Study of the New Testament: Supplement Series 269 (London: T&T Clark, 2004).

87. This letter is referenced in Martin Luther King Jr.'s classic response to it, known as "Letter from a Birmingham Jail." See http://www.thekingcenter.org/archive/document/letter-birmingham-city-jail-0.

88. Interestingly, Paul himself employs the language of "wisdom" in the opening chapters of 1 Corinthians, critiquing those who boast of special religious "wisdom" or "knowledge" (1:17–25; 2:6; 3:18–20).

89. Robert E. Allard, "'Freedom on your Head' (1 Corinthians 11:2–16): A Paradigm for the Structure of Paul's Ethics," *Word and World* 30 (Fall 2010): 402.

90. This is Michael Gorman's translation in *Apostle of the Crucified Lord*, 137.

91. Hays, *The Moral Vision of the New Testament*, 55. See also Alexandra R. Brown, "Creation, Gender, and Identity in (New) Cosmic Perspective," in *The Unrelenting God: God's Action in Scripture*, ed. David J. Downs and Matthew L. Skinner (Grand Rapids: Wm. B. Eerdmans Publishing Co., 2013), 173–93. Brown notes that throughout 1 Corinthians, "the division that marks humanity as male and female is strangely presented as both present and passing away" (176).

92. Hays, *The Moral Vision of the New Testament*, 55–56.

93. Polaski, *A Feminist Introduction to Paul*, 121.

94. Ibid., 75.

95. Ibid., 121.

96. Wire, "Response: The Politics of the Assembly in Corinth," 128.

97. Schüssler Fiorenza, "Paul and the Politics of Interpretation," 57.

98. Antoinette Clark Wire, "1 Corinthians," in *Searching the Scriptures*, vol. 2, *A Feminist Commentary*, ed. Elisabeth Schüssler Fiorenza (New York: Crossroad, 1994), 157.

99. Kirk, *Jesus Have I Loved, but Paul?*, 138.

100. David Rhoads, *The Challenge of Diversity: The Witness of Paul and the Gospels* (Minneapolis: Fortress Press, 1996), 8.

101. Fee, *The First Epistle to the Corinthians*, 530.

102. See Kirk, *Jesus Have I Loved, but Paul?*, 138.

103. As support for this position, Watson appeals to the story of Judah and Tamar in Gen. 38:15 and the story of Susanna in the Apocrypha. At Susanna's trial, wicked men command her to be unveiled so that they might gaze upon her beauty; see *Agape, Eros, Gender*, 49–52.

104. Ibid., 41.

105. Ibid.

106. Ibid., 2.

107. Ibid., 53–54.

108. Ibid., 2, 71.

109. Ibid., 54.

110. Ibid., 56–57.

111. Ibid., 54, 57.

112. E.g., Caroline Vander Stichle and Todd Penner, *Contextualizing Gender in Early Christian Discourse: Thinking beyond Thecla* (London: T&T Clark, 2009), 209.

113. Bailey, *Paul through Mediterranean Eyes*, 313; Garland, *1 Corinthians*, 521.

114. Davis, "Critical Traditioning," 168–69.

115. See, e.g., Michael Lakey, *Image and Glory of God*, 135; Dale Martin, *The Corinthian Body*, 232–33.

116. Polaski, *A Feminist Introduction to Paul*, 75.

117. Ibid., 121.

118. Anne J. Lane, "Do Women Have a History? Reassessing the Past and Present," in *With Both Eyes Open: Seeing Beyond Gender*, ed. Patricia Altenbernd Johnson and Janet Kalven (Cleveland: Pilgrim Press, 1988), 59.

119. Elisabeth Schüssler Fiorenza, "Feminist Theology and New Testament Interpretation," *Journal for the Study of the Old Testament* 22 (1982): 42.

120. Wire, *The Corinthian Women Prophets*, 130.

121. Ibid., 129.

122. Bassler, "1 Corinthians," 563.

123. Polaski, *A Feminist Introduction to Paul*, 121.

Chapter 4: Women and Worship Wars (II)

1. Deborah Krause, *1 Timothy*, Readings: A New Biblical Commentary (London: T&T Clark, 2004), 9.

2. Ellen F. Davis, "Critical Traditioning: Seeking an Inner Biblical Hermeneutic," in *The Art of Reading Scripture*, ed. Ellen F. Davis and Richard B. Hays (Grand Rapids: Wm. B. Eerdmans Publishing Co., 2003), 178.

3. N. T. Wright, *Paul for Everyone: 1 Corinthians* (Louisville, KY: Westminster John Knox Press, 2004), 200.

4. On this point see Carol Meyers, *Rediscovering Eve: Ancient Israelite Women in Context* (Oxford: Oxford University Press, 2013), 93–102.

5. Quoted in Marlene Crüsemann, "Irredeemably Hostile to Women: Anti-Jewish Elements in the Exegesis of the Dispute about Women's Right to Speak (1 Cor 14.34–35)," in *Journal for the Study of the New Testament* 79 (2000): 31–32; the quotation appears in the essay *Coniugalia praecepta* from Plutarch's *Moralia* 138–48; quotation from 142 D/E.31–33.

6. Since early Christians gathered for worship as "house churches," many have supposed that ambiguity about whether they were in private, domestic space or public space might have contributed to the dispute over appropriate norms of decorum, as reflected in both 1 Cor. 11:2–16 and 1 Cor. 14:33b–36.

7. Antoinette Clark Wire, *The Corinthian Women Prophets: A Reconstruction through Paul's Rhetoric* (Minneapolis: Fortress Press, 1990), 156.

8. Elisabeth Schüssler Fiorenza, *In Memory of Her: A Feminist Theological Reconstruction of Christian Origins* (New York: Crossroad, 1983), 233.

9. Jouette M. Bassler, "1 Corinthians," in *The Women's Bible Commentary*, ed. Carol A. Newsom, Sharon H. Ringe, and Jacqueline E. Lapsley, 3rd ed. (Louisville, KY: Westminster John Knox Press, 2012), 564.

10. E. Earle Ellis, e.g., contends that a woman's ministry is to be consistent with, and qualified by, her marriage obligations, and that this accords with Paul's teaching on marriage in 1 Cor. 7 (e.g., 1 Cor. 7:33–34; see Ellis, "The Silenced Wives of Corinth (1 Cor. 14:34–35)," in *New Testament Textual Criticism: Its Significance for Exegesis; Essays in Honour of Bruce M. Metzger*, ed. Eldon J. Epp and Gordon D. Fee [Oxford: Clarendon Press, 1981], 217). See also Elisabeth Schüssler Fiorenza, *In Memory of Her*, 230–33.

11. See, e.g., Kenneth E. Bailey, *Paul through Mediterranean Eyes: Cultural Studies in 1 Corinthians* (Downers Grove, IL: IVP Academic, 2011), 409. Conversely, John Chrysostom resolved the contradiction between 1 Cor. 11:2–16 and 1 Cor. 14:33b–36 by arguing that the former addresses female speech in a private, domestic setting, and the latter addresses female speech in a public, liturgical setting. The exercise of public liturgical leadership by women is prohibited. However, the entire section of 1 Cor. 11–14 is quite plainly focused on various divisive aspects of the Corinthians' public worship practice; thus few have found this distinction in setting to be convincing.

12. Bailey, *Paul through Mediterranean Eyes*, 410. Bailey speculates that multiple factors may account for the Corinthian women's chattering: the short attention span of "simple, uneducated women," lack of facility in Greek language, the problem of accent when speakers were functioning in a second language, lack of amplification for the speakers, and chatting as a methodology for learning in an oral culture (413–16). This speculation is grounded in his personal experience of contemporary Mediterranean culture.

13. L. Ann Jervis, "1 Corinthians 14:34–35: A Reconsideration of Paul's Limitation of the Free Speech of Some Corinthian Women," *Journal for the Study of the New Testament* 58 (1995): 61.

14. C. K. Barrett, *A Commentary on the First Epistle to the Corinthians*, Harper's New Testament Commentaries (New York: Harper & Row, 1968; repr., Peabody, MA: Hendrickson Publishers, 1993), 332.

15. Margaret M. Mitchell, "1 Cor 14:33b–36, Women Commanded to Be 'Silent' in the Assemblies," in *Women in Scripture: A Dictionary of Named and Unnamed Women in the Hebrew Bible, the Apocryphal/Deuterocanonical Books, and the New Testament*, ed. Carol Meyers et al. (Boston: Houghton Mifflin, 2000), 478. Sandra Hack Polaski, e.g., inclines toward the view that Paul addresses "recognized leaders" in 1 Cor. 11 and "disruptive chatterers" in 1 Cor. 14; see Polaski, *A Feminist Introduction to Paul* (St. Louis: Chalice Press, 2005), 59.

16. See, e.g., David E. Garland, *1 Corinthians*, Baker Exegetical Commentary on the New Testament (Grand Rapids: Baker Academic, 2003), 667–73; Anthony Thistleton, *1 Corinthians: A Shorter Exegetical and Pastoral Commentary* (Grand Rapids: Wm. B. Eerdmans Publishing Co., 2006), 251; and James D. G. Dunn, *Beginning from Jerusalem* (Grand Rapids: Wm. B. Eerdmans Publishing Co., 2009), 824.

17. Jervis argues that the use of *lalein* in 14:34–35 is to be distinguished from its use earlier in the chapter because it is unqualified: "In ch. 14, in all but one instance other than vv. 34–35 (i.e., v. 11), the word λαλεω is qualified so as to make it refer to spiritual speaking: tongues (14.2, 4, 5, 6, 9, 18, 23, 27, 29), prophecy (14.3, 29), speaking in connection with revelation, knowledge, prophecy and teaching (14.6), and speaking, presumably in connection with interpreting tongues (14.19). The unqualified use of λαλεω is distinctive. It is best to understand Paul censuring a type of speaking which he regards as unspiritual and uninspired" ("1 Corinthians 14:34–35: A Reconsideration," 61).

18. Gillian Beattie, *Women and Marriage in Paul and His Early Interpreters*, Journal for the Study of the New Testament: Supplement Series 296 (London: T&T Clark, 2005), 57.

19. Joseph A. Fitzmyer, *First Corinthians*, Anchor Yale Bible (New Haven, CT: Yale University Press, 2008), 533. Proponents of the quotation theory also include Raymond E. Collins, *First Corinthians*, Sacra pagina (Collegeville, MN: Liturgical Press, 1999), 514–17; Michel Gourgues, "Who Is Misogynist: Paul or Certain Corinthians?," in *Women Also Journeyed with Him*, by Gérald Caron et al. (Collegeville, MN: Liturgical Press, 2000), 123; and David Odell-Scott, *A Post-Patriarchal Christology* (Atlanta: Scholars Press, 1991), 186–87.

20. Polaski, *A Feminist Introduction to Paul*, 58.

21. However, Gourgues raises the question: "Why should Paul be obliged to adhere always to the same response pattern?" See "Who Is Misogynist?," 124.

22. Proponents of the interpolation theory include Bassler, Fee, Hays, Horsley, Jewett, and Sampley. For a comprehensive discussion, see Gordon D. Fee, *The First Epistle to the Corinthians*, New International Commentary on the New Testament (Grand Rapids: Wm. B. Eerdmans Publishing Co., 1987), 699–708.

23. However, Wire and Jervis contend that an abstract, positive appeal to law

can also be observed in 1 Cor. 7:19; Wire, *The Corinthian Women Prophets*, 154; Jervis, "1 Corinthians 14:34–35: A Reconsideration," 58.

24. It could be argued that 1 Cor. 14:33b–36 influenced 1 Tim. 2:11–15, rather than vice versa. Alternatively, both could have been influenced by a common tradition. But Ann Jervis calls attention to differences between these two texts: e.g., 1 Cor. 14:34–35 prohibits women from learning in public, while 1 Tim. 2:11 commands women to learn, presumably in the assembly. See Jervis, "1 Corinthians 14:34–35: A Reconsideration," 54.

25. J. Paul Sampley, "The First Letter to the Corinthians," in *The New Interpreter's Bible*, ed. Leander E. Keck (Nashville: Abingdon, 2002), 10:969.

26. Philip B. Payne initiated discussion and debate about these markings; see Payne, "Fuldensis, Sigla for Variants in Vaticanus, and 1 Cor 14.34–5," *New Testament Studies* 41 (1995): 240–61. For a helpful summary of scholarly discussion and debate about this matter and others related to the textual authenticity of vv. 34–35 (including attention to Codex Fuldensis, dated 546, and minuscule 88), see Eldon Jay Epp, *Junia: The First Woman Apostle* (Minneapolis: Fortress Press, 2005), 15–19.

27. Antoinette Clark Wire, "1 Corinthians," in *Searching the Scriptures*, vol. 2, *A Feminist Commentary*, ed. Elisabeth Schüssler Fiorenza (New York: Crossroad, 1994), 187.

28. Beattie, *Women and Marriage in Paul*, 60.

29. Wire, *The Corinthian Women Prophets*.

30. Ibid., 157.

31. Wire, "1 Corinthians," 187.

32. Richard B. Hays, *The Moral Vision of the New Testament: A Contemporary Introduction to New Testament Ethics* (San Francisco: HarperSanFrancisco, 1996), 55.

33. Wire, *The Corinthian Women Prophets*, 155.

34. E.g., one of the most intriguing aspects of Wire's reconstruction is her attention to the way in which theological differences between Paul and the Corinthian women prophets are intertwined with very different social trajectories. Paul's conversion to faith in Christ led to a loss in his social standing, while the Corinthian women's conversion led to a reversal of low social status. As Wire puts it, "Paul thinks they are subverting God's transvaluation of all values for their own social advantage. They think Paul is subverting God's transformation of social reality to legitimate his own losses" (*The Corinthian Women Prophets*, 61).

35. Elisabeth Schüssler Fiorenza, "Paul and the Politics of Interpretation," in *Paul and Politics: Ekklesia, Israel, Imperium, Interpretation*, ed. Richard Horsley (Harrisburg, PA: Trinity Press International, 2000), 57.

36. Margaret M. Mitchell, "1 Cor 14:33b–36," 478; see also Mitchell, *Paul and the Rhetoric of Reconciliation: An Exegetical Investigation of the Language and Composition of 1 Corinthians* (Tübingen: J.C.B. Mohr [Paul Siebeck], 1991), 280–83.

37. Jorunn Økland, *Women in Their Place: Paul and the Corinthian Discourse of Gender and Sanctuary Space,* Journal for the Study of the New Testament: Supplement Series 269 (London: T&T Clark, 2004), 246.

38. Jean-Paul Sartre, "What Is Literature?" (1947), translated by Bernard Frechtman and reprinted in *"What Is Literature?" and Other Essays* (Cambridge: Harvard University Press, 1988), 56. I am grateful to my colleague Sam Balentine for bringing this quotation to my attention.

39. Holly E. Hearon, "1 and 2 Corinthians," in *The Queer Bible Commentary,* ed. Deryn Guest, Robert E. Goss, Mona West, and Thomas Bohache (London: SCM Press, 2006), 617.

40. It is puzzling to hear Fee argue that since the text was not authored by Paul, "it is not binding on Christians" (*The First Epistle to the Corinthians,* 708).

41. Hays, *The Moral Vision of the New Testament,* 56.

42. Antoinette Clark Wire, "Response: The Politics of the Assembly in Corinth," in Horsley, *Paul and Politics,* 128.

43. Ellen Davis's summary of this important point is worth noting again: "If we disagree with a certain text on a given point, then it must be in obedience to what we, in community with other Christians, discern to be the larger or more fundamental message of the Scriptures. In other words, disagreement represents a critical judgment, based on keen awareness of the complexity of Scripture and reached in the context of the church's ongoing worship, prayer, and study" ("The Soil That Is Scripture," in *Engaging Biblical Authority: Perspectives on the Bible as Scripture,* ed. William P. Brown [Louisville, KY: Westminster John Knox Press, 2007], 39).

44. Richard B. Hays, *First Corinthians,* Interpretation (Louisville, KY: John Knox Press, 1997), 248–49, with original emphasis.

45. "A Brief Statement of Faith," in *The Constitution of the Presbyterian Church (U.S.A.), Part I: Book of Confessions,* lines 64, 70–71, http://www.pcusa .org/resource/book-confessions/.

46. *Presbyterian Understanding and Use of Holy Scripture,* A Position Statement Adopted by the 123rd General Assembly (1983) of the Presbyterian Church in the United States, 11, http://www.pcusa.org/media/uploads/_resolutions/ scripture-use.pdf.

47. See Elaine Wainwright, "The Gospel of Matthew," in *Searching the Scriptures,* vol. 2, *A Feminist Commentary,* edited by Elisabeth Schüssler Fiorenza (New York: Crossroad, 1994), 651–54; and "A Voice from the Margin: Reading Matthew 15:21–28 in an Australian Feminist Key," in *Reading from This Place,* vol. 1, *Social Location and Biblical Interpretation in Global Perspective,* edited by Fernando Segovia and Mary Ann Tolbert (Minneapolis: Fortress Press, 1995), 132–53.

48. *Presbyterian Understanding and Use of Holy Scripture,* 13. This document further explicates the "rule of love" as follows: "Any interpretation of Scripture is wrong that separates or sets in opposition love for God and love for fellow human

being, including both love expressed in individual relations and in human community (social justice). No interpretation of Scripture is correct that leads to or supports contempt for any individual or group of persons either within or outside of the church. Such results from the interpretation of Scripture plainly indicate that the rule of love has not been honored. This rule reminds us forcefully that as the rule of faith and life, Scripture is to be interpreted not just to discover what we are to think or what benefits we receive from God in Christ, but to discover how we are to live."

49. Jervis, "1 Corinthians 14:34–35: A Reconsideration," 65.

50. See Ann Jervis on this point, who contends that "Paul wrote these words out of concern that some women's speech was detrimental to the Corinthian assembly's exercise of prophecy, not because it was spoken by women, but because it was self-focused rather than loving" (ibid., 73).

51. Quoted in Scot McKnight, *The Blue Parakeet: Rethinking How You Read the Bible* (Grand Rapids: Zondervan, 2008), 207.

52. Frances A. Maher and Mary Kay Thompson Tetreault, *The Feminist Classroom* (New York: Basic Books, 1994), 92.

53. Ibid. A quotation from Carol Gilligan, Nona Lyons, and Trudy Hanmer, *Making Connections: The Relational Worlds of Adolescent Girls at Emma Willard School* (Cambridge, MA: Harvard University Press, 1990), 4.

54. Hearon, "1 and 2 Corinthians," 617. The abbreviation GLBTI refers to gay, lesbian, bisexual, transgender/transsexual (intersex) persons.

55. Deborah Krause, "Paul and Women: Telling Women to Shut Up Is More Complicated Than You Might Think," in *Paul Unbound: Other Perspectives on the Apostle* (Peabody, MA: Hendrickson Publishers, 2010), 172–73.

56. "A Brief Statement of Faith," lines 64, 70–71.

57. Hearon, "1 and 2 Corinthians," 617.

Chapter 5: Reining In Rambunctious Widows

1. Elsa Tamez, *Struggles for Power in Early Christianity: A Study of the First Letter to Timothy* (Maryknoll, NY: Orbis Books, 2007), xxii.

2. Ignatius, *Letter to the Smyrnaeans* 13.1.

3. Joanna Dewey, "1 Timothy," in *Women's Bible Commentary*, ed. Carol A. Newsom, Sharon H. Ringe, and Jacqueline E. Lapsley, 3rd ed. (Louisville, KY: Westminster John Knox Press, 2012), 600.

4. Ellen F. Davis, "Critical Traditioning: Seeking an Inner Biblical Hermeneutic," in *The Art of Reading Scripture*, ed. Ellen F. Davis and Richard B. Hays (Grand Rapids: Wm. B. Eerdmans Publishing Co., 2003), 178.

5. Luke Timothy Johnson uses this phrase in *Letters to Paul's Delegates: 1 Timothy, 2 Timothy, Titus* (Valley Forge, PA: Trinity Press International, 1996), 177.

6. Marianne Bjellend Kartzow, *Gossip and Gender: Othering of Speech in the Pastoral Epistles*, Beihefte zur Zeitschrift für die neutestamentliche Wissenschaft 164 (Berlin: Walter de Gruyter, 2009), 155.

7. Carolyn Osiek, "The Widow as Altar: The Rise and Fall of a Symbol," *Second Century* 3 (1983): 160.

8. Jouette M. Bassler, "Limits and Differentiation: The Calculus of Widows in 1 Timothy 5.3–16," in *A Feminist Companion to the Deutero-Pauline Epistles*, ed. Amy-Jill Levine with Marianne Blickenstaff, Feminist Companion to the New Testament and Early Christian Writings 7 (Cleveland: Pilgrim Press, 2003), 122, 136–37 n. 54.

9. Raymond F. Collins, *I and II Timothy and Titus: A Commentary*, New Testament Library (Louisville, KY: Westminster John Knox Press, 2002), 13.

10. There is some debate about the phrase translated "married only once" (1 Tim. 5:9 NRSV), which is rendered more literally as a "one-man woman." Does a "one-man woman" refer to being "married only once" or to fidelity during marriage (but not necessarily during only one marriage)? If it means "married only once," any previously married widow who follows the author's counsel and (re)marries would thereby disqualify herself from ever entering the order of widows, given the prerequisites the author enumerates. But if the "widow" is one who has never married (that is, a celibate woman among the "virgins called widows"), marrying would not disqualify her for future enrollment.

11. Sandra Hack Polaski, *A Feminist Introduction to Paul* (St. Louis: Chalice Press, 2005), 107.

12. Kartzow, *Gossip and Gender*, 144.

13. Jouette M. Bassler, *1 Timothy, 2 Timothy, Titus*, Abingdon New Testament Commentaries (Nashville: Abingdon Press, 1996), 97.

14. Deborah Krause, *1 Timothy*, Readings: A New Biblical Commentary (London: T&T Clark, 2004), 102.

15. Kartzow, *Gossip and Gender*, 147.

16. Gail P. C. Streete, "Bad Girls or Good Ascetics? The *Gynaikaria* of the Pastoral Epistles," in *Women in the Biblical World: A Survey of Old and New Testament Perspectives*, ed. Elizabeth A. McCabe (Lanham, MD: University Press of America), 1:158.

17. David Horrell, "Disciplining Performance and 'Placing' the Church: Widows, Elders and Slaves in the Household of God (1 Timothy 5,1–6,2), in *1 Timothy Reconsidered*, ed. K. P. Donfried, Colloquium Oecumenicum Paulinum 18 (Leuven: Peeters, 2008), 122.

18. Kartzow, *Gossip and Gender*, 160–62.

19. Margaret Y. MacDonald reports: "With respect to women, the laws promulgated by the Emperor Augustus and his successors made marriage mandatory between 20 and 50 years of age. Divorcees and widows were required to remarry after brief periods which ranged from six months to two years. Unmarried and childless women experienced restrictions on inheritance and were denied certain privileges of legal independence. In contrast, freeborn women who had three children and freedwomen who had four children were rewarded with the privilege of being able to conduct their legal affairs without a male guardian." See her "Reading Real Women through the Undisputed Letters of Paul," in *Women and*

Christian Origins, ed. Ross Shepard Kraemer and Mary Rose D'Angelo (New York: Oxford University Press, 1999), 212.

20. Margaret Y. MacDonald, *Early Christian Women and Pagan Opinion: The Power of the Hysterical Woman* (New York: Cambridge University Press, 1996), 159.

21. Bassler, *1 Timothy, 2 Timothy, Titus*, 97.

22. Bassler, "Limits and Differentiation," 143.

23. M. MacDonald, *Early Christian Women and Pagan Opinion*, 128.

24. Jouette M. Bassler, "1 Corinthians," in *Women's Bible Commentary*, ed. Carol A. Newsom, Sharon H. Ringe, and Jacqueline E. Lapsley, 3rd ed. (Louisville, KY: Westminster John Knox Press, 2012), 561.

25. Krause, *1 Timothy*, 103.

26. *Acts of Paul and Thecla*, in *New Testament Apocrypha*, vol. 2, *Writings Relating to the Apostles, Apocalypses and Related Subjects*, ed. Wilhelm Schneemelcher, rev. ed., English translation ed. R. McL. Wilson (Cambridge: J. Clarke & Co.; Louisville, KY: Westminster John Knox Press, 1991–92), 242 (see 3.20).

27. *Tertullian's Homily on Baptism*, text and commentary by Ernest Evans (London: SPCK, 1964), 17.

28. Dennis MacDonald, *The Legend and the Apostle: The Battle for Paul in Story and Canon* (Philadelphia: Westminster Press, 1983).

29. Francine Cardman, "Women, Ministry, and Church Order in Early Christianity," in *Women and Christian Origins*, ed. Ross Shepard Kraemer and Mary Rose D'Angelo (New York: Oxford University Press, 1999), 302.

30. M. MacDonald, *Early Christian Women and Pagan Opinion*, 176.

31. Margaret MacDonald, *The Pauline Churches: A Socio-Historical Study of Institutionalization in the Pauline and Deutero-Pauline Writings* (New York: Cambridge University Press, 1988), 183.

32. Gillian Beattie, *Women and Marriage in Paul and His Early Interpreters*, Journal for the Study of the New Testament: Supplement Series 296 (London: T&T Clark, 2005), 104–5.

33. Cardman, "Women, Ministry, and Church Order in Early Christianity," 305.

34. Sondra Wheeler, "Contemporary Ethics from an Ambiguous Past," *Christian Bioethics* 11 (2005): 73.

35. Osiek, "The Widow as Altar," 168–69.

36. David Horrell, "Disciplining Performance and 'Placing' the Church," 109–10.

37. Polaski, *A Feminist Introduction to Paul*, 109.

38. Kartzow maintains that "a woman was considered 'young' between twenty and menopause, which, according to the second century doctor Soranus, occurred after the age of forty and not later than fifty" (Kartzow, *Gossip and Gender*, 145 n. 554). She also observes that the age limit would be more understandable if it had been fifty rather than sixty, as the Augustan marriage laws required remarriage of

widows between twenty and fifty (ibid., 145). Sixty was an advanced age in the first-century world, in contrast with our own day.

39. Bassler, "1 Corinthians," 561.

40. Richard B. Hays, *The Moral Vision of the New Testament: A Contemporary Introduction to New Testament Ethics* (San Francisco: HarperSanFrancisco, 1996), 390.

41. Kartzow, *Gossip and Gender*, 203.

42. Ibid., 204.

43. Ibid., 208.

44. *Presbyterian Understanding and Use of Holy Scripture*, 13, with added emphasis.

45. Elisabeth Schüssler Fiorenza, "Feminist Theology and New Testament Interpretation," *Journal for the Study of the Old Testament* 22 (January 1988): 5–6.

46. James M. Houston and Michael Parker, *A Vision for the Aging Church: Renewing Ministry for and by Seniors* (Downers Grove, IL: IVP Academic, 2011), 19–20.

47. Interestingly, this same tension may be reflected in another NT text related to the care and support of widows in the life of the early church: Acts 6:1–7 narrates the story of a conflict that emerges between the "Hellenists" and the "Hebrews" over the fact that the Hellenist "widows were being neglected in the daily distribution of food" (6:1). But what, exactly, is the conflict about? Barbara Reid's compelling reading of the text makes this important observation: "What remains unclear in Acts 6 is whether the problem is that the widows of the Hellenists are not receiving their due in the 'daily distribution' or whether they are being overlooked in the assignment of ministries, that is, not being given their proper turn to serve. It is notable that nothing in the text indicates that these widows were poor, and thus in need of goods distributed by the community." Reid maintains that it is much more likely that at issue in Acts 6 is a conflict over the exercise of ministry *by* widows. See Reid, "The Power of the Widows and How to Suppress It (Acts 6.1–7)," in *A Feminist Companion to the Acts of the Apostles*, ed. Amy-Jill Levine with Marianne Blickenstaff (Cleveland: Pilgrim Press, 2004), 83.

48. Luke Timothy Johnson, *The First and Second Letters to Timothy: A New Translation with Introduction and Commentary*, Anchor Bible 35A (New York: Doubleday, 2001), 273–74.

49. Krause, *1 Timothy*, 109–10.

50. Ibid., 110.

51. Ibid., 111–12.

52. M. MacDonald, *Early Christian Women and Pagan Opinion*, 178.

53. Bassler, *1 Timothy, 2 Timothy, Titus*, 107.

54. Frances M. Young, *The Theology of the Pastoral Letters*, New Testament Theology (New York: Cambridge University Press, 1994), 147.

55. Ibid., 146–47. Elsa Tamez makes a very similar point: "Obedience to the domestic codes that keep women in their households and excluded them from leadership and from their self-realization as human beings in other areas outside the home never can be a basis for the proclamation of the gospel and the reign of God, which speak of equality and justice. That would be an insurmountable contradiction" (*Struggles for Power in Early Christianity*, 55–56).

56. Carl R. Holladay, *A Critical Introduction to the New Testament: Interpreting the Message and Meaning of Jesus* (Nashville: Abingdon Press, 2005), 438.

57. Ibid. One of the ways in which the author endeavors to undermine the false teachers is by feminizing them—by emphasizing their close association with idle, gadabout, gossipy, female busybodies and their deviant speech.

58. Krause, *1 Timothy*, 110.

Chapter 6: Women in Ministry

1. Michael J. Gorman, *Apostle of the Crucified Lord: A Theological Introduction to Paul and His Letters* (Grand Rapids: Wm. B. Eerdmans Publishing Co., 2004), 338.

2. Peter Lampe, *From Paul to Valentinus: Christians at Rome in the First Two Centuries* (Fortress: Minneapolis, 2003), 156.

3. Luke Timothy Johnson, *Reading Romans: A Literary and Theological Commentary* (New York: Crossroad, 1997), 217.

4. Brendan Byrne, *Romans*, Sacra pagina (Collegeville, MN: Liturgical Press, 1996), 450.

5. N. T. Wright, "Romans and the Theology of Paul," in *Pauline Theology*, vol. 3, *Romans*, ed. David M. Hay and E. Elizabeth Johnson (Minneapolis: Fortress Press, 1995), 35.

6. N. T. Wright, "The Letter to the Romans," in *The New Interpreter's Bible*, ed. Leander E. Keck (Nashville: Abingdon, 2002), 10:406.

7. Paul S. Minear, *The Obedience of Faith: The Purposes of Paul in the Epistle to the Romans* (London: SCM Press, 1971), 6–7.

8. Byrne, *Romans*, 450–51. See also Lampe, *From Paul to Valentinus*, 165–67.

9. Florence Morgan Gillman, "Phoebe," in *The Anchor Bible Dictionary*, ed. David Noel Freedman (New York: Doubleday, 1992), 5:348.

10. John N. Collins argues that *diakon*-words, while not common in the first century, denoted "activity of an in-between kind," engaged in by a spokesperson, by one who acts on behalf of another, or by one commissioned to a special task (*Diakonia: Reinterpreting the Ancient Sources* [New York: Oxford University Press, 1990], 335). Thus they have "no determinate or constant reference" (John N. Collins, "Did Luke Intend a Disservice to Women in the Martha and Mary Story?," *Biblical Theology Bulletin* 28 [1998]: 110). *The Exegetical Dictionary of the New Testament* (*EDNT*) acknowledges a range of meaning, noting that in

the life of Pauline churches, the word group (*diakoneō, diakonia,* and *diakonos*) is used especially of charitable care for the needy, either in local churches (Rom. 12:7; 1 Cor. 16:15) or for the Jerusalem Church in the form of a collection (Rom. 15:25, 31; 2 Cor. 8:4, 19–20; 9:1, 12); but it can also be used comprehensively for all of the church's ministries (1 Cor. 12:5). The *EDNT* further states that the office of deacon, mentioned for the first time in the NT in Phil. 1:1 (and later in 1 Tim. 3:8–13), probably had as its primary tasks both proclamation and charity (*EDNT,* ed. Horst Balz and Gerhard Schneider [Grand Rapids: Wm. B. Eerdmans Publishing Co., 1978–80]: 1:303).

11. As Antti Marjanen notes, Phoebe is introduced with a clause in which the term *diakonos* is connected with a genitival construction ("of the church in Cenchreae"). This conveys a church office in the same sense as Phil. 1:1, rather than a general willingness to serve ("Phoebe, a Letter Courier," in *Lux Hama, Lux Aeterna: Essays on Biblical and Related Themes in Honour of Lars Aejmelaeus,* ed. Antti Mustakallio [Helsinki: Finnish Exegetical Society, 2005], 503).

12. Robert Jewett, "Paul, Phoebe, and the Spanish Mission," in *The Social World of Formative Christianity and Judaism: Essays in Tribute to Howard Clark Kee,* ed. Jacob Neusner, Peder Borgen, Ernest S. Frerichs, and Richard Horsley (Philadelphia: Fortress Press, 1988), 142–61.

13. As a presumably prosperous woman, Phoebe may well have been educated and literate and able to read the letter herself; or she could have been accompanied by someone able to do so. Robert Jewett, for example, argues that Tertius, the scribe who recorded the letter (16:22), would have been in a position to do so (*Romans: A Commentary,* Hermeneia (Minneapolis: Fortress Press, 2007), 23, 978–79.

14. Allan Chapple, "Getting *Romans* to the Right Romans: Phoebe and the Delivery of Paul's Letter," *Tyndale Bulletin* 62 (2011): 213.

15. In addition to Chapple (ibid.), Antti Marjanen identifies her as such ("Phoebe, a Letter Courier," 506), as does Beverly Roberts Gaventa ("Romans," in *Women's Bible Commentary,* ed. Carol A. Newsom, Sharon H. Ringe, and Jacqueline E. Lapsley, 3rd ed. [Louisville, KY: Westminster John Knox Press, 2012], 555).

16. Jerome Murphy O'Connor suggests as much, noting that Luke's consistent use of the diminutive form of her name "might be interpreted as a putdown" ("Prisca and Aquila: Traveling Tentmakers and Church Builders," *Bible Review* 8 [December 1992]: 40).

17. F. Scott Spencer, *Journeying through Acts: A Literary-Cultural Reading* (Peabody, MA: Hendrickson Publishers, 2004), 188. Linda Belleville observes, "When New Testament writers refer to their occupation of tentmakers and to 'their house,' the order is 'Aquila and Priscilla' (Acts 18:2; 1 Cor 16:19). But when ministry is in view, the order is 'Priscilla and Aquila' (Acts 18:18; Rom 16:3; cf. 2 Tim 4:19). This is also the case with the introduction of Apollos (Acts 18:26), suggesting that Priscilla possessed the dominant ministry and leadership

skills of the duo" (Linda L. Belleville, "Women Leaders in the Bible," in *Discovering Biblical Equality: Complementary without Hierarchy*, ed. Ronald W. Pierce and Rebecca Merrill Groothius [Downers Grove, IL: IVP Academic, 2005], 122).

18. David Noy, *Foreigners at Rome: Citizens and Strangers* (London: Duckworth with the Classical Press of Wales, 2000), 259.

19. See Lampe, *From Paul to Valentinus*, 187–95, for a detailed discussion of the nature of this work, which he contends entailed working with linen rather than leather, sewing awnings for protection from the sun. See also Murphy-O'Connor, "Prisca and Aquila," 44–45; and Marie Noël Keller, *Priscilla and Aquila: Paul's Coworkers in Christ Jesus*, Paul's Social Network (Collegeville, MN: Liturgical Press, 2010), 14–16.

20. Lampe, *From Paul to Valentinus*, 187–95.

21. While women are more visible in Luke–Acts than in other NT documents, recent scholarship has noted Luke's tendency to circumscribe their roles. As Scott Spencer points out, Priscilla's teaching of Apollos is the closest we come to encountering a woman as a minister of the Word in Luke–Acts, not a hearer only (*Journeying through Acts*, 194).

22. Jouette M. Bassler, "Prisca/Priscilla," in *Women in Scripture: A Dictionary of Named and Unnamed Women in the Hebrew Bible, the Apocryphal/Deuterocanonical Books, and the New Testament*, ed. Carol Meyers (Boston: Houghton Mifflin: 2000), 137.

23. E.g., Keller, *Priscilla and Aquila*, 51; and Peter Lampe, "Prisca," in Freedman, *Anchor Bible Dictionary*, 5:468.

24. Jewett, *Romans*, 957.

25. Carolyn Osiek and Margaret Y. MacDonald, with Janet H. Tulloch, *A Woman's Place: House Churches in Earliest Christianity* (Minneapolis: Fortress Press, 2006), 32.

26. Keller, *Priscilla and Aquila*, 67–68.

27. Ivoni Richter Reimer, *Women in the Acts of the Apostles: A Feminist Liberation Perspective* (Minneapolis: Fortress Press, 1995), 212.

28. Osiek and M. MacDonald, *A Woman's Place*, 5.

29. Near the close of Rom. 16, Paul also identifies Lucius, Jason, and Sosipater as "my relatives" when he conveys their greetings (along with Timothy's) to the church at Rome (16:21).

30. Because the name appears in Rom. 16:7 in the accusative singular form (*Iounian*), it can refer to a woman named Junia or a man named Junias. The difference in Greek between "Junia" or "Junias" in Rom. 16:7 depends on how the name is accented: an acute accent would indicate a feminine name; and a circumflex accent would indicate a masculine name. Since accents were not employed in Greek manuscripts before the seventh century, the earliest manuscripts do not feature them. When the use of accents became common practice, the extant Greek manuscripts consistently accent the name as feminine. A few ancient manuscripts feature the feminine name "Julia" as a variant reading.

31. Elizabeth A. Castelli, "Romans," in *Searching the Scriptures*, vol. 2, *A Feminist Commentary*, ed. Elisabeth Schüssler Fiorenza (New York: Crossroad, 1994), 279.

32. Bernadette Brooten, "'Junia . . . Outstanding among the Apostles' (Romans 16:7)," in *Women Priests: A Catholic Commentary on the Vatican Declaration*, ed. Leonard Swidler and Arlene Swidler (New York: Paulist Press, 1977), 142.

33. See Eldon Jay Epp, *Junia: The First Woman Apostle* (Minneapolis: Fortress Press, 2005); Joseph A. Fitzmyer, *Romans*, Anchor Bible 33 (New York: Doubleday, 1993), 737–38; and Brooten, "Junia," 141.

34. John Chrysostom, "Homily 31," *The Epistle to the Romans* (on 16:7); quoted from *A Select Library of the Nicene and Post-Nicene Fathers*, ed. Philip Schaff (New York: Christian Literature Company, 1888–90), 11:554–55. Also noted by Brooten, "Junia," 141.

35. Brooten, "Junia," 141.

36. Luise Schottroff, *Let the Oppressed Go Free: Feminine Perspectives on the New Testament* (Louisville, KY: Westminster John Knox Press, 1993), 36.

37. Jewett, *Romans*, 962.

38. James D. G. Dunn, *Romans 9–16*, Word Biblical Commentary 38B (Dallas: Word Books, 1988), 894.

39. Brooten, "Junia." See also Peter Lampe, "Iunia/Iunias: Sklavenherkunft im Kreise der vorpaulinischen Apostel (Röm 16,7)," *Zeitschrift für die neutestamentliche Wissenschaft* 76 (1985): 132–34.

40. Epp, *Junia: The First Woman Apostle*. In a blurb on the back cover of Epp's book, Edgar Krentz rightly claims, "If anyone could say the 'last word' on a matter of New Testament interpretation, Epp certainly has. *Junia* covers all bases, including the history of interpretation, lexicography, grammatical analysis, and text criticism."

41. The New Revised Standard Version (NRSV, an update of the RSV) and the Revised English Bible (REB, an update of the NEB), both published in 1989, were the first translations to reinstate Junia in Rom. 16:7 (albeit with unfortunate footnotes giving "Junias" as an alternative), and others have followed suit.

42. Richard Bauckham, *Gospel Women: Studies of the Named Women in the Gospels* (Grand Rapids: Eerdmans, 2002), 172.

43. The debate hinges on construal of Greek grammar. The description of Andronicus and Junia as "prominent among the apostles" (NRSV) features a dative construction (*episēmos* with *en* + dative); and some argue that if Paul had wanted to convey that Andronicus and Junia were outstanding *among* the apostles, he would have employed a genitive construction (*episēmos tōn apostolōn*). For a thorough discussion of the "exclusivist" view (the view that Andronicus and Junia were not members of the circle of apostles), see Michael H. Burer and Daniel B. Wallace, "Was Junia Really an Apostle? A Reexamination of Rom 16.7," *New Testament Studies* 47 (2001): 76–91. For a refutation of their argument and

discussion of the "inclusivist" view (the view that Andronicus and Junia were included among the circle of apostles), see Epp, *Junia: The First Woman Apostle,* 69–78; Bauckham, *Gospel Women,* 172–80; and Linda Belleville, "Ἰουνιᾶν . . . ἐπίσημοι ἐν τοῖς ἀποστόλοις: A Reexamination of Romans 16:7 in Light of Primary Source Materials," *New Testament Studies* 51 (205): 231–49.

44. Craig S. Keener, *Romans,* New Covenant Commentary Series (Eugene, OR: Cascade Books, 2009), 186.

45. Arland Hultgren, *Paul's Letter to the Romans: A Commentary* (Grand Rapids: Wm. B. Eerdmans Publishing Co., 2011), 582.

46. Elisabeth Schüssler Fiorenza, "Missionaries, Apostles, Coworkers: Romans 16 and the Reconstruction of Women's Early Christian History," *Word and World* 6 (1986): 431.

47. Epp, *Junia: The First Woman Apostle,* 70.

48. Dunn, *Romans 9–16,* 894.

49. Keller, *Priscilla and Aquila,* 51; and Keith A. Gerberding, "Women Who Toil in Ministry, Even as Paul," *Currents in Theology and Mission* 18 (1991): 285.

50. Schüssler Fiorenza, "Missionaries, Apostles, Coworkers," 430. Dunn observes that while Paul refers to his own apostolic labors with the language of hard work (*kopiaō*), this language does not denote a leadership function here in Rom. 16 but rather "tasks voluntarily undertaken at their own initiative—that is, denoting a sensitivity to needs within a new congregation and willingness to expend energy and time in meeting them" (Dunn, *Romans 9–16,* 894). In his view, leadership entails "specific tasks or tasks formally given" and is to be distinguished from "tasks voluntarily undertaken." But is this not a narrow view of leadership? Could not discerning communal needs and taking the initiative to ensure that they are met be described as acts of "leadership"? And does Rom. 16 specifically indicate that the hard labor undertaken by Mary, Tryphaena and Tryphosa, and Persis was "voluntary" rather than formally assigned? The text does not provide enough information to make such distinctions.

51. For a discussion of women (including Tryphaena and Tryphosa) as missionary partners in the NT, see Mary Rose D'Angelo, "Women Partners in the New Testament," *Journal of Feminist Studies in Religion* 6 (1990): 65–86.

52. Mary Rose D'Angelo, "Tryphaena," in Meyers, *Women in Scripture,* 165.

53. Jewett, *Romans,* 968. See also W. Bauer, W. F. Arndt, F. W. Gingrich, and F. W. Danker, *A Greek-English Lexicon of the New Testament and Other Early Christian Literature,* 3rd ed. (Chicago: University of Chicago Press, 2000), 1018.

54. D'Angelo, "Tryphaena," 165.

55. See Lampe, *From Paul to Valentinus,* 179–83.

56. Ibid., 174–75.

57. Jouette M. Bassler, "Persis," in Meyers, *Women in Scripture,* 134. Also, Dunn, *Romans 9–16,* 894.

58. Bassler, "Persis," in Meyers, *Women in Scripture,* 134.

59. Jewett, *Romans,* 969.

60. Fred B. Craddock, sermon on Rom. 16, "When the Roll Is Called Down Here," www.youtube.com/watch?v=X20Sd8NKLsk.

61. Steven Croft, "Text Messages: The Ministry of Women and Romans 16," *Anvil* 21 (2004): 90.

62. Jewett, *Romans*, 969.

63. Jouette M. Bassler, "Julia," in Meyers, *Women in Scripture*, 106–7.

64. As Fred Craddock notes in his engaging sermon on Rom. 16 ("When the Roll Is Called Down Here")!

65. See Gorman, *Apostle of the Crucified Lord*, 582–83.

66. Luke Timothy Johnson, *Reading Romans*, 208.

67. Gaventa, "Romans," 556.

68. An important caveat may be needed here. Scholars have established that women played corresponding roles in Greco-Roman religions, routinely exercising cultic leadership. Thus it is no longer possible to claim that Christianity provided "unique" or advanced opportunities for women to exercise religious leadership, in contrast to women in the synagogues or Greco-Roman cults. In its early stages, Christian feminists themselves, in apologetic mode, propagated misconceptions of this sort, portraying Jesus and the early Christian movement as uniquely "liberating" for women (a stereotypically misogynistic Judaism usually providing the negative point of comparison). Jewish feminist critique has since had a significant corrective impact on the whole enterprise of feminist biblical interpretation, but that impact still needs to be felt within the church's enterprise of Christian education and proclamation, where regrettably inaccurate caricatures of Judaism as deeply misogynistic continue to be propagated as a negative foil for the "good news" in Jesus Christ. This misconception does not square with the literary, political, and archaeological evidence, for increasingly social historians are discerning "movement toward greater social freedom for women already happening in the Roman Empire independent of the influence of Christianity" (Osiek and M. MacDonald, *A Woman's Place*, 2). Indeed, a good case has been made that the church "rode the wave" of this social development (ibid.). In short, it may well be that many women entering early Christian communities expected to play significant leadership roles because they were accustomed to such in their former lives in Roman religious cults or Judaism.

69. Elisabeth Schüssler Fiorenza, "Feminist Theology and New Testament Interpretation," *Journal for the Study of the Old Testament* 22 (1982): 42.

70. Sandra Hack Polaski, *A Feminist Introduction to Paul* (St. Louis: Chalice Press, 2005), 46.

71. Beverly Roberts Gaventa, in the foreword to *Junia: The First Woman Apostle*, by Eldon J. Epp, xii.

72. See chap. 16, "The Roman Christians of Romans 16," in Lampe, *From Paul to Valentinus*, 153–83. Epigraphy is the study of ancient inscriptions. For a condensed version of Lampe's striking insights on Rom. 16, see "The Roman Christians of Romans 16," in *The Romans Debate*, ed. Karl P. Donfried (Peabody, MA: Hendrickson Publishers, 1991), 216–30.

73. As Lampe notes, we do not know the exact percentage, but "in Italy alone, one could estimate that about 40 percent of the total population were living in slavery" (*From Paul to Valentinus*, 172).

74. Andrew D. Clark, "Jew and Greek, Slave and Free, Male and Female: Paul's Theology of Ethnic, Social, and Gender Inclusiveness in Romans 16," in *Rome in the Bible and the Early Church*, ed. Peter Oakes (Grand Rapids: Baker Academic, 2002), 108, 123.

75. Richard B. Hays, "Whether We Live or Die, We Are the Lord's," in *The Art of Reading Scripture*, ed. Ellen F. Davis and Richard B. Hays (Grand Rapids: Wm. B. Eerdmans Publishing Co., 2003), 322.

76. N. T. Wright, "The Letter to the Romans," 749.

77. Douglas J. Moo, *The Epistle to the Romans*, New International Commentary on the New Testament (Grand Rapids: Wm. B. Eerdmans Publishing Co., 1996), 927.

78. William M. Greathouse with George Lyons, *Romans 9–16: A Commentary in the Wesleyan Tradition*, New Beacon Bible Commentary (Kansas City, MO: Beacon Hill Press of Kansas City, 2008), 275.

79. Again, thanks to Phyllis Trible for this striking Old Testament metaphor for engagement with Scripture.

Epilogue

1. See Ellen F. Davis's exquisite reflection on the "wondrous depth" of Scripture and the interpretive virtues of humility, charity, and patience in her essay "The Soil That Is Scripture," in *Engaging Biblical Authority: Perspectives on the Bible as Scripture*, ed. William P. Brown (Louisville, KY: Westminster John Knox Press, 2007), 36–44.

Author Index

Allard, Robert, 66

Bailey, Kenneth E., 180n12
Bassler, Jouette M., 37, 51, 57, 79–80,
    88, 131, 147, 153
Beattie, Gillian, 94–95
Belleville, Linda L., 189–90n17, 192n43
Billings, J. Todd, 61
Bokedal, Tomas, 178n83
Brooten, Bernadette, 54, 149, 150
Brown, Alexandra R., 178n91
Brown, Raymond, 15
Bruce, F. F., 104
Brueggemann, Walter, 13
Burer, Michael, 191–92n43
Burgess, John, 21
Byrne, Brendan, 140

Calvin, John, 22
Cardman, Francine, 122
Carroll, Robert P., xi
Case-Winters, Anna, 169n20
Castelli, Elizabeth, 149
Chapple, Allan, 143–44
Chrysostom, John, 180n11
Collins, John N., 188–89n10
Craddock, Fred, 153, 193n64

D'Angelo, Mary Rose, 152–53,
    192n51
Davis, Ellen F., 1, 2, 4, 9, 14, 59–60,
    74, 183n43, 194n1
Dewey, Joanna, 111
Dunn, James D. G., 150, 192n50

Ellis, E. Earle, 180n10
Epp, Eldon, 150, 151, 182n26, 191nn40,
    43

Fee, Gordon, 47, 49, 52, 71, 172–73n11,
    181n22, 183n40
Fiorenza, Elisabeth Schüssler, 79, 173n17

Garland, David, 43, 171n3, 173n13
Gaventa, Beverly Roberts, 156, 189n15
Gilligan, Carol, 105
Gorman, Michael, 174n27, 178n90
Gourgues, Michel, 181n21
Gray, Patrick, 172n8
Greathouse, William, 160
Green, Joel, 4, 177n83
Gundry, Judith, 50–51

Hays, Richard, 40, 47, 55, 62, 67–68,
    100–101, 124
Hearon, Holly, 97, 106, 108, 165n7
Horrell, David, 123
Houston, James, 128–29

Ignatius of Antioch, 111, 114, 115

Jacobus, Mary, 165n2
Jervis, L. Ann, 47, 65, 103, 178n84,
    181nn17, 23; 182n24, 184n50
Jewett, Robert, 143, 154, 189n13
Johnson, E. Elizabeth, 43
Johnson, Luke Timothy, 129, 184n5

Kartzow, Marianne Bjelland, 116, 125,
    186–87n38
Keller, Marie Noël, 147
King, Martin Luther, Jr., 66, 178n87
Kirk, Daniel, 14, 70
Kittredge, Cynthia Briggs, 55–56
Krause, Deborah, 5–6, 83, 106–7, 116,
    120, 130, 134
Krentz, Edgar, 191n40